YOU KNOW WHO THEY ARE . . .

The people who claim that the CIA killed Kennedy, that elections are rigged, that the presidency is controlled by a secret brotherhood. Everybody says they're crazy. But a lot of their claims make sense. And can be proven. How do *you* know for sure?

CONSPIRACIES, COVER-UPS AND CRIMES
Jonathan Vankin

CONSPIRACIES, COVER-UPS AND CRIMES

From JFK to the
CIA Terrorist Connection

BY

JONATHAN VANKIN

A DELL BOOK

Published by
Dell Publishing
a division of
Bantam Doubleday Dell Publishing Group, Inc.
666 Fifth Avenue
New York, New York 10103

ISBN: 0-440-21385-1

Printed in the United States of America

Published simultaneously in Canada

November 1992

10 9 8 7 6 5 4 3 2 1

OPM

To my parents,
LARRY AND JEAN VANKIN,
with love, for everything.

CONTENTS

Acknowledgments

When you go to the library and look up "conspiracy theories," you don't find much. The research for this book, therefore, was more a process of accumulation than systematic investigation. I relied almost as much on people chatting with me and handing me stuff as on my own digging. The list of those people is very long, and I don't remember everyone, but thanks to you all.

There are a few people I must single out by name, two in particular. Ken Swezey was so essential to developing my ideas and direction for this book that he deserves more than just a humble thank-you. He did even more than help. It must sound like a terrible cliché to say that without Ken this book never would have been possible. But it's true. Without Ken this book would never have been written. I was originally writing the book for Ken's small imprint, Blast Books. Not only was he willing to encourage me to write my first book, he had enough faith in the project to bring it to the attention of Paragon House.

That brings me to Evelyn Fazio, my editor at Paragon. About Evelyn, too, I can truthfully say that this book wouldn't have been written without her. She was enthusiastic about the project from the start. Her confidence in me was something I never thought I'd experience as a first-time book writer. She was always there with reassuring words, and I needed many.

Also at the top of my list is Don Kennison, of both Blast Books and Paragon House. He offered research help, ideas, and all-important moral support.

Of all the people who helped with my research, my colleague John Whalen, media columnist at *Metro,* deserves top billing. Much gratitude also to Eric London, who read my rough draft and gave me exactly the type of criticism I needed.

Thanks to Gary Sherman for encouragement and legal advice and a special note of gratitude to my employer, Metro Newspapers Inc., for allowing me the flexibility to write a book while holding down a full-time newspaper job, and for its logistical support.

Finally, thanks to my sister, Laura Vankin, for being proud of me, thanks to Dan Reichert for being my friend for an extremely long time; to Hal March for the same thing (and for innumerable hours of conversation in the world's coolest record store); and to Brent Filson, my mentor.

Saving the best for last, my most special thanks to Coleen Curran, who read every chapter as soon as it came out of the word processor, and did the impossible through this entire ordeal: She lived with me. Most remarkable of all, she still does.

Jonathan Vankin
Santa Clara, California
December 1990

Introduction

THE THRESHOLD OF BELIEF

> *Ignorance . . . brought about anguish
> and terror. And the anguish grew solid
> like a fog and no one was able to see.*
>
> The Gospel of Truth, 17:10
> NAG HAMMADI BIBLE

Is there something rotten in America? Ever since the political assassinations of the 1960s, Vietnam, Watergate, and, more recently, the Iran-Contra affair and the Persian Gulf War, there has been a growing feeling among many Americans that something is terribly wrong. But what is it?

Conspiracies, Cover-ups and Crimes is a journey through the blood-red and midnight-blue netherworld where governments mingle with gangsters, and democracies enter secret partnerships with Nazis; where presidents deal drugs, respectable businessmen run billion-dollar rackets, and shadowy secret societies pull the strings of public officials. It is about the dark area usually covered by the term, "conspiracy theory."

Conspiracies, Cover-ups and Crimes is the first comprehensive and objective exploration of "conspiracy theory," the last real political heresy. Who really killed J.F.K.? Were we told the truth about the "mass suicide" at Jonestown? Did the CIA have a hand in bombing Pan American flight 103? Did the Nazis ever really surrender? Is the government manufacturing human robots to carry out assassinations? Is there a secret, evil force manipulating our everyday lives?

Crazy questions, perhaps. But in writing this book, I've interviewed a variety of Americans who have devoted their lives to answering those questions nonetheless. Are they crazy people? The answers may surprise you. After profiling a number of "conspiracy theorists," I'll explain the conspiracies themselves, presenting the evidence gathered by conspiracy researchers, and letting the reader decide where fact becomes fiction and fiction all too factual. While the book tries to present no final answers, I came away from this project asking questions about America and my own place in it that I'd never dared ask before.

Between 1963 and 1981, there were six attempts on the lives of presidents or presidential candidates. When that happens in other countries, we shake our heads at the primitive ways of "banana republics." Here, every recent assassination attempt has been attributed to madmen (or madwomen) acting alone. Get rid of the crazy people, and the system still works. Perhaps we should change a law or two, make it tougher for them to get guns, but otherwise the country is stable.

To maintain this belief, we must also place faith in the institutions that comprise the amorphous entity called "the system"—government, business, media, academia. Those institutions provide us with our way of life and all the information we need to live it, but lately an unshakable faith in their benevolence and stability has been hard to justify.

There is something about America that makes conspiracy theories inevitable. Something that makes them necessary. The word conspiracy derives from Latin roots which translate roughly as "breathing together." Sounds healthy, but the idea is heresy. In America, the word used to describe conspiracy theories is "paranoid." Conspiracies are delusions. Believe in them and you are mentally ill.

But is there value to these ideas after all? Would we be shutting ourselves off to a fuller understanding of America by understanding conspiracy theory as a symptom of mental illness?

Stalinist as it sounds, treating unorthodox ideas as psychiatric ailments, this diagnosis of conspiracy theories is distinctly American. We like to believe that our American system is unique, that unlike most countries around the world we have a system that works. Things may go wrong, sometimes terrible things, but they are caused by minor malfunctions, not by flaws in the system itself.

That is why, when we face awesome crises like the savings and loan robbery, the defense-contracting scam, or even constitutional collapses like Iran-Contra or Watergate, we never ask the obvious question: How in our democracy could these things happen? Instead, we change a few laws, prosecute a few villains, then declare that the system is repairing itself. Nevertheless, participation in politics has never been lower, because, I believe, people have a gut-level feeling of helplessness.

I've heard it said that the most dangerous thing about conspiracy theories is that they create a feeling of helplessness. If everything that goes wrong is caused by a conspiracy, then there is nothing anyone can do about it. The people in this book are evidence to the contrary. They are activists, constantly working on, thinking about, and searching for the real causes of helplessness gripping America.

In the past century, we have experienced an overwhelming social transformation. We are moving toward what one scholar, Bertram Gross, calls "friendly fascism." We may already be there. When the difference between lies and truth no longer means anything, we become easy to manipulate—fair game for "mass media, world spanning corporations, armies and intelligence agencies," he wrote. "Meanwhile, the majority of people have little part in the decisions that affect their families, workplaces, schools, neighborhoods, towns, cities, country, and the world."

In the first part of this book I've profiled a variety of Americans who reject the illusion of "friendliness," what appears to be a new insidious form of control. In the second part, I explore the ideas of these Americans. My intention is not to endorse—and certainly not to discredit—any one conspiracy theory or the broad conspiracy that seems to emerge throughout Part Two.

This book is an attempt to delve into a way of seeing the world that is far different from the one we're all used to. In this strange and not very comforting view, fantasy and fact shift positions with disconcerting, but delightful, regularity. I've attempted here a kind of mental new journalism of total immersion into the subject. I've steeped my mind in conspiracy theories, figuring the only way to truly understand them is to see the world from their point of view. Despite the pervasive paranoia that can result from these explorations, I'm fairly confident that I've emerged with my sanity intact.

So consider this a voyage, like Darwin on the *Beagle*, through environments rarely explored, stopping to take samples along the way and coming back to port with a new understanding of our environment, our history, and ourselves.

In a scolding editorial about a congressional committee's finding in 1979 that President John F. Kennedy was assassinated by a conspiracy, the *New York Times* declared that the problem was not the committee's finding but its choice of vocabulary. "The problem," said the paper of record, "is the word. The word is freighted with dark connotations of malevolence."

The *Times*'s attitude toward *conspiracy,* though typical, is disheartening. As scary as some of this stuff is, I also find it exhilarating. As important as I believe it is to explore dangerous ideas, I also find it fascinating. The word "conspiracy" may be a "problem" for some, but only because it represents the unknown, mystery, and risk. Those are the things that grip the human mind and bring it to life. These ideas can only be a problem for those who wish to keep our minds under control.

Part One

THE
RESEARCHERS

1

"I Am a Breeding Experiment"

"Did you shoot the President?"
"I didn't shoot anybody. No, sir."

Exchange between a newsman
and Lee Harvey Oswald shortly
after Oswald's arrest.

Sometime around Easter 1959, a young marine named Kerry Wendell Thornley struck up a friendship with his company's resident misfit. The misfit was sometimes called "comrade" by the other marines at El Toro Annex just outside Santa Ana, California, because he was unreserved in his admiration for Karl Marx and communism. His real name was Lee Harvey Oswald.

Oswald openly subscribed to communist newspapers. On a Marine base, that was more than enough to make him an outcast. His introverted personality and penchant for cracking jokes in an exaggerated Russian accent secured his position as what Thornley called "the outfit eightball . . . what in the Army they called a yard bird and in the Marine Corps a shit bird." He had no true friends, but among his acquaintances on the base Thornley was one of the steadiest.

Oswald was "a jarhead private with a swab in hand, slopping soapy water over the wooden plank porch of the operation hut," Kerry wrote in 1965. "With this picture there is a vague feeling of sympathy that might find expression in the question: Why are they picking on that poor guy?"

And who was Kerry Thornley? Kerry Thornley is still trying to figure that out more than thirty years later. In 1959, he was an aspiring writer from Los Angeles, a barracks intellectual serving his tour in the military after a year at the University of Southern California.

In retrospect it was a propitious pairing—Thornley and Oswald. The next four years of Oswald's life, which were also its last four years, marked him as one of the most bizarre figures in American history. And Thornley, in a different and far more obscure way, would leave his own palm print on the cultural brainscape. The assassination of President Kennedy would change them both profoundly, more even than it altered the American consciousness forever. It ended the existence of Lee Harvey Oswald, accused of the crime and murdered on national television two days later.

For Kerry Thornley, on the other hand, the assassination at first seemed a stroke of morbid good fortune. At first. He was no admirer of Kennedy and admits to celebrating at the news of Kennedy's death. More important, the sudden if posthumous fame of his eccentric marine buddy appeared to be a remarkable coincidence that would give Thornley's literary career a big break.

Thornley had already written a novel, a story of a marine's disillusionment with his country. The protagonist of Thornley's novel, *The Idle Warriors*, was a fictionalized version of Lee Harvey Oswald.

The manuscript yellowed in the National Archives, among other "evidence" collected by the Warren Commission, for almost three decades. Finally, in 1991, a small publisher called IllumiNet Press, in Atlanta where Thornley now lives, extracted it and brought it into print. Kerry Thornley's odd distinction of being the only author to write a book about Oswald *before* the Kennedy assassination finally brought him a smattering of publicity—including a segment on "A Current Affair."

Thornley's association with the president's alleged assassin has long ceased to seem a coincidence to him, or particularly good fortune (though it did get him a commission to write a nonfiction book called *Oswald*, which was published in 1965). He has come to believe that he was, against his will and without his knowledge, part of the conspiracy that killed Kennedy. And not only that. The plot, or rather the master plot of which the assassination was but one result, was hatched before he was born. He has been a coerced conspirator since his prenatal days.

Thornley and Oswald, too. This plot still continues. In 1981, Thornley wrote another book—as yet unpublished —about what he believes was his part in the conspiracy. At the time he wrote it, Thornley thought that the conspirators first began to manipulate him when he became friendly with Oswald. He now believes that this association was a part, not the start, of the operation.

"Since then, I've realized that I'm the product of a German breeding experiment. My mother and father were spies for Japan during the war. I learned enough about intelligence community cant and so forth that I can decipher what was going on in my early environment," Thornley said to me, once I had tracked him down by phone.

"What I think they were trying to do was create a monarchy in this country. I think they came over here originally with that purpose."

A breeding experiment?

"Oswald was, too," Thornley says. "We both were."

This would be a good time to take a step back. Let's leave the "breeding experiment" thing for a while, because even more than most conspiracy theorists, Kerry Thornley is an easy guy to poke fun at. His ideas can't be done justice in pithy snippets like "he thinks he's a breeding experiment." When I last tried to make contact with Thornley, after being out of touch for about a year, he said that he didn't want to talk on the phone because the only phone he can use is in his landlady's living room and "last time we talked she and her son sniggered at the far-out things I was saying through the whole conversation."

Writer Bob Black once remarked to Thornley, "You used to satirize conspiracy theories; now you believe in them." Black reports that Thornley "solemnly agreed." Nonetheless, I still wonder if it's all a put-on. Is Thornley's intricate conspiratorial autobiography an elaborate mind game he plays with himself and anyone who'll join in? Or is he really an intelligence agent, with a macabre cover story for his role in the J.F.K. conspiracy? Or could the story be true? Is Kerry Thornley a helpless pawn in a game beyond anyone's comprehension, who somehow figured out what has been happening to him? If it could happen to him, what about the rest of us?

I raise these questions not because Thornley's theories are remarkably strange. For the most part, they're no stranger than a lot of the other stuff I've come across in researching this book. But unlike some of the other characters herein, whose stone-faced sincerity is unimpeachable, Thornley has a history as something of a philosophical jester. This history makes his encounter with Oswald and its aftermath all the more a conundrum.

In the 1950s, during a philosophical argument in a bowling alley, Thornley and his friend Greg Hill invented a bogus religion they called "The Discordian Society." To be a Discordian, one must worship Eris, the Greek goddess of chaos and discord. Most religions are unworkable because they impose order on the senseless course of human events. Discordianism, Thornley and Hill therefore resolved, would worship disorder.

This seems a commonsense proposition, if a rather

Swiftian one. Thornley and Hill wrote a little Bible (Hill wrote most of it) called *Principia Discordia*. The book became a kind of underground classic. It gained in stature when Robert Anton Wilson and Robert Shea quoted liberally from it in their best-selling science fiction novel *The Illuminatus! Trilogy* (a satire of conspiracy theories, in which the Illuminati are, fittingly, sinister conspirators and the Discordian Society must rescue the world). Wilson and Shea dedicated the first book of the *Trilogy* to Thornley and Hill.

The *Principia Discordia* gained enough notoriety to propel it through five editions, and it's still in print today. In what must surely be one of the most twisted examples of synchronicity in this whole tale, for reasons which will soon become evident, Hill is reported to have first run off the *Principia* on a Xerox machine in the office of New Orleans District Attorney Jim Garrison a few months before the Kennedy assassination in 1963.

To readers of what is sometimes described as the "marginal" press—the busy subculture of fanzines and similar self-published tracts—Thornley is known for his impassioned and occasionally incoherent (though always funny) rants that appear in every issue of *Factsheet Five* magazine and on his own irregularly published broadsides, *Kultcha* and *Decadent Worker*. In these highly unusual writings, Thornley reveals himself as an anarchist thinker with a heavily conspiratorial perspective unique even among anarchists. But anarchism is just the culmination of a long intellectual quest.

Despite the subversive wit of Discordian "guerrilla ontology" (as Discordian dabblers like to call that particular line of thought), Thornley classified himself as an "I-Like-Ike" conservative during the late 1950s. He slithered out of that phase, through traditional liberalism and into Marxism during his marine stint. While he was immersed in his "Marxist" period, Thornley heard a news report about a young ex-marine who defected to the Soviet Union.

The defector, as is etched in the brain of every Kennedy conspiracy aficionado, was Thornley's former buddy Lee Oswald.

Oswald's defection was ostensibly the result of his growing disaffection with the American way after serving at a Marine base in Japan. It echoed the alienation Thornley was feeling at the time. He served at the same Japanese base after Oswald had been there and left: Atsugi, home of the supersecret U-2 spy plane (an odd assignment for a sympathizer like Oswald). Observing how Americans interacted with their hosts in a foreign land, Thornley seethed. Oswald's defection to the USSR gave Thornley the inspiration for *The Idle Warriors,* and he promised whoever would listen that the book would be "a poor man's *Ugly American* which would 'blow the lid off' the situation resulting from peacetime stationing of troops in the Far East."

The Idle Warriors would turn out to be the center of Thornley's life for the next few years. But its ideological theme changed even before he began writing it. On the ship back to the States once his tour in Japan was up, Kerry picked up *Atlas Shrugged,* the philosophical novel by Ayn Rand. Pitting diametrically opposed Randian "Objectivism" and degenerate "collectivism" against each other and a backdrop of melodrama, *Atlas Shrugged* changed Kerry's outlook once again.

Thornley was now a confirmed *"laissez-faire* capitalist." In theory. Not in practice. Honorably discharged from the marines, he adopted a Bohemian life-style—prided himself in it, actually. He supported himself as a waiter, a doorman, and later a hobo. When I first reached him, he was washing dishes in a Mexican restaurant. His reliance on menial jobs or no job at all, despite his noteworthy intellect, has stirred suspicion of Kerry Thornley, as we shall soon see.

Thornley's service at Atsugi was just one of the many times Kerry Wendell Thornley stepped in the footprints of Lee Harvey Oswald. Back in the states, after some time in his native California, Kerry moved to New Orleans. His stay in New Orleans was to be the crucial episode of his life. Some of what happened to him at that time did not take on significance until a decade later. There was one incident that would begin to haunt him sooner.

According to Thornley, in the fall of 1963, when he had just returned from a few months out of town, he was in a restaurant called the Bourbon House in the French Quarter. He was at a corner table talking to a man. He can't remember who.

As Thornley told it in 1976, a woman named Barbara Reid, "whose reputation as a voodoo worker had reached my ears but with whom I was not then well acquainted," came over to him.

"Have you ever been in radio work?" she asked.

Thornley said that he hadn't.

"Well, you should be in radio," said the voodoo lady. "You have a lovely voice."

Kerry, unmoved by flirtation, said thanks. He went back to his conversation. With whom was he talking? After the Kennedy assassination, Barbara Reid said that Thornley was conversing with Lee Harvey Oswald. She told this to New Orleans District Attorney Jim Garrison. Five years later, on February 8, 1968, Garrison called Thornley to testify before a grand jury. Garrison's investigation into the J.F.K. assassination was by then national news, and the subject of national controversy. Garrison quizzed Thornley about his alleged acquaintance with Oswald in New Orleans. Thornley maintained, as he always had and still does, that he had not seen Oswald since 1959.

Thornley and Oswald's rather casual friendship came to a screeching halt when Thornley made a sarcastic remark, in response to one of Oswald's incessant gripes about life in the marines, in America, or something. "Come the revolution," Thornley chided, "you will change all that."

Oswald, looking "like a betrayed Caesar," as Kerry told the Warren Commission, shrieked at him "Not you too, Thornley!" and stalked away. Thornley never spoke to him again.

That was Thornley's recollection, noted as early as two days after the assassination, when the FBI interviewed him at Arnaud's Restaurant in New Orleans, where he was a waiter. He repeated the same account to the Warren Commission in his testimony of May 18, 1964. He still tells the same story.

Garrison wasn't buying it. As Thornley repeatedly denied meeting Oswald in New Orleans, Garrison just as doggedly prodded him. He had arrived at a conclusion about Thornley in advance, and the twenty-nine-year-old free-lance writer wasn't confirming it. Garrison still holds to that conclusion with the same conviction that Thornley still refutes it.

Garrison's conclusion was, and is, that Thornley was the man calling himself "Oswald" who, accompanied by a big, scary-looking Cuban tried to buy ten pickup trucks from a Ford dealership in New Orleans in early 1961. The real Lee Oswald was still in the Soviet Union. In all likelihood, the trucks were going to be used in the Bay of Pigs raid, or some such covert anti-Cuban operation, because the fake Oswald and his tough-guy cohort said they were from a group called "Friends of a Democratic Cuba."

This was one of many "second Oswald" incidents prior to the assassination, and Garrison thought Thornley was playing Oswald in this one and possibly others. The D.A. even calls Thornley an Oswald "look-alike."

Judging by photos of Thornley from back then, that's a real stretch. The resemblance is passing at best—imaginary, if you ask me. In any case, Garrison or at least people around him were so keen to prove Thornley could have impersonated Oswald that a reputed Garrison associate, Harold Weisberg—a writer who by 1968 had already written four conspiracy books about the assassination—asked a California artist to "touch up" photos of Thornley to make him look more like Oswald. Weisberg's letter making this suspicious request was typed by one of Garrison's secretaries. When the letter was leaked to the press, Garrison's office denied having anything to do with it.

"Was Thornley an agent of the intelligence community?" Garrison asks in his most recent book. "Had he impersonated Oswald or coached others to do so?"

That was what Thornley was up against when he encountered Jim Garrison. At first, Thornley thought he would be helping Garrison. When he refused to admit meeting Oswald in New Orleans, Garrison indicted him for perjury. It was not exactly a secret indictment. Garrison spared nothing in smearing Thornley well before any trial. He sent forth a press release on February 21, 1968, stating flatly that "Kerry Thornley and Lee Oswald were both part of the covert federal operation operating in New Orleans." He noted that Thornley was one of "a number of young men who have been identified as CIA employees."

"I can tell you this flatly: I'm not a CIA agent," said Thornley when he was arrested at his home (then in Tampa) the next day. "Why does he think I am? One of the reasons is that I went to Arlington, Virginia, after leaving New Orleans. Another is that I have the education to hold white collar jobs, but don't."

Garrison was also intrigued by *The Idle Warriors.* "As luck would have it," Garrison snidely observed, "the man he wrote about ended up being charged with assassinating the president."

If only Garrison had known that the insane Bible of Discordianism had been first published on a Xerox machine in his very own office. What would his reaction have been then? Thornley mentions that, for a while, Garrison theorized that the Discordian Society itself was a CIA operation. In 1976, Thornley said that he thought that was "very funny and completely absurd" of Garrison. In 1989, he might not have been so sure.

Garrison eventually dropped the perjury charges. Thornley never stood trial. The ordeal was a jarring one. Extremely disturbing to Thornley were the numerous apparent coincidences, seen as highly sinister by Garrison, between his travels and Oswald's. Or those of an Oswald impersonator.

Though Thornley denied meeting Oswald in New Orleans, it was undeniable that they were there at the same time in late 1963. This baffled Kerry. Oswald had made headlines that summer, when Thornley was out of the city. Oswald was passing out leaflets for the "Fair Play for Cuba Committee," a real organization of which he was the only New Orleans member. It is now widely believed, and was by Garrison, that Oswald's New Orleans chapter was a front—some sort of government operation with Oswald as its agent.

Whatever Oswald's real motives, he had been in a street corner brawl with an anti-Communist Cuban. In retrospect, it's likely that this incident was staged. Again, whatever its real reason, it put Oswald in the news and made him briefly a local celebrity, appearing on local newscasts as a spokesman for Marxism.

Yet when Thornley returned to New Orleans in September, no one thought to mention to him, "That marine buddy of yours who you're writing a book about is in town," though most of his friends knew the gist of his work in progress. This was all the more strange because Thornley, from news reports of Oswald's return from the Soviet Union, knew he'd gone to Dallas and was considering a trip there to see him. Thornley hoped to elicit some details that would flesh out the ending of *The Idle Warriors.*

Another convergence: While Thornley was out of New Orleans, after visiting his parents in Whittier, California, he traveled to Mexico City. He returned from Mexico, he told the Warren Commission, on September 3 or 4, 1963. About three weeks later, in Mexico City, Lee Harvey Oswald, or someone claiming to be him, appeared at the Cuban consulate and threw a very conspicuous tantrum. He wanted to travel to Cuba, and he wanted a visa right away. When he couldn't get it, he had a fit.

In a book called *High Treason,* Robert J. Groden, who was a photographic consultant to the House Select Committee on Assassinations, published what he says are photos, presumably taken by the CIA, of the man identified as Oswald in Mexico City. They are not photos of Oswald (and they sure aren't Kerry Thornley), so this incident may also be part of a frame-up.

Garrison points out that when Thornley moved to New Orleans, he moved directly to a neighborhood occupied by a cadre of intelligence agents. Some of the most startling coincidences came from Thornley himself, in his 1976 recollections.

Oswald's "Fair Play for Cuba" address was 544 Camp Street, the same building as the offices of Guy Bannister, ostensibly a private investigator. Actually Bannister was a right-wing crazy who appears to have been working for some intelligence agency on anti-Cuban subterfuge. His secretary reported that Oswald often visited the office, and on the very day that JFK was murdered one of Bannister's employees told the FBI that Bannister and David

Ferrie—another far-right CIA operative, who also worked for the Mafia—were somehow involved in the assassination. Even the House Select Committee on Assassinations, reluctant as it was to find any conspiracy, found these two characters worth investigating. Oswald's almost certain link to Ferrie went back to when Oswald was a teenager when they were both in a unit of the New Orleans Civil Air Patrol.

Without going through all of the evidence amassed by a phalanx of researchers over the years (Garrison not least among them), suffice to say that it indicates that Bannister and Ferrie were coordinating some kind of intelligence operation out of 544 Camp Street, an operation that was probably intended to target Castro, but may well have turned against Kennedy. And the consensus is that Lee Oswald, possibly without knowing all of what he was involved with, was part of that operation. Was Kerry Thornley?

Garrison is convinced of it. Thornley protested, but by the mid-1970s he didn't know what to believe. He recalled meeting Bannister at the Bourbon House as early as 1961. Bannister, Thornley recalled, was introduced as "a man with a great interest in literature." So Thornley, remarkably, began to tell him all about his book in which Oswald was the main character. Thornley also remembered going to a party where he met David Ferrie. Was he being manipulated?

When he appeared before the Warren Commission, Thornley was quite satisfied that Oswald was Kennedy's lone killer. He was still convinced a year later when his book *Oswald* came out. A tabloid in Los Angeles ran some excerpts from the book. A graduate student at UCLA named David Lifton saw the excerpts. Lifton's avocation was collecting evidence to criticize the Warren Report. He tracked down Kerry, who was then a doorman at an L.A. high rise called Glen Towers.

This apartment building posed another puzzle that had

significance to Thornley only in retrospect. According to Thornley, "the most colorful resident" of Glen Towers was John Roselli. One of the country's most powerful mobsters, Roselli, it would later be revealed, was part of the CIA's assassination plot against Castro. His intimacy with the CIA's dirtiest dealings made Roselli a posthumous object of suspicion in the Kennedy assassination. Shortly before he was to testify before the House Select Committee on Assassinations, which assembled in the mid-1970s, Roselli was found chopped into pieces, floating in a metal drum off the Florida coast.

Thornley said that Roselli told him the CIA "killed their own president."

Thornley didn't know quite what to make of his casual conversations with Roselli, but with David Lifton's help, his thought was going through troubling transformations at that time. Lifton and Thornley had a series of meetings and struck up a friendship. Lifton confronted Thornley with enough evidence that Thornley felt he could "no longer hide from myself the probability that either Lee Oswald was innocent or he had not acted alone."

The evidence Lifton laid out would soon become standard stuff in writings by the many critics of the Warren Report. When Lifton showed it to Thornley, it was revolutionary. By the time Thornley met with Jim Garrison, he believed that there was a conspiracy in the assassination. He did not believe that he had played any part in that conspiracy, even unwittingly. It was Lifton, then, who thought Thornley had been "set up previous to the assassination as an alternate patsy."

It was largely at Lifton's urging that Thornley cooperated with Jim Garrison. Before Thornley got involved with Garrison, Lifton held high hopes for the New Orleans D.A.'s investigation. But a couple of meetings with Garrison, followed by the indictment of Kerry Thornley, left Lifton bitterly disillusioned. Thornley as well. But where Lifton went on to pursue his own rigorously factual assassination investigation, which culminated in his 1980 best-seller *Best Evidence,* Thornley was personally involved in the drama, and rather than investigate, he meditated.

In the course of Thornley's reflections, something that he had not told the Warren Commission, and certainly not Jim Garrison, began to take on drastic importance. Besides his chat with the alleged Oswald at the Bourbon House in September, 1963, Thornley had other mysterious conversations in New Orleans.

In 1961, a friend of Thornley's introduced him to a pipe-smoking, bald man named (Thornley was told) Gary Kirstein. Like Thornley, Kirstein was a writer (again, this is what Thornley was told). At the time, the only thing memorable about Kirstein, who was kind of a Neanderthal racist, was that he was planning to write a book with the curious title *Hitler Was a Good Guy.*

Thornley recalled the content of his more notable conversations with Kirstein. The rekindled memory was astonishing: They had debated how to assassinate President Kennedy. Hypothetically, of course. They were talking as two writers discussing how it would be done in a novel. Kerry had blotted out this macabre recollection for a decade.

"I was so bored," Thornley now recalls. "He basically predicted everything to me that was going to happen in the next twenty years, including the Manson family, the war in Vietnam, and so on and so forth. All of which at the time I did not believe a word of. If I'd known that I was making history I would have been so excited. I was actually just bored to tears.

"I thought he was a nut," Thornley says, remembering his initial impressions of Kirstein. "I just didn't think he had it together. I thought he was just some asshole who was probably a little bit sadistic and didn't have anything

lse to do, so he was just playing with my mind. That's
what I thought. To me, his whole worldview was so foreign to my nonconspiratorial worldview at that time that
he just seemed to me like a psychologically degenerate
individual."

This gossamer "Gary Kirstein" is the catalyst of
Thornley's conspiratorial scenario. Thornley still isn't
sure who Kirstein really was. He believes he might have
been E. Howard Hunt, the CIA master spook who became a public figure as a shadow dweller of the Watergate
scandal. Playing around with this possibility, Thornley
authored an article in 1973 called, "Did the Plumbers
Plug J.F.K., Too?" After the piece was published in an
Atlanta underground newspaper, Thornley received a
couple of strange anonymous phone calls.

One of the callers asked, "Kerry, do you know who
this is?"

Thornley said he didn't.

"Good," said the caller, and hung up. The voice on the
other end of the line brought back eerie memories. It
sounded similar to the voice of that man Thornley had
talked to in New Orleans a decade before. He decided he
could keep his recollections to himself no longer.

Two years later, after searching his memories for every
bit of information they would yield, Thornley went to
the Atlanta police, who were then looking into new allegations about the murder of Martin Luther King, Jr. He
remembered Kirstein had also talked about killing King.
The idea, Thornley remembered, repelled him and he
didn't want to discuss it even hypothetically. In 1975, he
was beginning to see connections between the assassinations of Kennedy and King.

Twelve days after making his statement to the police,
Thornley was attacked by two men in ski masks who
pistol-whipped him in the face and, weirdly, stole all of
his identification.

Thornley had nothing solid to prove that the robbers

attacked him with the intention of stealing his I.D. But he
had his suspicions. He wondered if his I.D. might be used
—by whom?—to create a "second Thornley," not unlike
the "second Oswald," who Jim Garrison still suspect
may have been, at least once, played by Kerry Thornley.

The mysterious phone call. The stolen I.D. The re-
freshed memories of Gary Kirstein. The series of coincidences linking Thornley to Lee Harvey Oswald. Things
coalesced in Thornley's brain.

"He was always repeating himself," Thornley recall
of his "Conversations with the Devil of Sauerkraut and
Philosopher-Kings" (the title of Chapter 1 of Thornley's
book about his Kirstein experience). "There were things
he wanted me to remember. What the CIA calls programming somebody."

In 1981, Thornley thought Kirstein was the first intelligence agent who tried to program him. His readings and
meditations have caused him to dig deeper in the decade
since he wrote his unpublished book about Gary Kirstein. He now believes he knows who his first controller
was.

"There were five or six things that my mother always
said over and over all the time," Thornley reminisces.
(Mother? Mother!) "One of them is that, when they put a
child out for adoption, they usually pick parents that
physically resemble the natural parents. Whenever she
could, she brought that up. And another was, 'Kerry's
not very observant.' And I gradually realized that what
she was saying over and over was not evidence of senility.
There were certain things she wanted me to remember."

By studying his own genealogy, Thornley says he has
found that instead of Irish, as his name sounds, his family
is actually of German and Swiss descent. He also believes
they were part of the Vril Society. The Vrils were a proto-
Nazi occult group that had connections to Aleister
Crowley's Golden Dawn. They tried to make contact
with a race of alien gods who lived in the center of the

Earth, believing that the gods were fathers of the "master race." Kerry Thornley takes it from there. Like all good Nazis, he says, the Vrils are working "to create a super race." That is the purpose of their "breeding experiments."

"The Vril Society isn't technically genocidal," he says. "As far as I've been able to tell, the philosophy behind it is to breed people the same way that other animals are bred, to create ones that are more intelligent, healthier etc., etc., etc. Within every race, they're breeding. It's not quite such a simpleminded type of thing as was going on under Hitler."

The experiment that produced both him and Oswald, Thornley concludes, was a Vril-Nazi attempt at eugenics. Thornley, however, says that he is "what they call a mutant, because I didn't turn out to be a racist. . . . I wasn't turning out to be the good Nazi they hoped I would be."

Because he is the output of what must be a very important process to Nazi cultists carrying out these experiments, Thornley has been under surveillance since birth, he says. A "bugging device" was planted on his body when he came into the world. He came to that realization after being teased by strangers for an embarrassing sexual experience that could only have been recorded by some device hidden on his person.

People have been checking up on him, monitoring and terrorizing him all along. The enigmatic "Gary Kirstein" may have been foremost among his controllers.

"Whatever it is, I've lived this long because the Nazis happen to like my genes," he says. "Twenty years ago, the guy I talked to in New Orleans predicted a lot of the stuff I've been going through, particularly once I realized that I was somehow involved in the Kennedy assassination. Basically, he told me I'd be persecuted to the end of my life. I probably will be. I'm getting used to it, I guess."

So there is the tale of Kerry Thornley, first known as footnote to one of the century's pivotal episodes, wh now believes he is one of the "Boys from Brazil." Hi own introspection has been supplemented by ceaseles reading, and among his readings are expositions by Ma Brussell. Brussell's article, "Nazi Connections to the JF Assassination," rings familiar after Thornley's account c his meetings with "Gary Kirstein." Frankly, Thornley' theory would explain a lot of the anomalies that hav cropped up in Thornley's life, although it's hardly th most concise and probable explanation.

I still wonder, and have never really answered for my self, whether Thornley means his theory literally. Thorn ley is always the intellectual explorer, but his one dogm appears to be this, as stated in a recent scribbling (he still a voluminous writer, *compelled* to write): "Every hu man being is—either because of evolution or an innat way of nature—born into this world with an enlightene consciousness that is curious, loving, ecstatic, freedor loving and erotic, and early social conditioning obliter ates and fractures it."

In the dark reality of Thornleyism, I wonder if th conspiracy against Kerry Thornley is a metaphor for th larger conspiracy against human nature. Social condition ing taken to ghastly extremes. Perhaps a metaphor com true.

Robert Anton Wilson, whose *Illuminatus! Trilog* gave Thornley a dose of underground acclaim, once ex plicated Thornley's satirical Discordian religion. On achieves "Discordian enlightenment," Wilson states when one realizes that Discordian doctrines are not liter ally true, *"but neither is anything else."* Reality is deter mined by its interpreter.

Thornley's memories and speculations are his evidenc for his own current version of reality. His "breeding ex periment" hypothesis fits his evidence as well as any other. Is it literally true? If not, what is?

"A lot of order is projected, according to Greg Hill," Thornley says, referring back to his old cohort in Discordianism from the days of bowling-alley philosophy debates.

"I think there's some truth to that. And Greg is probably, I think, an arch-conspirator, you know."

2

VOTESCAM

O good voter, unspeakable imbecile,
poor dupe . . .

OCTAVE MIRBEAU,
Voter's Strike!

On election night, when the three major television networks announce the next president, the winner they announce is not chosen by the voters of the United States. He is the selection of the three networks themselves, through a company they own jointly with Associated Press and United Press International.

That company is called News Election Service (NES). Its address is 212 Cortland Street, New York City. Its phone number is (212) 693-6001. News Election Service provides "unofficial" vote tallies to its five owners in all presidential, congressional, and gubernatorial elections. NES is the only source Americans have to find out how they, as a people, voted. County and city election supervisors don't come out with the official totals until weeks later. Those results are rarely reported in the national media.

The U.S. government does not tabulate a single vote. The government has granted NES a legal monopoly, exempt from antitrust laws, to count the votes privately.

Those are the facts.

Even an average citizen should be a bit unsettled by the prospect of a single consortium providing all the data

used by competing news organizations to discern winners
and losers in national elections. To Kenneth F. Collier
and his equally obsessed older brother James, the possibilities are apocalyptic.

Ken and Jim Collier's discovery of NES in 1988 was
the apex of a pyramid they had been assembling for
nearly twenty years. Other stones in the awesome structure: Richard Nixon, John F. Kennedy, George Bush, the
CIA, Supreme Court Justice Antonin Scalia, Washington
Post publisher Katherine Graham, "60 Minutes" reporter
Mike Wallace, and just about everyone who has anything
to do with administering, tabulating, reporting on, and
running in American elections.

In their self-proclaimed crusade to prove "Votescam"
(as they've pithily christened the conspiracy) the Colliers
have filed a string of lawsuits, *pro se,* against the Republican National Committee and other big-time defendants.
The RNC offered a reward for evidence of vote fraud.
The Colliers say they have evidence, but the RNC won't
pay up, depriving the brothers of both the reward money
and, they claim, a Pulitzer Prize with all its attendant
benefits. So they sued for $250 million.

They've traveled from coast to coast, depending on the
kindness of strangers—people who believe their own local election officials are cheaters. The Colliers come in
and offer to prove it. They've haunted warehouses, slept
in VW buses, set up their office in the middle of a side-
walk, and for a while lived in the Library of Congress.
One person who lodged Ken Collier for a period of
weeks told me he finally had to kick Collier out of the
house. The person called Collier a "con man," but it
seems to me that if the Colliers are trying to engineer a
get-rich-quick scheme, they've picked a funny way to go
about it.

Almost all of the Colliers' writing on Votescam has
been published by two newspapers. The Liberty Lobby
tabloid *Spotlight,* voice of the ultraright "Populist Party,"

ran a continuing series of Votescam articles from 1984 until 1988 (the Colliers insist that Votescam is a "nonpartisan" issue, and indeed there seems to be no detectable ideology in their writing, even in *Spotlight*). A small community newspaper in Hialeah, Florida, called the *Home News* is also a regular outlet. Collier articles with headlines like "Herald Fabricates Story," "The Case against Judge Scalia," and "The Real Roots of Watergate" break up the folksiness of the forty-four-year-old *Home News,* which mostly fills its columns with city council debates, high school sports, and garden club meetings.

In 1989, the brothers compiled the entirety of their research into 326 pages of manuscript—including a plethora of reprinted memos, clippings, court transcripts, and magazine articles. Their unpublished book is called, appropriately enough, *Votescam.* The ordinary person's one chance to take part in democracy, the vote, has been stolen, says the book. Every significant election in the country, the Colliers believe, is fixed. And not by rogue opportunists or even Boss Tweed-style strong-arm "machines," but by a sophisticated web of computer experts, media executives, and political operatives, all under the coordination of the Central Intelligence Agency.

"There isn't one single person in public office who earned their way there," said Ken Collier, when I interviewed him. "That's why the environment sucks. That's why there's the drug scene. That's why there's so many criminals and crooked politicians. Everything that's happened is because the vote is totally rotten. Rotted through to the core."

Like many conspiracy researchers, the Colliers can trace their life's mission back to one single event. Unlike many researchers, that event was not the J.F.K. assassination. Later, they would find a place for the pivotal assassination in their scenario. But the Colliers' revelation came on a date that lives in infamy for them alone: September 8, 1970, in Dade County, Florida.

The events of that day appeared innocent enough. The Democratic party in Dade County held its primary election for the U.S. House seat held by veteran congressman Claude Pepper. Pepper, who remained in Congress up to his death in 1989, was entrenched. He had no Republican opponent. The Democratic primary between Pepper and a hopelessly obscure opponent was *de facto* the final election, and a mere formality even in that regard.

The shock, to the Collier brothers, came soon after the polls closed at 7:00 P.M. Two of Miami's three television news stations projected Pepper the winner almost immediately. Nothing spectacular about that. They could have picked Pepper to win days before the election. What was remarkable were the exact predictions of Pepper's victory margin, and of the total voter turnout. At 7:24, one station projected a turnout less than 550 votes away from the eventual count of 96,499. In that same time span, less than half an hour, the stations called several other races on the ballot to within a percentage point of the final totals.

Unbelievable accuracy. But perhaps explainable as a marvel of technology, the genius of statisticians, or at least a mind-boggling stroke of luck. Until a University of Miami professor overseeing the projections announced one other fact: The projections were based on numbers from a single, computerized voting machine. Not one precinct, but one lone machine.

There was a third television station in Miami, but it was reported to suffer a computer malfunction on election night and waited until late in the evening to broadcast election results phoned in from county headquarters. By that time, televisions were off. Dade County received its results not from the courthouse, but from a single machine somewhere. Not even the professor who collected the spewing data knew where that machine was.

Most voters in Dade County watched the election returns with indifference. There were no big political sur-

prises, least of all in the Claude Pepper race. The dazzling
speed and precision of the local stations' projections went
largely ignored. Except, of course, by the Colliers, who
were mortified. They had more than an average voter's
interest in the race. Claude Pepper's hopelessly obscure
opponent was Ken Collier.

The brothers Collier, sons of a Royal Oak, Michigan,
businessman, were both journalists. Jim had worked for
the Miami *News* (though like so many impoverished reporters, he has already defected to public relations). Ken
wrote features for the New York *Daily News.* In 1970,
they caught the ear of an editor at Dell Publishing with a
book proposal about running a grass-roots political campaign. The main chunk of research, they proposed, would
consist of actually running such a campaign. And so Ken
decided to take on the venerable Claude Pepper with Jim
as his campaign manager and with no fund-raising. The
whole campaign cost $120 and consisted mainly of gum-
shoe canvassing, talking to nearly every voter in the eighteenth congressional district.

"It was a random thing that I happened to decide to
run in the year 1970," Ken told a radio interviewer in
1988. "But they had never used prognostications like this
prior to that time in Florida. And when they did, it seems
like we stumbled into the pilot project of the methodology that has since 1970 absolutely, completely, taken
over the United States voting system."

According to the Colliers, the process used on a limited scale that evening in Miami has been expanded into
an Olympian system that allows the three major television networks to "monolithically control" any election
worth controlling—that is, most of them.

"What do they do? They wait 'til the polls close. They
announce who's going to win in virtually every race, they
announce what percentage these people are going to get.
They are virtually *never* wrong. And the key to remember is once you have been named, you can rest assured

you will be the winner. And later on, if only these networks can have some sort of mechanism whereby they could make the actual vote turn out the way they projected it nationwide, they would have the same setup they had down in Dade County, where they would announce who won early on, then meddle with the election results later to make sure they turned out that way."

Into the picture steps News Election Service, the only mechanism in existence for counting national votes on election night, the only one in contact with every voting jurisdiction in the nation. The Colliers are the only researchers I've come across who make an issue out of NES, but the company is a conspiracy theorists' dream—or nightmare.

As mentioned above, NES operates exactly the way the most imaginative conspiracy theorists believe all media operate. The ABC, NBC, and CBS networks, together with the AP and UPI, own the company jointly. Associated Press is a nonprofit co-op of a large number of daily newspapers, and UPI serves many of the rest. Local television and radio stations take most of their election returns from network tabulations. NES is a very real "cabal." Every media outlet in the United States acts in concert, at least on election nights.

NES has a full-time staff of fourteen. On election nights, that number swells to approximately ninety thousand employees, most of them posted at local precincts phoning in vote totals as they're announced. Others answer the phones and enter these totals into the NES computer. The government has no such computer. Only the privately held NES counts the votes. I called NES's executive director, Robert Flaherty, and asked him whether his company was run for profit. He wouldn't answer. His only response was "I don't think that's part of your story."

The Colliers find the existence of a "master computer" that records every vote in the United States more than coincidentally reminiscent of that single, mysterious voting machine in Dade County whose printouts were the basis for preternaturally precise vote-total predictions. The Colliers hold an even more ominous suspicion that the NES computer can "talk back" by phone lines to vote tabulation computers in cities and counties across the country.

"I don't know for sure that they're all connected to one. The immutable fact is that if they can do it, they will do it," Collier explains. "Computers are all linked. If you have a telephone number, you can get into most computers."

NES was conceived in 1964, in part as a cost-saving measure by the three major television networks (it was originally called Network Election Service), but largely to solidify the public's confidence in network vote tallies and projections by insuring uniformity. In the California Republican primary that year, television networks projected Barry Goldwater the winner on election night, while newspapers reported Nelson Rockefeller victorious in their morning editions. The networks themselves could vary widely in their return reports.

"Many television executives believe the public has been both confused and skeptical over seeing different sets of running totals on the networks' screens," the *New York Times* reported.

The networks (the two print syndicates were soon added to the setup) wanted the figures transmitted over their airwaves to be irrefutable. With all the networks—and later the print media—deriving their information from a central computer bank, with no alternative source, how could they be anything but?

"The master tally boards . . . would probably come to be accepted as the final authority on the outcome of races," the *Times* declared.

The "news media pool" was first tried in the 1964 general election. Most of the 130,000 vote counters were volunteers from civic groups. Twenty thousand newspaper reporters acted as coordinators. NES central was located at New York's Edson Hotel. Vote-tallying substations were set up in such select sites as an insurance company headquarters and a Masonic temple. When polls closed, the newly formed system shaved almost ninety minutes off the time needed to count votes in the 1960 election.

News Election Service had its goal *circa* 1964 to report final results within a half hour of final poll closing time. Now, of course, they go much faster than that. In the 1988 election, CBS was first out of the gate, making its projection at 9:17 Eastern time, with polls still open in eleven states. ABC followed just three minutes later.

All of these light-speed results are, naturally, "unofficial." The Collier brothers would say, "fraudulent." County clerks take a month or more to verify their counts and issue an official tally. Plenty of time, the Colliers say, for any necessary fudging and finagling. And there may be none needed. Discrepancies are a matter of course throughout the nation's thousands of voting precincts. The major networks rarely bother to report on such mundane matters. So who's going to know? The idea, according to Ken and Jim Collier, is to get the predetermined winner announced as speedily and authoritatively as possible. NES provides the centralized apparatus to do just that.

One rationale behind maintaining a vote-counting monopoly is to insure "accuracy," but in 1968, when Richard Nixon defeated Hubert Humphrey by a margin that could be measured in angstroms, the role of NES became a good deal more shadowy.

At one point in the tally, the NES computer began spewing out totals that were at the time described as "erroneous." They included comedian/candidate Dick

Gregory receiving one million votes when, the New York *Times* said, "His total was actually 18,000." The mistakes were described as something that "can happen to anyone."

NES turned off its "erroneous" computer and switched on a backup system, which ran much slower. After much waiting, the new machine put Nixon ahead by roughly forty thousand votes, with just six percent of the votes left to be counted. Suddenly, independent news reporters found over fifty-three thousand Humphrey votes cast by a Democratic splinter party in Alabama. When the votes were added to Humphrey's total, they put him in the lead. Undaunted, the Associated Press conducted its own state-by-state survey of "the best available sources of election data" (presumably, NES also makes use of the "best available sources") and found Nixon winning again. And that's how it turned out.

What exactly was going on inside the "master computer" at NES? The company's director blamed software, even though the machine had run a twelve-hour test flawlessly just the day before using the same programming. Could the software have been altered? Substituted? Or was the fiasco caused by a routine "bug," which just happened to appear at the most inconvenient possible time? At this point, it's more a question of what we *can* know than what we *do* know.

My own feeling is that with all the snafus and screwups, the real winner of the 1968 presidential election will never be certain. I do know this: Liberal warhorse Humphrey died without fulfilling his dream of becoming president, while Nixon is still hanging around, his loyal crony George Bush in the White House.

"Nixon has more power now than when he was president," proffers Ken Collier. "He's the elder statesman."

The Colliers look at "The Great Dade Election Rig" of 1970 as a trial run for a new, streamlined method of election rigging. Could the presidential election two years before have been the nearly botched rig job that convinced the conspirators of election banditry to concoct a slicker modus operandi?

Computers tabulate fifty-four percent of the votes cast in the United States. Sure, paper ballot elections were stolen all the time, and lever voting machines are invitations to chicanery. But there's something sinister about computers. Though most professionals in the field, as one would expect, insist that computers are far less vulnerable to manipulation than old ways of voting, the invisibility of their functions and the esoteric language they speak makes that assertion impossible to accept.

Even executives of computer-election companies will admit that their systems are "vulnerable," although they're reticent to make public statements to that effect. One executive told me, right after asserting that there's never been a proven case of computer election fraud, "there's probably been some we don't know about."

Even if "we" do find out, there's still little chance that the fraud will be prosecuted. A former chief assistant attorney general in California points out that without a conspirator willing to inform on his comrades or an upset so stunning as to immediately arouse suspicion, there's little hope of ferreting out a vote fraud operation.

There are very few elections that qualify as major upsets anymore. Preelection polling tempers the climate of opinion effectively enough to take care of that. As for turncoat conspirators, if the conspiracy works there are no turncoats. A good conspiracy is an unprovable conspiracy. It remains a conspiracy "theory." To even talk about it is "paranoid."

"If you did it right, no one would ever know," said the same state prosecutor, Steve White. "You just change a few votes in a few precincts in a few states and no one would ever know."

Maybe it's already happened, say the Collier brothers. In their unpublished book, they note that a turnaround of just 535,000 votes distributed correctly in eleven states would have handed Massachusetts Governor Michael Dukakis the 1988 presidential election, defeating George Bush in the electoral college.

Bush may have received an earlier Votescam benefit, the Colliers hypothesize, a rare election that *was* a significant upset. According to the Colliers, the favor came courtesy of New Hampshire Governor John Sununu, who had staked his political future on Bush before the then-vice president was a clear people's choice (if he ever was).

Bush had lost the Iowa Republican Caucus, the first round of the 1988 presidential primaries, to Senate Majority Leader Bob Dole. As Bush entered the New Hampshire primary, pollsters placed him behind Dole in that state, too. These were "days when things were darker," Bush said in his acceptance of the Republican presidential nomination six months later. His campaign was fizzling.

Despite his apparent deficit in public opinion, Bush won a decisive nine-point victory in the New Hampshire primary, reanimated his campaign, and more or less coasted to the nomination and presidency. The press attributed this remarkable turnaround to the contrary nature of New Hampshire voters and Dole's allegedly "mean" public image.

Ken and Jim Collier tell a different story.

Sununu was later rewarded with an appointment as Bush's chief of staff, often considered the second most powerful job in the country. He is a *computer engineer* who had been a member of the Center for Strategic and International Studies, a Washington think tank the Colliers believe to be linked to the CIA. The Colliers also posit the CIA as the umbrella over NES, for reasons we'll get to before the chapter is through.

"All John Sununu had to do," they write, "was get access to the on-air script of (the networks') election unit to *script-in* George Bush as the 'projected' winner based on exit polls; step two: commandeer the mainframe master computer (NES) . . . so that the final official totals in county and state computers can be manipulated over a sixty-day period to reflect the early projections of a Bush victory.

"It is the prescription for the covert stealing of America."

Even though Ken Collier insists that vote-fraud researchers who preoccupy themselves with computer voting are "obsolete," the New Hampshire primary-rig scenario turns on the "Shouptronic" voting machines used in Manchester, New Hampshire, from which early returns were taken. The Shouptronic's most advantageous feature is the speed with which it tabulates votes. Multiple machines can send results to a central computer instantly over telephone lines or even by satellite.

Shouptronic is essentially an automatic teller machine for voters. All votes are recorded by button pressing. The Shouptronic leaves no physical record of votes. Like all computer vote counters, its programming is top secret.

As solid a source as Robert J. Naegle, author of the federal government's national standards for computerized vote counting, is alarmed by the secrecy masking computer election software.

"They act like it was something handed down on stone tablets," he says. "It should be in the public domain."

The Shouptronic is named for its company's owner, Ransom Shoup II. In 1979, Mr. Shoup was convicted of conspiracy and obstruction of justice relating to a Philadelphia election under investigation by the FBI. That election was tabulated by old-fashioned lever machines, which also leave no "paper trail" of marked ballots. Shoup was hit with a ten thousand dollar fine and sentenced to three years in prison, suspended.

Another computer voting company, Votomatic, maker of Computer Election Services (now known as Business Records Corporation Election Services), emerged unscathed from a Justice Department antitrust investigation in 1981. The president of the company quipped, "We had to get Ronald Reagan elected to get this thing killed." The remark was supposed to be a joke. Forty percent of American voters vote on CES systems.

CES machines have been described as relying on "a heap of spaghetti code that is so messy and so complex that it might easily contain hidden mechanisms for being quietly reprogrammed 'on the fly.' " A computer consultant hired by the plaintiffs in a suit against CES described the way a CES computer runs its program as "a shell game."

Votomatic has one especially troubling drawback. On election night 1982 in Miami, Ken and Jim Collier captured the problem on videotape. This "Votescam Video" has been the Colliers' Exhibit A ever since. They've showed it to reporters at major television networks, and evangelical talk show host Pat Robertson paid them 2,500 dollars for broadcast rights to the tape. Robertson aired a portion of the tape.

The problem with Votomatic, captured on the Colliers' tape, is something called "hanging chad." The perforated squares on Votomatic computer ballot cards are, for some reason, called "chad." When a voter fails to punch it out completely, it hangs on the card.

To solve this problem and allow the computer to read the cards, election workers routinely remove hanging chad. The registrar of voters in Santa Clara County, California, says that "five percent or less" of all Votomatic cards have hanging chad, and election workers don't pull it off unless it is hanging by one or two corners.

The vision of local ladies from the League of Women
Voters deciding how voters have voted, putting holes in
perforated ballots with tweezers was an astounding proposition to the Colliers. When they talked their way into
the Miami counting room on November 2, 1982, toting
video camera with tape rolling, that's exactly what they
found. *Prima facie* evidence of tampering, they believed,
and Jim started shouting, "Vote fraud! Vote fraud!" for
the benefit of the camera. The Colliers were forced out of
the room.

The Votescam Video is the basis for James and Kenneth Collier's lawsuit against the Republican National
Committee. The video led them to Washington, where,
through sheer force of will, they convinced an ABC legal
reporter to screen it. But ABC never picked up the story.

The Colliers were not surprised. They added ABC to
their list of defendants in one of their *pro se* lawsuits,
along with the League of Women Voters and the RNC.
Then they invoked the federal RICO (Racketeer Influenced and Corrupt Organizations) statute to charge the
troika with a racketeering vote-fraud conspiracy.

Backed by the *Home News,* Ken and Jim sued
Antonin Scalia, whom President Reagan appointed to the
Supreme Court in 1986. Ken Collier testified at Scalia's
senate confirmation hearing, where, under oath, he accused Scalia of sandbagging his lawsuits against the RNC.
Scalia, say the Colliers, wrote a "killer memo" recom-
mending that aspects of the suit be dismissed. He placed
the memo in court records without following legal proce-
dure, the Colliers contend, thus using his authority as a
federal judge to shield Votescam from public scrutiny.

"He acted without jurisdiction to cause to come into
existence a 'counterfeit concurrence' which contained
self-serving prejudicial language exonerating friends and
colleagues who had been party-defendants in the three
cases, causing lower court judges to take judicial note of
the tainted document and summarily dismiss those

cases," Ken testified in the prepared portion of his statement.

The brothers' antipathy toward Scalia dates back to April 23, 1971, when they sent a telegram to then-president Nixon detailing the Great Dade Vote Rig. Scalia was in charge of the White House telecommunications office at that time, and the Colliers are convinced that he grabbed the telegram, took it to Nixon personally, and instead of suggesting an investigation of vote fraud persuaded the president to cover it up.

The telegram led to Watergate, the break-in compelled by Nixon's fear that the Democrats were going to use some Votescam connivance of their own and he would be cheated out of reelection in 1972.

"He never invoked that as a reason for Watergate," says Ken Collier. "But, instead, he had his brother buy into the company that was putting out all the software back when that's the way they were doing it." The California company was CES.

For a while, Watergate was the cornerstone of Votescam, but the Colliers seem to replace cornerstones rather frequently without letting the edifice of their Votescam scenario crumble. After linking Watergate to Votescam, they took the big leap back to the muddy pool from which all contemporary American conspiracy theory crawls: the Kennedy assassination.

The creation of NES was part of a CIA operation to control the media. The agency needed to hush up its involvement in the killing of J.F.K., so it created its own "media desk," which maintains hegemony to this day. The Colliers last year shot a new video in Dealy Plaza revealing a sewer grating in the grassy knoll—the area from which assassination researchers have long believed the shot striking Kennedy in the head was fired.

Beneath the sewer grating is a "sniper's nest" says Ken

Collier, concealed by grass and brush. The drain leading out of the grassy knoll is a perfect escape route.

And Votescam spirals on through time.

The Colliers have now spent two full decades tracing Votescam. They've been flat broke most of the time, and Jim lay for a while near death with a stomach tumor. The tumor was diagnosed not as cancer, but as an outgrowth of stress. Killed—almost—by Votescam.

When I contacted the Colliers, they were somewhere in New York, trying to find a publisher for their finished book. They've packaged the manuscript replete with cover graphic. An American eagle, its beak is curled in a sinister sneer. They wanted me to help them. They wanted me to call the editor of the *New Yorker* on their behalf to recommend that he publish an excerpt from *Votescam.* I told them that, somehow, I didn't think my opinions would carry much clout with the *New Yorker*'s management, if I could even get through on the phone (it was tough enough just tracking down the elusive Ken and Jim Collier).

"It's not even a quest," said Ken of their twenty-year endeavor. "It's a simple report. The book will blow your mind because if you didn't have some reason not to publish it, you'd publish it because it's so vital. It goes right to the core, heart of the democracy. The vote. The winners, the senators, the congressmen, the ones that go ninety-eight to ninety-nine percent incumbency every single time—it's all because it is truly a clique, a club.

"Ultimately it might come out. I don't see how though. Everyone with anything to hide is at the top with billions to gain. Even if we had the book out, you would never see an interview on network television. You couldn't publicize it. Why? Because the networks are the ones that do it. The networks are the ones that count all the votes for senate, for the president, for congress. You don't necessarily even believe it until you see it yourself. Why twenty years? I don't know."

I had the feeling, talking to Ken, that the Colliers were nearing the desperation point. I couldn't worry about them. They'd been there, and past it, before. The Colliers still hope that Votescam will be their road back. At the same time, strangely, they know they have no hope. Once Votescam hit them like a gnostic vision, there was no returning to the world of consensus.

In the course of one conversation, Ken Collier recoiled from the label "conspiracy theorist," then turned around and announced, "The newspapers are all corrupt, and at this point I'll say that and I don't care what anyone thinks." The Colliers' pessimism is as confirmed as their perseverance.

That may be the final paradox of Votescam.

3

GET LaROUCHE!

*The stealthiness of the enemy
and his ubiquity!
I saw that we must copy it.
In our own way of course.*

ADOLF HITLER

Lyndon Hermyle LaRouche, Jr., could have stepped fully formed from the pages of Marvel Comics. His devotees see him as the lone hero who can save the world from forces of evil raging out of control. To adversaries, he is a sinister genius bent on global domination. In the real world these days, he's a federal prisoner.

LaRouche has spent immeasurable energy constructing an aura of personal importance. Every studied nuance says "executive": meticulously tailored suits, salon-clipped thinning hair, a fixed smirk of contempt for all those intellectually inferior (which is everybody), and a tight circle of disciples, who, far more than a "cult," are an efficient machine converting his innumerable schemes to reality. How it all came crumbling around him is a story whose plot is helical to say the least, leading from the school yards of Lynn, Massachusetts, to the secret chambers of British aristocracy, through the fertile ferment of Lyndon LaRouche's mind.

LaRouche began life as the son of New Hampshire Quakers. The family moved to Lynn, an industrial, ethnic burg, when Lyndon, Jr., was ten. When World War II hit, he was a conscientious objector, as the family religion demanded. Then he suddenly changed his mind and enlisted in the Army anyway. His tours of duty were spent in medical units around India and Burma.

There's some speculation that LaRouche may actually have been an Office of Strategic Services (OSS) intelligence agent—an intriguing hypothesis, considering that he was also a Marxist. He claimed to be, anyway. Somewhere along the line, he became a hardened anti-Stalinist and swayed toward Trotskyism. Never satisfied with the Marxist groups he encountered, put off by their hypocrisy and vacillation, he started his own group. In the late 1960s, LaRouche's no-prisoners style of leftism attracted a few radical academics, but most were repulsed in 1973 when LaRouche began his "Operation Mop Up" baseball-bat attacks against members of the more traditional left. His henchmen raided more than seventy gatherings of groups like the American Communist Party and the Socialist Workers Party (a little irony there—LaRouche had been a full-fledged SWP member from 1948 to 1963).

By then, leftists were convinced that LaRouche belonged nowhere in their ranks, that he was at least a provocateur, at worst a dedicated fascist. He did nothing to alter that impression. His writings and speeches in the mid-1970s mark a mutation in LaRouche's public thinking, usually characterized as a swing from the radical left to the extreme right.

His alliance in 1977 with CIA-connected mercenary and "security specialist" Mitch WerBell, who ran a paramilitary training camp for LaRouchians, as well as later contacts with KKK big shot Roy Frankhouser and others of that ilk, confirmed LaRouche's "swing to the right." But the physiognomy of LaRouchism displays characteristics evolved far beyond most known species of right-wing extremism. LaRouche transcends classification and scoffs at "left-right" distinctions. "I don't believe," he sneers, "the seating arrangements of the French National Assembly of 1793 have permanently frozen politics for the end of time."

While most kids his age were preoccupied with the exploits of Babe Ruth or Gary Cooper, young LaRouche, shunned by his schoolmates, was a pennant-waving fan of German philosopher Immanuel Kant. While this failed to win him a date to the junior prom, it did provide LaRouche with the philosophical basis for his swelling *weltanschaung*.

"The problem with most of the conspiracy buffs is Americans don't know much about history, and they don't understand historical processes. Therefore they come up with simplistic kinds of conspiracies and they don't understand what the word conspiracy really means," says LaRouche. "Since I had a philosophical background as a young man, I recognized what the problem was. It was philosophical. I always look at these things from a political, philosophical standpoint, rather than how most people look at them. So that takes me to the evidence a little more directly than most people."

LaRouche's "philosophical background" is like a pair of X-ray specs. It lets him see through the shroud of politics, history, and current affairs to the naked truth, which is an eternal struggle between two philosophies—rationalism (good) and empiricism (evil). Their adherents are united in two opposed conspiracies.

LaRouche starts with Kant's "moral imperative," that the only moral "maxim" is one that could be formulated as universal law. Stated simply, if an action is not right for everybody, it isn't right for anybody. Or, to look at it another way, if something is morally right for anyone, then it must be right for everyone. Murder, to take an example, is morally wrong, because "Thou shalt murder" could never be a universal law.

LaRouche, who has an acute techno fetish, updated

Kant for the postindustrial world, composing the prime directive of LaRouchism: "the promotion of scientific and technological progress not only in our own country, but the right of developing nations to the same principles that we're committed to."

LaRouche sees technocracy as the proper goal of global politics. The title of LaRouche's book, *There Are No Limits to Growth*, says it all. We don't need less industry; we need more. We shouldn't be phasing out nuclear power; we should be accelerating it. We shouldn't be trying to curtail the world's population; we need *more* people to make technology work. All limits to growth are artificial and unnatural. There is no danger to the environment. Technology *is* ecology.

Technology is also morality. As societies become technological, LaRouche believes, they place more cultural value on rational thinking. As they place more value on rationality, they become more moral. Kant says that all moral laws can be discovered through the rational process. LaRouche extrapolates from Kant: Technology is rationality in action, *ergo* technological development equals moral action.

"Wherever populations have become more rational in this fashion they have become more moral," LaRouche wrote. "The converse is more emphatically true. Technological pessimism . . . promotes cultural pessimism [which] unleashes all of the devils of which a population is capable of becoming."

One of the terms in the LaRouchian lexicon, a language that sounds something like conventional political discourse, but not quite, is "Malthusian." What LaRouche calls "neo-Malthusianism" is close to what's usually called "Social Darwinism." LaRouche loathes Thomas Malthus, the British economist who coined the phrase "survival of the fittest," later appropriated by Charles Darwin, who turned what was supposed to be an economic principle into a hypothetical natural law. In

LaRouche's technotopia, there's an abundance of industrial-produced everything, so there's no competition for resources—no "survival of the fittest."

This thinking leads LaRouche to include in his dogma support for "beam weapons," the Strategic Defense Initiative—"my proposal" he calls it—as well as nuclear power, especially the as-yet-untamable fusion variety. He really pushed the limits with his latest cause. When he was running for president in 1988, his fourth campaign, he bought a half hour of network prime time to explain his plan for colonizing Mars. He called it the "Mars driver project," and declared it the only conceivable means to unite the country, accelerate technological innovation, restore the economy, and save the planet.

The naysayers to these brilliant ideas, the "pessimists," are the empiricists: David Hume, John Locke, John Stuart Mill, Thomas Hobbes, Bertrand Russell. They and their philosophical ilk, in LaRouche's interpretation, base their moral reasoning not on rationality but on experience (empirical facts, hence the term, "empiricism").

Experience is a muddy thing. If we base our moral judgments on our experience, then we'll confuse things that *feel* good with things that *are* good, morally. Empiricist morality, as LaRouche reads it, is governed by "irrational hedonism."

So repelled by empiricism was schoolboy LaRouche, and so convinced by Kant, that when his adolescent schoolmates taunted him—they called him "big head"— he lashed back by calling them "unwitting followers of David Hume."

Thus was born the LaRouchian conspiracy theory. History's bad guys have been the "irrational hedonists" of empiricism, whose "pessimism" has spawned all of the evils mankind has endured in its nasty, brutish, and, so far, short existence. If their conspiracy succeeds, the human race will plunge into an anarchic abyss. The LaRouchian term is "New Dark Ages." The tool they'll use to cast us into darkness, he believes, just may be a nuclear holocaust.

One shouldn't get the idea that this awesome and complex conspiracy is perpetrated by a bunch of dead philosophers. Hume and the empiricists are no more than shills for evil ideology. The conspiracy predates these British philosophers, but it is uniquely British. Lately, its deadliest exponent, in LaRouche's view, is Henry Kissinger.

"Henry's career has always been, since he got out of the war as a tool of Chatham House, that section of British Intelligence . . . Kissinger is essentially an agent of Chatham House. He's essentially a British agent or an agent of British influence who has been funded to a large degree and sponsored by Nelson Rockefeller and to some degree, less so I think, by David (Rockefeller)."

Chatham House is headquarters of and another name for the Royal Institute of International Affairs, a British counterpart to the Council on Foreign Relations. LaRouche says that Kissinger's government training at Harvard came under the auspices of Chatham House.

The British have been keepers of this "irrationalist" flame for centuries. LaRouche traces the conspiracy's British lineage back to fourteenth-century Scottish King Robert Bruce. Bruce was the originator of Scottish Freemasonry. He was under the heavy influence of the Knights Templars, whom he seems to have been harboring from the persecution they faced in Europe at that time.

The Templar connection links Bruce with the ancient tradition of gnosticism—or, to put it in LaRouche's terms, irrationalism. Oddly, LaRouche considers the Templars "humanists," that is to say, on the right side. Bruce's Templar faction were "renegades," and Bruce himself is "the direct ancestor, by unbroken lineage, of all the men of evil in England."

When LaRouche says that Bruce is forefather to the present-day irrationalist conspiracy—the conspiracy responsible for the world's opium traffic and its resulting subjugation of entire nations, including the United States —he means it. "The leading controllers of the opium war against the United States are not only connected by interlocking directorates and other business ties, but by ties of 'blood' that constitute this web under *one* family."

Rationality, he believes, will save the world from the British conspirators. In LaRouche's opinion, the world's leading rationalist now sits in Lyndon LaRouche's jail cell in Rochester, Minnesota. A political prisoner of the forces of darkness.

From the rationalist vs. empiricist premise, LaRouche's reasoning behind such conclusions as his widely publicized "Queen of England pushes drugs" zinger is relatively clear—as clear as anything can be in the fog that hangs over a battleground of dueling conspiracies.

LaRouche combats the conspiracy with an intricate counterconspiracy of his own devising. Now, he believes, he is suffering for it. He began serving a fifteen-year sentence for federal tax and credit fraud convictions on January 27, 1989. He was sixty-six years old when he reported to prison.

"Who's the conspiracy theorist," asks LaRouche's Boston lawyer, Odin Anderson. "LaRouche or the U.S. government?"

Though the numbers of LaRouche's followers are usually estimated at around one thousand (domestically— there are overseas LaRouchians as well), his network has consisted of at least sixteen political organizations and twelve publications—even a software company. His "Fusion Energy Foundation" and its now-defunct magazine, *Fusion*, gained a readership of respected scientists and dealt seriously with nuclear fusion technology. The newsweekly, *Executive Intelligence Review*, sometimes beats the mainstream press to major stories and reports on regions of the world most ethnocentric American media ignore.

His private intelligence organization has the respect of even LaRouche's harshest detractors, sometimes rivaling the official intelligence community. "That doesn't mean we're running the biggest spy net in the world. It means we are able to think better than they are," LaRouche boasts.

Boston was the site of his first trial, where the government sought to expose LaRouche's underworld financial-political machine, devouring the life's savings of little old ladies to underwrite the vaulting political ambition of its central figure, LaRouche.

LaRouche's lawyers countered by outlining a government conspiracy to destroy LaRouche, a "Get LaRouche Task Force" created at high levels of the administration. While most media had made a practice of dismissing LaRouche's theories, to their bemusement LaRouche's "paranoia" began to look more and more like reality as the Boston trial progressed. Eventually, it became such a morass that the judge declared a mistrial.

"The government got caught with its hand in the cookie jar, failing to disclose exculpatory evidence," says Anderson.

Just as LaRouche had suspected, there was a full trough of internal government memos—including one between Iran-Contra conspirators Richard Secord and Oliver North—showing an apparently concerted effort to keep LaRouche under surveillance. LaRouche surmised that he'd been framed.

The LaRouche defense team tried to show that the credit-fraud and tax crimes LaRouche faced were the result of government skulduggery. The government, they said, had placed infiltrators deep in LaRouche's organization. Numerous documents came out to support that claim. LaRouche claimed that more than informants, these infiltrators actually committed the various illegalities and improprieties that he was being tried for.

Among the motives proposed by LaRouche's lawyers for this government operation was that LaRouche and Oliver North were apparently competing for the same pool of cash. While North and his surrogates were smooth talking wealthy senior citizens and right-wing tycoons for funds to ship to the Nicaraguan contras, LaRouche's supporters were doggedly combing that same constituency to fund their leader's presidential campaign.

The government's true motives were much darker and deeper, says Lyndon LaRouche. Though LaRouche, who affects the image of a high-tech CEO, must now don undignified jailhouse skivvies, his confidence remains regal. He experiences not the slightest doubt as to the origins of his current predicament. The mastermind of the frame-up, he's certain, is that Chatham House chiseler, Henry Kissinger.

On August 19, 1982, Kissinger wrote a brief note to William Webster, then director of the FBI. In its entirety, the two-paragraph letter with the salutation "Dear Bill" reads: "I appreciated your letter forwarding the flyer which has been circulated by Lyndon LaRouche, Jr. Because these people have been getting increasingly obnoxious, I have taken the liberty of asking my lawyer, Bill Rogers, to get in touch with you to ask your advice, especially with respect to security.

"It was good to see you at the Grove, and I look forward to the chance to visit again when I am next in Washington."

The "flyer" could have been any one of a number of LaRouchian anti-Henry tracts. Undoubtedly this particular flyer was "Kissinger: The Politics of Faggotry." In it, LaRouche drew connections between the Roman Empire,

Studio 54 (famed hangout for coke-snorting squalid socialites), Red-baiting homosexual mob lawyer Roy Cohn, and Kissinger. The purpose, apparently, was to demonstrate how Kissinger's policies are shaped by the overriding fact that he is a "faggot." Or at least by the fact that he has "the personality of a faggot," as LaRouche later testified when he realized that he'd have a hard time certifying his claims about Kissinger's sexual orientation.

Kissinger signed his letter to Webster with "warm regards," but to LaRouche this was hot stuff. Kissinger's letter, he believes, started the FBI on its "get LaRouche" campaign of spying and persecution that eventually led to his incarceration.

The creepy thing is, he's right.

At least it looks that way. Just a few months later, Webster asked one of his underlings to figure out how the FBI could start a probe of LaRouche, "under the guidelines or otherwise."

One of his many problems, LaRouche says, is that he opposed the administration's Nicaraguan contra war. "We opposed it because it stank, not for any other reason. I said, 'What do you want to do, start a war with the Jesuit order? You idiots!' "

Not that LaRouche had any sympathy for the Sandinistas or Catholic Liberation Theology under which "the Soviets came in very happily and merrily." He felt that politically there were better ways to handle the problem than the contra operation. As he put it, in a flash of common sense, "You don't just go in there and start shooting up Jesuits."

How LaRouche's reasoning runs from the Jesuits to Oliver North to Henry Kissinger is not simple. North was a "throwaway" for CIA director William Casey, who was "covering for somebody." That "somebody" may have been Reagan. Not Ronnie (as the chummy LaRouche likes to call him). Nancy. She was supposedly "under the very strong influence of the circles of Armand

Hammer. . . . She's an idiot," LaRouche offers, genteel as always. "This is one of the problems I ran into. The president is pussy whipped."

Hammer, the pro-Soviet industrialist, provides the necessary link to the New Dark Ages ideology of which Soviet foreign policy is an embodiment. Kissinger, as an agent of Chatham House, comes from the same "irrationalist" skein.

Unlike the John Birchers, who view Kissinger as a traitor and commie mole but no more than that, LaRouche sees Kissinger as his nemesis in a most personal sense. Kissinger was "coordinating most of the dirty operations run against me internationally," since the spring of 1975, when LaRouche, who dabbles in the foreign policy game himself, began stepping on Kissinger's diplomatic toes.

To hear LaRouche tell it: "The indicated prompting of this is that I made a trip to Baghdad and from Baghdad back to Germany in April of 1975. What I launched at that point were two projects. One, to attempt to set up a new approach to Israeli-Palestinian relations, to secure a negotiated peace based on something like that which has been called the Middle East Marshall Plan. Shimon Peres and others in Israel were interested in that. Some Arabs were interested, particularly some of the so-called moderate PLO people. We thought we had something going and Kissinger didn't like that.

"At the same time I had proposed that as part of doing business in the Middle East, this was the time to make a general monetary reform, to go back to a gold-reserve basis rather than a floating exchange rate system, which was in effect at that time. So Kissinger from that period was on my tail. So at that point I began to take notice of Kissinger. I took notice of him as a person who was personally committed to being my adversary."

LaRouche also claims to have angered Kissinger by investigating the real reasons behind Israel's 1982 invasion of Lebanon. LaRouche assumes it was Reagan's secretary of state Alexander Haig who gave the Israelis the go-ahead, and because Haig is a Kissinger protégé, "we assumed this had to be a Kissinger scenario that was used."

So LaRouche and his crew of civilian spies set out on what he calls "a journalistic sort of investigation." As usual, they came back with bedazzling results.

"What we caught them at was a land scam operation. We got Henry Kissinger Associates and Henry personally deeply involved in this. What they were doing was using thuggery to induce Palestinians to give up their land at bargain prices on the West Bank. Then [Ariel] Sharon over at the [Israeli] defense ministry was certifying this land as Israeli defense territory. . . . It was the most profitable real-estate swindle in the world. I said, 'Look, we've got to turn this stuff over to our friends at the National Security Council. It's a matter of national security.' But Henry found out about this and became furious."

One supposes that even Henry Kissinger at his wiliest would have a tough time driving up property values on the West Bank—the view's not bad, but the neighborhood's a little shabby. Oddly enough, LaRouche's "discovery," that Kissinger induced the invasion of Lebanon to make a quick killing off rigged real estate, is one of his more mundane postulates.

On the wilder side, there's his assertion that the Grateful Dead, rather than simply an aging, boring rock band, is actually "a British Intelligence operation." The British, it seems, have been using sex and drugs and rock 'n' roll to pave the way for a postnuclear population.

"That was an Allen Dulles-period operation which was run, together with the Occult Bureau types in British Intelligence, such as Aldous Huxley," he calmly explains. "This is part of this satanism business. Call it the counterculture. Call it the Dionysius model of the counterculture. Rock is essentially a revival of the ancient Dionysic,

Bacchic ritual. It does have a relationship to the alpha rhythms of the brain. If combined with a little alcohol and more, shall we say, mood-shaping substances, with youth, with funny sex, this does produce a personality change of a countercultural type."

"This satanism business" has become LaRouche's latest pet peeve. He alleges that the canon of New York's Episcopal archdiocese "was a regular visitor of a notorious Manhattan homosexual and satanic cult-practicing club called the Mineshaft. Here (the canon) had his own room where little boys were shamelessly abused."

In the preceding brief passage are three of LaRouche's more noxious themes: Anglophobia (the Episcopal church, the U.S. version of the Church of England), satanism, and homosexuality, with special attention paid to pederasty. It was shouted accusations that "your husband sleeps with little boys" that once prompted Nancy Kissinger to throw a right to the jaw of a vociferous LaRouche follower in Newark Airport back in 1982. That incident prompted Kissinger to worry about LaRouche's people becoming "increasingly obnoxious."

A fixation on sexuality, or, perhaps more correct to say, a revulsion at sexuality, was once one of LaRouche's main themes. For public consumption at least, he has toned it down as of late, but his charge that Kissinger is a "faggot" is hardly atypical. He's branded entire movements, the Puerto Rican nationalists, for example, as "sexually impotent." Reportedly, masturbation is in violation of LaRouchian tenets and can get a follower kicked out of the group. He has also insisted on sanctioning all relationships into which his followers enter, and "unauthorized" liaisons have been dealt with cruelly.

Sex, drugs, Dionysian revelry—anything that can be broadly defined as "countercultural"—is to LaRouche not a natural rebellion of youth, not an expression of real alienation, but a deliberately planned attack on modernity (i.e., morality) by forces who want to create a malleable populace, ready to follow orders once the structure of rational-technological society has been obliterated.

"Another word for it: New Age," he says. "The longer term: Age of Aquarius. People were experimenting with various utopian models, constructing small groups experimentally which were considered New Age types. How to create experimental types that might survive the aftermath of a general nuclear war."

"Conspiracy essentially means either a common purpose, a common philosophical and practical purpose, or a set of common and conflicting purposes which cause people to work together for common ends as well as conflicting ones," explains Lyndon LaRouche. "And conspiracy is a general term which can mean a great number of things. One can't say, 'There is a conspiracy.' One has to say, 'What do you mean by a conspiracy? What kind?' "

As LaRouche battles empiricists, British imperialists, and spaced-out touchy-feely types united by the common purpose of creating a primitive, hedonistic neo-Roman Empire, he has done well in forming his own allegiances with people in high places.

For that reason, and others, he is often the subject of speculation by other conspiracy researchers, who are given to mistrusting one another, who wonder if LaRouche himself is an agent of something . . . larger.

"He was in army intelligence," says conspiracy researcher John Judge, whom we'll meet in Chapter 7. "I've thought that for many years from the earliest stuff he did. I also felt he was put up by the Rockefellers, because you know some of the Rockefellers are Navy intelligence."

LaRouche has met with heads of state in Mexico and India (he somehow worked his way in to hold talks with Indira Gandhi) and has sold himself in Latin America as a respectable advocate of debt relief—something Latin

American leaders are only too happy to hear. While he was on the outs with Jimmy Carter, a president who was the consensus selection of the Trilateral Commission (he is said to have once mulled over the possibility of assassinating Carter), LaRouche was received kindly by the Reagan administration. At least in the beginning.

There was a taint of double-cross to the Reagan administration's prosecution of LaRouche. LaRouche and his supporters met often with important officials in the Reagan administration and the CIA. He was even admitted to the CIA's sanctified Langley, Virginia, headquarters on at least one occasion.

Confronted with the administration's frequent contacts with LaRouche, the president's press secretary Larry Speakes allowed only that the administration would meet with "any American citizen" who could provide "helpful" information. The ability of LaRouche's private intelligence operation to come up with a helpful hint here and there is hard to deny.

LaRouche also helped to get Reagan elected. He popularized George Bush's Trilateral Commission membership and "blue blood" pedigree, which devastated then-front-running Bush in the 1980 New Hampshire primary. The LaRouchians embrace attack politics like a holy crusade. Their eagerness to smear Bush let Reagan reap its benefits without soiling his hands.

LaRouche claims to have been "very much involved with the National Security Council" in 1982, developing his "beam weapon" proposal. Whether his influence was as profound as he wants the world to believe, who knows? What does seem certain is that the Reaganites saw something they liked in LaRouche. He met with several high-level NSC aides, and even had one over for dinner at his mansion in Leesburg, Virginia. Even in the days before Reagan, LaRouche used his friend Mitch WerBell to cultivate a network of contacts in the CIA.

LaRouche's own followers were a formidable intelligence gathering force. They spent endless hours on the phone, displaying the kind of perseverance that the hungriest cub reporter only dreams about. Throwing in healthy doses of deception (sometimes posing as journalists from more respectable news organizations), their untiring labor paid off in interviews with a wide range of policy makers. But they had the mentality of spies, not conventional journalists who never try to break the parameters of credibility. With information gleaned from their telephone conversations, they are often able to come up with intelligence data even professionals find quite useful.

Supreme Court justice David Souter, when he was attorney general of New Hampshire, used information passed to him by LaRouche's private spies to help cripple the Clamshell Alliance, an antinuclear group fighting to stop construction of the Seabrook nuclear power plant. New Hampshire's state police recommended the LaRouche agents to Souter as "very well-informed gentlemen." Philadelphia mayor Frank Rizzo found the LaRouchies useful as he prepared for "terrorists" to attack bicentennial celebrations back in 1976.

There is no doubt that LaRouche's effort to construct a counterconspiracy is the reason he now serves what amounts to a life sentence in federal prison.

He was convicted after his second trial, in Alexandria, Virginia. The judge in that trial would not allow LaRouche's lawyers to use government sabotage as his defense. That issue is what made the Boston mistrial an epic.

I'm in no position to pass judgment on LaRouche's guilt or innocence on the charges of credit fraud and tax evasion. His jurors, I would say, are. When his four-month Boston trial on those charges ended with the judge calling the whole thing off, the jury decided they had to settle things in their own minds, and they took a straw poll. Unanimously, they agreed that there was "too much question of government misconduct," and that government plants "may have been involved in some of this fraud to discredit [LaRouche]."

Their verdict was completely unofficial, of course. But they found Lyndon LaRouche not guilty.

4

UFOs in the Garden of Eden

As flies to wanton boys are we to the gods;
They kill us for their sport.

WILLIAM SHAKESPEARE
King Lear, Act Four, Scene One

William Bramley's law office is an uncharismatic cubicle in a cozy complex tucked away on the outskirts of San Jose, California. A desk, a couple of chairs, sparsely decorated white walls, and a window are all the amenities his modest practice requires, along with the portable computer and copy machine he keeps at home where he would much rather work.

Bramley keeps his office as understated as his ambitions. Driven not by the desire to pull down six figures as a partner in some heavy-hitting urban firm, the thirty-six-year-old Bramley, who has lived in and around San Jose since he was a teenager, dreams instead of salting away just enough to buy a plot of land along the Oregon coast and move to quieter climes.

Even his demeanor seems too temperate for the contentious civil courtrooms where he makes his living. With a calm voice and light blue eyes that don't always rise to meet yours, Bramley is ill fitted to the mold of a big-city attorney. As unlikely as he is a model for "L.A. Law," William Bramley is even less suited for the role he assumed early in 1990: prelate to an American underground of UFO believers.

"I guess I've become kind of the historian of the movement," drawls a bemused Bramley. His unfamiliar cult status leaves him unimpressed, and a little uneasy. In fact, "William Bramley" isn't even his real name. Rather, it's a *nom de plume* the lawyer assumed for the book that has conferred upon him his newfound renown, a fat volume he published himself and embossed with the grandiose title *The Gods of Eden.*

He doesn't want his secret identity revealed because he worries that judges, on whose whim his success in the legal profession depends, would take him less than seriously if they knew he had spent seven years devising an all-encompassing conspiracy theory in which the masterminds of the plot are . . .

Well, let's put it this way: One of the reasons the book has become so popular among hard-nosed UFOlogists is that *Gods of Eden* is not another slavish paean to the great saucer faith. There is only one chapter in Bramley's book—the first—that addresses the question of whether UFOs are real. The book contains but a single example of those familiar could-be-anything photos purporting to depict a flying saucer.

Most of the illustrations chosen by Bramley are plates lifted from an old edition of Milton's *Paradise Lost.*

Bramley's 535-page tome, which includes a fifteen-page bibliography, is not another cumbersome catalogue of close encounters, an awestruck account of alien abduction or a New Agey prophecy of messianic star children come to save us from ourselves. Instead, this camera-shy attorney has formulated a unified field theory of human history, tying virtually every turn of events since the garden of his book's title to an unseen oligarchy of UFO overlords Bramley identifies only as "The Custodians."

Here is his thesis: "Human beings appear to be a slave race breeding on an isolated planet in a small galaxy. As such, the human race was once a source of labor for an extraterrestrial civilization and still remains a possession today. To keep control over its possession and to maintain Earth as something of a prison, that other civilization has bred a never-ending conflict between human beings, has promoted spiritual decay, and has erected on Earth conditions of unremitting physical hardship."

Pretty potent stuff, for a torts lawyer. Bramley is acutely aware that, as he says in his book, he is "wide open to ridicule for expressing such a hypothesis." Hence, he keeps his real name under wraps. He takes pains to maintain a decidedly nonwacky tone in his prose, has never seen a UFO, and protests that he was never a UFO true believer nor particularly fascinated by conspiracy theories. When he started working on the book, he insists, UFOs were not even on his outline.

The question, then, is how a levelheaded member of the bar like Bramley can devise such a bleak, belief-defying theory. But first, it is necessary to digress. We need to discuss the whole question of UFOs. Most conspiracy theories have their basis, at least, in something undeniably real: assassinations, big banks, intelligence agencies, or whatever. With UFO theories, the footing is not so firm. Are they real? Are they a massive hoax? A delusion? If real, what are they? Spaceships from another world? Projections of the collective unconscious? Sinister and supersecret government experiments?

Whatever they are, or aren't, UFOs always lead into the idea of conspiracy. While there are many serious students of, say, CIA malfeasance, who are not conspiracy theorists, anyone who approaches the UFO "problem" finds a conspiracy of some sort. But that is only one reason why this book, which is about exploring territory where the possible melts into the unthinkable, contains a chapter about a topic that many serious observers and scientists find utterly unbelievable.

Another, more important reason is the simple lesson

UFO theories can teach us: What we know about the reality we have to deal with every day is nothing compared to what we don't know. And to what we can never know.

More than most conspiracy theories, UFOs are an intellectually treacherous subject. Credibility is precious currency, and it is quickly spent when UFOs are the topic of discussion. There are many things about the world we just don't understand completely yet; that should be an innocuous and self-evident statement. But even suggest that the UFO phenomenon may be one of those things, and suddenly you'll find yourself the target of suspicious glances and skeptical innuendo. Are you one of those believers? they wonder. One of those nuts? This despite the fact that a majority of the American people believe that extraterrestrial spacecraft actually visit li'l ol' planet Earth. Like truth, credibility is not a democracy.

With my own somewhat tenuous credibility at stake for including a chapter on UFO conspiracies in a book whose subject already tiptoes on the fringe, I want to answer here the same question I get—and anyone else gets—when trying to talk about the topic with the slightest hint of seriousness. "Do you believe in UFOs?"

If I could, I'd strike the word "believe" from the English language. Since what we understand about the empirical world is based on probability and supposition, not certainty, "belief" is a faulty state of mind, except when dealing with the obvious.

To the question "Do you believe in UFOs?" the answer, therefore, has to be yes. Obviously, there are flying objects that go unidentified. That, of course, is not what the question really means. When people ask, "Do you believe in UFOs?" what they're really asking is "Do you believe that space creatures patrol the planet in flying saucers?"

That's an empirical question. So my answer has to be no, I don't believe in UFOs, but I don't completely disbelieve in them either. I find it highly unlikely that spacemen from another planet have traveled to Earth. There are too many factors against it, not least of which are the laws of physics. On the other hand, even though the vast majority of UFO encounters appear explainable, a few are not. Can I say for sure that these few are not actual brushes with visitors from another world? No, I can't. I'm pretty confident that they are not, but I can't be *certain*. To be certain is to be dishonest.

What I do know is that there are thousands, millions of people convinced that UFOs are space aliens. Why? Any supposition we make about the physical world comes from our experience. We are convinced gravity exists because things fall. We stick to the ground. *Ergo,* gravity is real.

We all experience gravity. Not as many of us have experienced UFO contact (I never have, in case you were wondering). People who are convinced that UFOs are real have been convinced by experience. Discounting out-and-out hoaxes (of which there are undoubtedly plenty), the question becomes: *what* have these people experienced?

Attempts at objective investigations of UFO sightings, abductions, crashes, and so on have gone nowhere over the years. The physical evidence is usually ambiguous, pseudoscientific, or subsumed by the politics of this touchy topic. Yet we're still left with these "contactees" and their experience.

John Keel, mentor to many a UFO theoretician, posed the apt question in his book *UFOs: Operation Trojan Horse:* "How do you investigate something that doesn't exist?"

"The answer," Keel continued, "is that you investigate

and study the people who have experienced these things. You don't investigate them by checking their reliability. You study the medical and psychological effects of their experiences."

Essentially, that was William Bramley's approach. Not to investigate contemporary cases, but historical ones. Tracing the written record back to Mesopotamia and Sumeria, Bramley noted what people throughout history actually said about celestial phenomena, how they actually reacted to lights in the sky and "gods" flying down from heaven.

Bramley did not begin by looking for UFOs. He started with a single question, one that could be answered any number of ways, and finished with his Grand Theory. He got from the first point to the rather distant second much the same way many conspiracy researchers come to their unorthodox conclusions.

Clichés to the contrary, most conspiracy theories are born not of "paranoia" but from a kind of hopeful curiosity. Conspiracy theorists usually get started by trying to understand the inequities and horrors that have fogged the human spectacle for all of recorded time. Why are things this way, they wonder, and must they be this way?

"I got interested in the problem of war," says the matter-of-fact Bramley. As an undergraduate in the early 1970s, he majored in sociology at the University of California, Santa Barbara. He says he was "always what you'd call liberal," but never highly active politically, especially by the standards of that era. A decade after he graduated, whiling away his time wondering where his life was headed (he hadn't got his law degree by then), he succumbed to perpetual student syndrome and embarked on a book project that would be an extension of his collegiate focus.

"My idea was to kind of go through history and see

where you have people profiting and benefiting from war who were not directly involved in it. Just do a sociological study of that problem and maybe offer a solution to resolving it—some way to take the profit out of it."

Applying the intellect of a future lawyer, Bramley figured that all wars must have some motive. There had to be something in it for someone. He quickly shot down his own preliminary hypothesis, however. He came across numerous wars in history that appeared to be motivated by no tangible objectives.

"I started getting into these bizarre things where there didn't seem to be anything more than ideology," Bramley says. "You look for the profit and you look for the political advantage, and it's just not there. That's when you start to get into religion. So you ask, 'Where did these religions start?'

"I started looking into how these religions all seem to have a common nexus: secret societies," Bramley explains. "That's when things started getting a little off the track."

Secret societies: that inescapable theme. Bramley's "Gods of Eden" theory is a twist on the legend that secret societies have been the guiding force behind human history. There is, as Bramley notes, a religious component to secret societies and, therefore, to secret-society conspiracy theories. But even "secular" conspiracy theorists, who focus on such tangible (by comparison) entities as the U.S. intelligence community, attribute the qualities of a secret society to the CIA and like bodies.

Bramley turned up numerous historical personages linked to or belonging to secret societies. Freemasonry has been a preoccupation of more than a few American presidents: George Washington, Harry Truman, Theodore Roosevelt, Ronald Reagan, and others. Other politicians, too. Jesse Jackson, of all people, is a Masonic inductee.

While it's an axiom of conspiratoriology that secret

societies of one form or another are at the core of the story-behind-the-story, there's no agreement on who's behind the secret societies. Bramley's conjecture is that secret societies originated as a prehistoric cult of snake worshippers dedicated to freeing humanity from the snare of the brutal "Custodians." Defeated in this effort, the "Brotherhood of the Snake" was then infiltrated by Custodial agents, and turned against mankind. It survives today, in its diverse incarnations, as the secret societies that allegedly manipulate human events.

Bramley's theories of snake-worshipping cults and their relationship to secret societies are factual enough. The snake is one of the oldest religious symbols known to man. Hidden in the Bible is the surprising detail that Moses founded a snake-worshipping cult, and that a sect of Jews made sacrifices to the snake for several hundred years. As pagan symbols always are, the snake was redefined as a symbol of evil by modern religions. To continue their religion, snake cultists formed secret societies to dodge persecution. One of the few places the snake symbol survives with its original meaning, that of a healer, is on the emblem of the American Medical Association.

But we're getting ahead of ourselves again. Even when he hit on the secret society thesis, Bramley still had not uncovered the UFO connection that, unbeknownst to him, he was being drawn inexorably toward.

He hadn't been quite ready for his secret society revelation, so it was with a bit of trepidation that he pushed on through library stacks in search of details to flesh out this esoteric topic. All the secret societies—Masons, Rosicrucians, Persian and Asian sects, ancient mystery cults, pagans, snake worshippers—as different as they appeared on the surface, the more his intellectual adventure steamed ahead, the more Bramley found that the societies shared common beliefs and motifs.

The "All-Seeing Eye" was one frequently recurring

symbol. It now peers from the back of every U.S. dollar bill, as well as, oddly enough, from the emblem of the Marxist government of Ethiopia. Bramley found that, as all conspiracy mongers are aware, the eye is a sacred symbol in Freemasonry. But it goes back even further. It represented God's eye in early Christianity and the "Eye of Horus" in ancient Egyptian religion. The eye even appeared on early versions of the Confederate flag before the U.S. Civil War. Where was the link?

"Eventually you run into these things—people they call the gods," Bramley says. He traced mythology back to Sumerian tablets, then found that the same stories dated into prehistory. The characters in various stories had different names, but were disconcertingly similar.

"There were very human gods who used to fly around in the air," Bramley says. "Then, somewhere along the line, I read something about the ancient astronauts theory. Here were people who were speculating those gods were members of an extraterrestrial society."

When an amateur researcher finds himself whisked away by the chariots of the gods, that aged icon, credibility, begins to become a problem. "This is where I just ended my research," Bramley says. "I didn't want to get into it."

Bramley was not the first to conflate ancient mythology with modern UFOlogy. As Keel notes, "Many leading UFOlogists suspect that innumerable historical incidents branded as religious phenomena may actually be misunderstood UFO activity."

The Bible is the source of several such incidents. Ezekiel's "wheel," which according to the scriptural account dispatched four odd-looking creatures upon its descent from the sky, is most often cited, but there are quite a few others.

The "pillar of fire" that guided the Israelites out of

Egypt is another bizarre celestial phenomena recounted in the Bible. Elijah, another major prophet, was watched over by guardian angels in the form of flying fireballs and was finally carried away in a "chariot of fire." Could the brimstone barrage that flattened Sodom and Gomorrah have been a nuclear device from an alien spacecraft? And just what was that "burning bush" that held such detailed conversations with Moses, anyway?

No less an authority than Carl Sagan, who is one of the most dogmatic and—for some unknown reason—respected UFO debunkers, once called for an historical investigation of ancient myths to see if they yielded clues to early contact with extraterrestrial visitors.

These close encounters of the allegorical kind are not exclusive to the Bible. Almost every culture features religious myths involving strange creatures, gods, and chariots from the sky. There are innumerable explanations for the frequency of such stories. Fertile human imagination is certainly one. Take them at face value, however, and they are what they are: UFO reports.

While what we think of today as the UFO phenomenon began in 1947, the historical record of unusual heavenly happenings runs uninterrupted. Joseph Smith, founder of the Mormon church, received his life's mission in a visit from a heavenly messenger. The Book of Mormon is supposedly a translation of writings Smith found on a set of mysterious tablets he unearthed at a location given to him by this visitor. Also in the nineteenth century, coincidentally (or maybe not), there were a series of unexplained "airships" sighted over parts of the United States.

Charles Fort, the brilliant turn-of-the-century writer who invented the category of "unexplained phenomena," catalogued a handful of nineteenth-century "lights in the sky" incidents, which read exactly like more recent UFO sightings, even though Fort was writing over thirty years before the term "UFO" was concocted.

Fort's wonderful books dealt with the unexplained phenomena of nature—events that science refused to explain, because they did not fit. Fort didn't try to explain them, or debunk them. All belief systems exclude something, he thought. Strange phenomena were proof to Fort that there is a deeper reality that science has excluded.

Fort was an inspiration to Keel, who founded the New York "Fortean Society." Bramley, on the other hand, didn't discover Fort until he was into the third draft of *Gods of Eden,* and when I met him he hadn't even heard of John Keel. His journey to the heart of the conspiracy was a solo flight.

Bramley stopped his spare-time quest when he found no escape from the "ancient astronauts" theory. He came across so many of these historical UFO tales that he figured going on would only get him into trouble. After a hiatus from his project, Bramley began to squirm with curiosity. "I finally confronted it and said, 'That's strange, but that's what it seems to be.' "

Having traced the origins of secret societies back to age-old tales of aerobatic humanoid gods, Bramley decided to work forward again. He wanted to see if he could track the secret society network, the "Brotherhood of the Snake," from ancient times to the present, correlating its beliefs and activities with historical UFO stories. "And I was just stunned," Bramley says. "Because I could."

To do Bramley's book-length argument justice in a short summary is not possible. A selected example will have to suffice, even though the one I'm going to choose is one Bramley is sensitive about. His theories on the Black Death of the Middle Ages have been a popular topic of discussion on radio programs that have featured him as a guest. Bramley doesn't like to see them taken out of context.

"Anybody who has read the book, by the time they get to the chapter on the Black Death, they've understood all that stuff beforehand and they could see how I could arrive at that conclusion. But if you just launch into that with somebody who's not exposed to the earlier stuff, it becomes totally unreal to them," Bramley warns.

With that caveat—and with the hope that anyone reading *this* book already expects unreal conclusions—here is Bramley's theory on the Black Death, the plague that wiped out a sizable slice of the European population in the thirteenth and fourteenth centuries.

The generally accepted explanation is that the plague was spread by rats in the unimaginably unhygienic conditions of the times. Bramley's research contradicts the "rodent theory." A "minority of cases seem to be related to the presence of vermin," he found. Far more common, his research revealed, were reports of odoriferous "mists" preceding outbreaks of the disease. Also coinciding with certain outbreaks, Bramley discovered, were—lo and behold—reports of strange lights in the sky.

The foreboding aerial anomalies were described in contemporary writings as "meteors" or "comets." Bramley points out that back then anything moving across the sky not identifiable as a bird or the sun was called a "comet."

These "comets" left deadly trails that killed trees and vegetation as well as people. Bramley connects these accounts with Mesopotamian writings that mention flying "gods" who scorched the landscape, and quotes numerous historical passages describing "mists" and "fogs" that were blamed for outbreaks of disease going back to ancient Greece, where Hippocrates himself advocated communal bonfires as a method of clearing the air of the noxious clouds.

Other historical sources uncovered by the scholarly barrister from San Jose indicate that the mists were exuded by mysterious "demons" who strolled into villages clad in black, wielding instruments usually referred to as "scythes." The scythes, Bramley speculates, may actually have been some sort of spraying device that spewed toxins.

The "Grim Reaper" caricature derives from those descriptions. Seasoned UFO aficionados will recognize the archetype of the "Men in Black," those macabre agents whose alleged appearance often coincides with saucer sightings.

From those accounts, Bramley surmised that the plague was the result of something other than poor medieval municipal sanitation services. It was a deliberate act of biological warfare perpetrated by the Custodians. The ranchers, for some reason known only to themselves, were reducing the herd.

That's the best example I could find of how Bramley links historical events to the postulated airborne superrace. The plague episode is exemplary of his thesis that, as Charles Fort put it, "we are property." Bramley spent nearly a decade of his life devising this thesis and accruing evidence to support it. Then came decision time.

"I had to decide whether I wanted to publish all of this," Bramley laughs. "I mean, it could be embarrassing to be associated with ideas like that!"

For others, it could be more than embarrassing. I interviewed a pilot who claimed to have been employed by "a number of government agencies" in Southeast Asia. In his contact with various friends in the military and intelligence communities, he became aware that the U.S. government has already made contact with an extraterrestrial race, and that there were over one hundred people at a saucer landing on a U.S. Air Force base outside of London, England, in 1980.

He wondered, "If this stuff is going on, why don't I know more about it?" He "called in a few favors" from his shadowy buddies, and pieced together a story of massive government cover-ups and "programming of the population for the last forty years." After he dared to give a few public lectures on the topic, he was called in by his employer—he was then a cargo pilot—and asked, "Do you really believe this stuff?" He said that he did. He was fired.

I haven't given this particular fellow's name because he has a new job with a different company, and I have no desire to cost him that one, too. Suffice to say that he bears one of the best-known names in aviation. In any case, he is but one advocate of the widespread "government cover-up" UFO conspiracy theory.

It is true that the U.S. government took a strong interest in the UFO phenomenon. The now famous Air Force "Project Blue Book" compiled a thick compendium of UFO incidents. An eyebrow-cocking footnote to Project Blue Book: Despite its astonishing thoroughness, nowhere does it mention the "Roswell incident," the first and most exhaustively researched "saucer crash." Not surprisingly, there has never been definitive verification that a spacecraft, or any craft, crashed as alleged near Roswell, New Mexico, on July 2, 1947. But something weird did happen there, and the military at the time took more than a passing interest. The case still gets occasional publicity. Yet the Blue Book files are silent about it.

Government agencies have aroused ominous suspicions, perhaps rightly so, by going out of their way to discredit UFO reports. In 1954, the CIA set up the "Robertson Panel," named for its chairman, Dr. H. P. Robertson. The committee was at least a spiritual ancestor to the Warren Commission, as by all accounts it had reached its conclusions in advance.

Somewhat more candid than its Kennedy assassination counterpart, the Robertson Panel openly advocated a policy of "debunking" the UFO phenomenon with the stated aim of reducing public "susceptibility to hostile propaganda." The panel's frankness may or may not have something to do with the fact that, unlike the Warren Commission, which thrust its report with authority into the public forum, the Robertson Panel's full findings were secret for twenty-five years.

One of the most thoughtful and credible (there's that word again) UFO researchers, French astronomer Jacques Vallee, believes that the government may have good reason to obscure the truth behind UFOs. Like John Keel, Vallee sees little evidence to convince him that UFOs are probes from another planet. His scenario is even more frightening than the dark theories of malevolent extraterrestrial superbeings propounded by the reclusive William Bramley.

"UFOs are real," Vallee wrote in his 1979 manifesto, *Messengers of Deception.* "They are an application of psychotronic technology; that is, they are physical devices used to affect human consciousness."

Vallee takes Keel's advice and delves into the psychology of UFO contactees, and the cults they form and that form around them. The contactees are victims, he proffers, used by some controlling power to effect deep social changes in human society.

It is true that there are totalitarian overtones, and sometimes more than overtones, to the beliefs of many contactees. What's even more sinister, some of the early contactees, particularly the founders of a movement called "I AM" in the 1930s, were open fascists and anti-Semites who draped pro-Hitlerian "Jewish conspiracy" ideology in an extraterrestrial cloak. "I AM" was a forerunner to the more recently fashionable "New Age."

William Bramley doesn't fit in there anywhere. I've been cautioned to "be careful" when dealing with these suspiciously nazified UFO ideas, but to me what is remarkable about William Bramley is that he is the opposite of a zealot, ideologue, or zombie-faced cultist. His politics are, if anything, mainstream progressive. When last I spoke to him, he doubted that he would bother to write a follow-up to *Gods of Eden*, so casual is his commitment to the UFO cause. His desire for personal secrecy is a discretion to shield his "real life," not the clandestine tactic of a cryptototalitarian.

Bramley is interesting precisely because he is so boring. His is a normal intellect that came into contact with abnormal aspects of reality few people have the energy or courage to confront. When we do confront them, the world becomes, to borrow the title of a John Keel book, a "Disneyland of the Gods." Given how little human beings comprehend of what's really going on out there, anything, to the adventurous mind, can seem possible. The danger is not in trying to know more, no matter how wild the attempt, but in the conviction that knowledge is all but complete, with only details left to fill in. What we know is insignificant, and there is a human hunger for answers. A healthy hunger.

If a logical, meticulous trial lawyer like the pseudonymous William Bramley can reach such an outrageous conclusion after seven years of research, it proves not that he's crazy or a fascist, but that the limits of our understanding are exceeded only by the boundaries of curiosity.

5

THE INVISIBLE GOVERNMENT

> *Can you look in the mirror, or into the faces of your children or grandchildren, and say that you were too busy to become involved? Are you not willing to give your time and money when our Founding Fathers pledged their lives, their fortunes and their sacred honor to oppose the New World Order?*
>
> GARY ALLEN
> *Say "No" to the New World Order*

Much has changed for the John Birch Society since 1960, when it was the nation's most fearsome regiment of right-wing militants. They worked to impeach Earl Warren. They called Eisenhower a dirty Red. They staged a campaign to repeal the income tax. No more. By the late 1980s, the Birch Society was something closer to a preservation society of parochialism in an America long since mutated into a cultural black widow's web.

"There's hope that we can turn this thing around," says Jack McManus, the Birch Society's spokesman since 1973 (and a member since 1964). "We can accomplish the goals of saving our country and saving the constitutional republic our founding fathers gave us. And one of the reasons for hope is the fact that it is a conspiracy."

"**I**'ve been looking for a way to build and sell a house in a biblical way, without having to charge interest," mused the man behind the counter at the John Birch Society bookstore. He was a chunky fellow in a flannel shirt and a smile that said "Southern hospitality," even though he was in northern California. He held six paper dollars in his hand, fanning them like playing cards. They were the receipts from his one sale of the day, and he had nowhere to put them. No cash register, no counter, no change, except for a box of coins. It's a bright and clean little shop, uncontaminated by customers. "When you look at it, really, in this country, with all the interest we have to pay, we're all slaves," he said.

The gray-haired lady who'd stopped by to chat, looking like she'd come straight from telling Tom Sawyer to whitewash the picket fence, grabbed the six paper dollars in his hand and ruffled them disdainfully.

"*This* is credit," she warned. "See here where it says, 'Federal Reserve Note.' If they want to do away with credit, they'll have to do away with *that.*"

The "American Opinion" bookstores, though not actually operated by the society, are the only outlets devoted exclusively to Birch-sanctioned literature. So ready are they to spread the word, that a good chunk of their stock lists an asking price of "free." The four hundred American Opinion stores across America will still take your six bucks for a crisp new copy of *The Blue Book of the John Birch Society,* now in its twenty-third printing. They sell flags, too, and that brings in a little more of that paper money.

The folks who work in the shops—it just seems right to call them "shops" and "folks"—often work there for free. They're usually downright friendly. Their compensation is conversation, even in little bits. A tad here about Citibank forcing South Dakota to repeal its usury laws so it can set up a national credit card business. A morsel there about getting the truth out to the young generation, because they're the ones who need it most.

If not a conspiracy, the evils Birchers see perpetrated against our national heritage would be unstoppable forces of history. The America of John Birch and Robert Welch would be left pathetically in the dusty past.

Robert Henry Winborne Welch, Jr., Massachusetts candy and jelly magnate, was the founder and self-proclaimed "dictatorial boss" of the John Birch Society. John Morrison Birch, military intelligence officer, never knew of the society's existence. He was killed in 1945, at age twenty-seven, by Chinese Communists while on a spying mission in North China.

Welch, who died in January of 1985 at the age of eighty-five, was born in North Carolina. He claimed a lineage of farmers and Baptist preachers going back to 1720. He moved to Boston in 1919, after an eight-year education at the University of North Carolina, the U.S. Naval Academy, and Harvard Law School. He never received his law degree. He went into business and became one of the country's largest candy makers. Throughout his career, politics, not sucrose, was his passion.

Welch had long been fascinated by Birch, authoring a biography of the fundamentalist Baptist missionary turned anti-Communist spy, four years before founding the society. Welch never knew Birch, but for his original society "Council" Welch selected Lt. Gen. Charles B. Stone, III, Birch's military unit commander. Welch decided that Birch was not merely a spy killed on an espionage mission in hostile territory. He was the first American soldier to die in World War III, the struggle against world communism. If there was ever any doubt that Birch would have agreed, his parents gave the society their public support.

The John Birch Society began when Welch invited eleven well-to-do, conservative industrialists to a meeting in Indianapolis, on December 8, 1958. There, he harangued them for two days with the "incontrovertible and deadly" truth that had been cooking in his fudge maker's brain for years. On the first day, he outlined the aims of "the Communist conspiracy." On the second day, he detailed his plans for a new organization dedicated to battling the alleged conspiracy in the United States political arena. Curiously, Welch acknowledged that this plan involved using the same techniques used by the Communist conspirators themselves: letter-writing campaigns, propaganda publications, and front organizations.

These speeches were published as the *Blue Book*, often called Welch's *Mein Kampf*, which quickly became required reading for all Birch initiates. But it was an unpublished book, which, when the media discovered it, made Welch one of the country's most visible and controversial figures. That book was called *The Politician*, and it, too, is sometimes called Welch's *Mein Kampf*. (Likening Welch to Hitler was not uncommon in those days, and though he, like all Birchers, considered such rhetoric yet another element of the Communist smear campaign against him, his own statements about the Birch Society being a "monolithic organization" under "complete authoritative control," with Robert Welch as the authority, invited the comparison.)

The Politician was the book in which Welch made his instantly notorious allegations that President Dwight D. Eisenhower was a Communist agent, saying he had been "planted in (the presidency) by the Communists." He also called General George Catlett Marshall (he of the famous Plan), "a conscious, deliberate, dedicated agent of the Soviet conspiracy." He doled out likewise vituperation to numerous other political figures.

Even Barry Goldwater, a friend and admirer of Welch, advised Welch to "burn" the privately circulated manuscript, but Welch didn't listen and his unfinished book, which he claimed had nothing to do with the John Birch Society, turned this frumpy, bald little businessman into a national celebrity.

Celebrity was nothing Welch craved. He conceived of the John Birch Society as, if not a secret society, then at least one shy of media scrutiny. It took two years before any national media even noticed the society's existence. Welch himself has been described as a painfully shy man with absolutely no gift for public speaking, an odd trait in light of the hundreds of speeches he gave in his career as Bircher in chief.

His talks were nothing more than readings from his pamphlets and books. He'd drone on for up to three hours, convinced that his message was so important that listeners would endure any hardship to hear it. He once lectured to a group of businessmen in Florida in an enclosed lecture hall, forbidding, for some reason, any windows to be opened. He was dreadfully doctrinaire, refusing to answer questions from the audience when he found the questions too pointed.

Welch was a cantankerous sort, given to complaining about his bad accommodations when traveling and his incompetent underlings back at the office, but he could be oblivious to the oppressive conditions of sweltering gymnasiums and lecture halls where he delivered his gospel, eyes rarely glancing up from the text.

Unlikely as it seems, celebrity is what Welch got, and the Birch Society, embodied in his presence, became an object of national fascination. One newspaper asserted that the Birchers "provoked the most heated public controversy since the heyday of the late Senator Joseph R. McCarthy."

One of the most furious melees involved the Army's major general Edwin A. Walker. A highly decorated veteran, Walker was fired from his command of the 24th Infantry in Augsburg, Germany, in 1961, when an overseas newspaper reported that he was indoctrinating his troops with Birchian ideas. He later resigned from the Army.

Welch's *The Life of John Birch* was required reading for soldiers in Walker's "special warfare" program designed to teach them proper ideals of Americanism. Walker had also been lecturing his troops on who the real Americans were. He called former president Harry Truman "definitely pink," along with Eleanor Roosevelt, Edward R. Murrow, and Eric Sevareid.

This was the same General Walker who, two years later, would duck a bullet flying through the window of his Dallas home, allegedly fired by one Lee Harvey Oswald. If Walker staged his own attempted murder, and he may have—he was the original source for *the* claim that Oswald fired the shot—then the Birch Society itself is implicated in a significant and sinister conspiracy of its own.

For Robert Welch, celebrity brought criticism, even from friends. Barry Goldwater publicly disavowed Welch's more extreme positions, particularly the slur on Eisenhower contained in *The Politician*. Welch's allegations about Eisenhower's loyalty also led the conservative National Association of Manufacturers to censure the Birch Society, even though a Birch council member was also on the NAM board.

The Birch Society still protests that Welch's remarks on Eisenhower's alleged crimson tint were taken out of context, suggested only as a possible explanation for Eisenhower's upsettingly moderate (to Birchers) policies. Birchers insist that Welch generously granted Eisenhower the benefit of the doubt. He allowed that likable ol' Ike could have been a mere dupe or an outright fool, rather than a dedicated Communist agent.

Off the record, some of Welch's acquaintances questioned his practice of labeling everyone and everything not in sympathy with the society as part of the conspiracy. "We should use a rifle instead of a shotgun, perhaps," suggested one.

The John Birch Society still takes its shots, but no longer struts into the saloon guns drawn. "If you measured our strength in numbers, we're not doing well anywhere," says McManus. "But anyone who says anything and means it sounds like a crowd."

The society's headquarters moved in July 1989 to Appleton, Wisconsin, hometown of Birchian tragic hero senator Joseph McCarthy. "A delightful irony," quips McManus. The home base had been previously divided between San Diego, California (lair to many a right-winger), and Belmont, Massachusetts. Membership is loaded into places like Idaho, which has twenty percent more Birchers per capita than the union's other states and sixty John Birch Society chapters, at last report. There are eight chapters in Oklahoma City, with fifteen to twenty members apiece. Total Birch membership is reported to be down to about fifty thousand (from a high of twice that many in the 1960s) in three thousand chapters.

But the Birch Society is not letting itself die out like a clan of Shakers. At ten summer camps spread through the country, the society enrolls about one thousand children and teenagers. They're given a regime of softball, swimming, and conspiracy.

"We've got truth on our side, and there are more good people in this country than bad," says Jack McManus. "History is made by the dedicated few."

McManus's words would be anathema to political scientists who see history as a process of competing views struggling to reach an accommodation. History as a creation of the "dedicated few" is the mentality of crusaders and conspiracy theorists. In the idealized vision of political science, the "process" is paramount, in which two political parties, one "liberal" and one "conservative," share a total commitment to fair and open debate. Within that agreed-upon framework, they smooth their differences into a consensus. The product of this process, like noodles oozing from a pasta maker, is national policy.

John Bunzel, author of the 1967 book *Anti-Politics in America,* explained the right-wing conspiratorial mindset as opposed to that seamless system; therefore, it is not only antidemocratic, but "antipolitical" as well.

"Early in our history fear of a 'democracy of the people' was the motivating force behind those who lashed out against what they felt was the 'conspiracy of the immigrants,'" Bunzel wrote. Conspiracy mongers were motivated, he says, by a loathing of immigrants and the horror that their "foreign" culture would subvert the American way of life, whatever that may be.

Fear of foreign influence was the motivation for early "nativist" political parties, of which the so-called "Know-Nothings" were the first. Was the root of revulsion at foreigners a fear of "democracy of the people"? The question is rather more complicated than Bunzel makes it out to be.

The Know-Nothing Party was founded in the early part of the nineteenth century by writer Ned Buntline, whose only other achievement was fictionalizing the exploits of a cowboy named William Cody to create the American Hero "Buffalo Bill." Named the American Republican Party, they, like the Birchers more than a century later, modeled themselves along the agoraphobic lines of a secret society. When asked about the party's activities, a member was supposed to say, "I know nothing."

The Know-Nothings had one policy: to ban immigrants, especially Catholics, from holding any kind of public office or becoming U.S. citizens. The Vatican, they believed, was organizing a conspiracy to subvert the United States from within and thus "extend its sphere of influence." A typical pamphlet, "Startling Facts for Na-

tive Americans Called Know-Nothings," explicated how
the scourge of "Popery," led by its "Popish" priests,
would accomplish its goals.

"There is abundant proof," the pamphlet asserted,
"that a foreign conspiracy has been organized in Catholic
Europe to embarrass and overthrow the institutions of
this country. . . . The valley of the Mississippi has been
mapped as well as surveyed by the Jesuits of the Vatican,
and Popish cardinals are rejoicing in the prospect of the
entire subjection of this land of freedom and intelligence
to Papal supremacy."

The "Papists" realized that America was becoming the
"center of civilization," the Know-Nothings surmised,
and set their "Popish" designs on it to "compensate" for
their "losses in the old world," by conquering the new
one.

Know-Nothing anti-Catholic fixation never died,
though the party faded away. Manic Christian comic
books drawn by Jack Chick show the pope as a high-tech
anti-Christ, with a supercomputer keeping tabs on good
Christians, who are hunted down and tortured into re-
cantation.

The Know-Nothing Party in its day extended its influence beyond comic books—or whatever their nineteenth-
century equivalent would have been. No fewer than seventy-five Know-Nothings served in Congress, many
more in state legislatures. Millard Filmore, a former president, tried to reclaim the White House in 1856 as an
"American Party" candidate. He scored twenty-one percent of the vote.

Did all this success come to the nativists because of a
widespread fear of "democracy of the people"? If there
had ever been such a "people's democracy," as Bunzel
thought there was, there would be no nativism. The an-
ticonspiratorial struggle was not so much a struggle to
exclude certain people from the political process, as it was
a battle over control of political institutions, the perma-

nent institutions of power already in place in the then-fledgling U.S.A. They were unabashed servants of those institutions. They may have been antidemocratic, at least with regards to "democracy of the people," but they were not antipolitical. They were expressly political and, like the McCarthyites, used the political tools of the American system.

"Advocating the largest freedom in matters of religion, we view no sect with prejudice or favor. We are organized for political purposes and cannot recognize the existence of sects," the Know-Nothings wrote. The Know-Nothing claim to be bigotry free finds an echo in 1990, when Louisiana politician David Duke, a former Ku Klux Klan grand wizard, claims no animosity toward blacks or Jews. He merely seeks to protect white citizens—the citizens already in control of the nation's political and economic system.

Historical treatment of Know-Nothings as a prototypical "hate group," and the media's handling of Duke as a persistent, if noxious, outsider given to lying about his own racism miss a critical point. Conspiracy theories are not an aberration in American history. Conspiracy theories *are* American history.

Some form of "right-wing" conspiracy theory—which usually means a conspiracy theory in which the conspirators are some breed of social outsiders—has always been the fabric weaving together the sheer cloth of American political unity. To the Know-Nothings, the outsiders were Catholics. To the Birchers, they were Communists. To Christian fundamentalists, they are "secular humanists." To ultraright survivalists, they are Jews. In the common parlance of acceptable political debate, they are "special interests," which usually means minorities and ethnic groups. The conspiracy theory is constant.

The difference between mainstream Reaganite conservatives and John Birchers is that besides the "fringe groups" none dare call it conspiracy theory. The Birchers do dare, and by calling it conspiracy they make their targets not only outsiders, but insiders.

"We believe that the conspiracy we're fighting is a conspiracy above Communism," says McManus. "Communism is its chief arm, but at the heart of it is a powerful clique of individuals that mean to rule the world. They've created a lot of 'isms.' Communism, socialism, syndicalism, taking power with labor unions. Other isms."

The Birch version of the Illuminati story is actually one of the yarn's most sober spinnings. Adam Weishaupt founded the Illuminati on May 1, 1776, "which is why Communists and socialists celebrate May Day." Concerned more with contemporary politics than history, the Birch Society doesn't bother filling in the fluorescent colors that other tellers of the Illuminati tale swab on liberally.

Gary Allen touched on the Illuminati in his definitive rendition of the Birch theory, *None Dare Call It Conspiracy*. He discusses antecedents to the supposedly Illuminist Council on Foreign Relations, particularly the "secret society" of the Round Table established, Allen says, in the will of British colonialist diamond king Cecil Rhodes.

"It should be noted that the originator of this type of secret society was Adam Weishaupt, the monster who founded the Order of Illuminati . . . for the purpose of conspiracy to control the world. The role of Weishaupt's Illuminists in such horrors as the Reign of Terror is unquestioned, and the techniques of the Illuminati have long been recognized as models for Communist methodology."

The Illuminati, however, weren't always players in Birchian conspiracy theory. At the outset, Robert Welch was content simply to talk about "the Communist conspiracy" without delving into any more detail than that.

Allen apparently picked up the tale from Welch, who gleaned his ideas about the "monster" Weishaupt and his cabal from the writings of Nesta Webster, Victorian England's conspiratologist in residence, and the eighteenth-century journalist John Robinson.

For Welch and Gary Allen, "Illuminati" was too esoteric a term. They preferred "Insiders." In looking for a properly descriptive buzzword, Welch rejected "Luminist," but almost settled on the puzzling "Supercom" (apparently short for Super Communist). He dropped "Supercom" when he realized that its similarity to "Superman" gave it "a comic-page flavor which was not helpful."

The Insiders are the spiritual descendants of the Illuminati, inheritors of the conspiratorial crest. They have names like Rothschild, Ford, Morgan, and Rockefeller. "An *Insider* is consciously a member of an international Master Conspiracy of long standing," Welch wrote.

The most important of the Insiders' regular meeting places in the conspiracy's modern era is the Henry Pratt House, on West 68th Street in Manhattan, home to the Council on Foreign Relations (CFR). Since its founding in the aftermath of World War I, the CFR has been the preeminent intermediary between the world of high finance, big oil, corporate elitism, and the U.S. government. Its members slide smoothly into cabinet-level jobs in Republican and Democratic administrations. The policies promulgated in its quarterly journal, *Foreign Affairs*, become U.S. government policy.

Through the CFR and its offshoot, David Rockefeller's Trilateral Commission, the Insiders program a destructive course for America.

The goal of the Council on Foreign Relations is to establish a "One World Government," or a "New World Order," according to Birch theory. Sounds pleasant, but the reality, Birchers say, will be a commie/illuminoid nightmare with the Insiders in charge. The grand design of the Insiders is nothing short of total world power.

World government will redistribute the world's wealth among all nations, resulting in "a reduced standard of living for Americans." Worse yet, there will "no longer be any freedom of movement, freedom of worship, private property rights, free speech, or the right to publish." Finally, the New World Order will "be enforced by agents of the world government in the same way that agents of the Kremlin enforce their rule throughout Soviet Russia today."

Intimidating prospects, made more so by the council's own proclamations. Mixed in among articles on Peruvian political upheavals, international monetary policy, and East-West relations, *Foreign Affairs* occasionally carries a piece like "The Hard Road to World Order," which appeared in the April 1974 issue and was authored by Richard N. Gardner of Columbia University, sending tremors quaking through the Birch Society's ranks.

"In short, the 'house of world order' will have to be built from the bottom up rather than from the top down," says Professor Gardner. "An end run around national sovereignty, eroding it piece by piece, will accomplish much more than the old-fashioned frontal assault."

Gardner goes on to describe as "hopeful" the fact that "technological, economic, and political interests" are dragging individual governments toward some form of world government or world order. No matter that Gardner calls for a "world structure that secures peace, advances human rights, and provides the conditions for economic progress."

Nor that another CFR member protests that the council is an idyllic "marketplace of ideas related to American foreign policy . . . an exciting, creative, and intellectually stimulating institution," whose opposition comes from those egg-sucking unfortunates "not invited to be members." The Birchers are having none of it.

"The reality of socialism is that it is not a movement to divide the wealth, as its superrich promoters would have us believe, but a movement to consolidate and control wealth," wrote Gary Allen. "If you control the apex, the power pinnacle of a world government, you have the ultimate monopoly."

In *None Dare Call It Conspiracy,* Allen details how multinational cartels literally built the Soviet Empire. "The Federal Reserve–CFR Insiders began pushing to open up Communist Russia to U.S. traders soon after the revolution."

He details how the Rockefellers' Standard Oil and Chase Manhattan Bank bought into the young Soviet Union as early as 1922, purchasing huge swaths of oil fields and setting up an American-Russian Chamber of Commerce. With these early investments, Allen asserts, the Insiders literally purchased control of the Communist world. Their master plan was to use socialism, with its centralized economic control, to take over the rest of the world and set up their "One World Government," a "New World Order."

What ended up happening looks like exactly the opposite. The capitalist world took over the communist countries. But the end result is still the "New World Order." The Birchers see the whole series of shocking events as a scam.

Former CFR member George Bush and his military machinations in the Middle East are especially alarming to the Birchers, designed as they are to create a "New World Order."

"Remember, war is big government's best friend," said McManus on a radio interview during the Saudi Arabian troop buildup in late 1990. Most troubling to McManus was the role of the United Nations in guiding the operation—"the U.N., founded by a pack of Communists." If

Gary Allen were alive, he would share McManus's revulsion.

Allen, who died in 1986, was a former Stanford University football player, high school teacher, and self-proclaimed practicing leftist until he ran into John Stormer. The aptly named Stormer (whom we'll meet more formally in the next chapter) was a hard-line conservative polemicist whose book, *None Dare Call It Treason*, was the Goldwater Republican's bible. Allen was an instant convert; apparently, his reverence for Stormer's work was so great that Allen named his own most famous book—the above-mentioned *None Dare Call It Conspiracy*—after Stormer's.

Stormer's book contained the usual and numerous indictments of the CFR, but lacked the Illuminati angle. Allen added that later, inspired by Robert Welch. Stormer, in turn, derived much of his CFR information from Dan Smoot, a former FBI agent whose "Dan Smoot Report" newsletter continually updated the machinations of pinkos in power. Smoot's book *The Invisible Government* was one of the first to lay down the anti-CFR law. In his reasonably dry (for this sort of thing) account of the CFR network, Smoot never goes into the "Round Table" legacy to which the CFR, according to Allen, owes its existence. When Smoot wrote his book, the Birch theory hadn't developed its intricate nuances. Nonetheless, he does go into considerable detail about the "interlock" between the CFR and a formidable list of liberal organizations, including usual suspects such as the American Civil Liberties Union (ACLU), the National Association for the Advancement of Colored People (NAACP), Americans for Democratic Action, and SANE Nuclear Policy, Inc. The latter organization was connected with Bertrand Russell, whom Smoot calls a "British pro-Communist socialist." He also cites, approvingly, a newspaper editorial calling Americans for

Democratic Action "an organization strikingly like the British Fabian Socialists."

Birch-inspired or approved writings never go too far in singling out the "British" as masterminds of the conspiracy, but occasionally references to the conspiracy's "Anglophile" bent do crop up. Names like Cecil Rhodes and Lord Alfred Milner ("front man for the Rothschilds") figure prominently. The Anglophobic strains running through the Birch conspiracy theory erupt to the surface in the thinking of other theorists, particularly Lyndon LaRouche. As the Birch theory developed, it settled comfortably into that tradition.

The Birchers do not shy away from naming prominent Jews as conspirators, but, on an official level anyway, they recoil from any expressions of anti-Semitism. One former John Birch Society employee has criticized the Birch leadership for tolerating anti-Semites in the society's ranks so long as bigoted members don't spread their views around publicly or embarrass the organization. The society sees the charges of anti-Semitism and bigotry as part of an organized smear campaign, which peaked along with the society's notoriety in the early 1960s.

"Our Jewish members were very upset when they heard we were anti-Semites, and our black members said, 'This is ridiculous,' " says Jack McManus. "The smear campaign did its work. It was very effective, and we realize that."

During Welch's reign, several anti-Semites who later went on to become prominent in the always-active field of Jew hatred either left the John Birch Society in disillusionment with the society's refusal to attack the Jews, or in direct conflict with Robert Welch over the same issue. Willis Carto, who went on to found the Liberty Lobby and the Institute for Historical Review, was a member in the early days and wrote a couple of articles for Welch's *American Opinion* magazine. Others included William Pierce, who quit the society to link up with George Lincoln Rockwell's American Nazi Party, and Ben Klassen, author of *The White Man's Bible*, who upon quitting called the society "a smokescreen for the Jews." Paramilitary rightist (he founded the Minutemen) Robert DePugh was kicked out of the society in 1964, when the Birchers realized that he was plotting guerrilla warfare. And Tom Metzger, skinhead leader and former Ku Klux Klan grand dragon who somehow became the designated hater on national television talk shows such as "Oprah," "Donahue," "The Morton Downey, Jr., Show" and "Geraldo" (Metzger was on stage during the legendary Geraldo Rivera nose-breaking extravaganza), was also a Bircher for a while.

Though the society has fingered the Anti-Defamation League (ADL) of B'nai B'rith as an arm of the conspiracy because of the way the ADL monitors right-wing groups, it did start a "Jewish Society of Americanists" to make Jewish right-wingers feel more at home.

Welch and his heirs in the John Birch Society leadership have been scrupulous in avoiding any perceptible hints of anti-Semitism. Whether that's just a P.R. ploy I can't say, but I don't believe so.

Warns Jack McManus, "No one has anything to fear from us but the Establishment."

The irony of the ultraconservative Birch Society's rabid hatred for the Establishment is that the Establishment is by its nature conservative. By the time of the "Reagan revolution," conservatives had mastered the subterranean craft of public relations. The folks-and-shops American provincialism that binds the rank and file of the John Birch Society became official P.R. of the administration. Savvy conservatives learned to use conspiracy theory in subtle ways, resurrecting the nativism of the nineteenth century, adapting it shrewdly to the configurations of a mass, technological society. As they came to political power, their Birch-style "Insider" theory became more than a searching explanation for the puzzling American predicament. It is a tool of power, the quasi-official conspiracy theory of the United States.

6

NONE DARE CALL IT
TREASON

*The United States has had more light
than any other country on this planet.
God has placed his hand upon America.*

JIMMY SWAGGART

In a crisp blue blazer, sporting a smartly trimmed white handlebar mustache, the old man looked like a colonel from the First World War. John Stormer saw him approach. It was 4:30 in the afternoon. Stormer had finished a lecture a few minutes earlier. He'd been lecturing without much interruption since 10:30 that morning. He'd start up again after dinner.

He was taking a well-deserved break, alone in the corner of a large function room at the Sheraton-Lincoln Hotel in Worcester, Massachusetts. Worcester was but one stop on a perpetual tour with his traveling seminar "Understanding the Times." Each two-day conference may feature up to fourteen hour-long speeches by Stormer. He lectures on the encroaching presence of international communism, the Communist influence in the U.S. government, media, and education system, and what Americans can do to combat the menace.

Mr. Mustache, the colonel, was eager to consume that message, and to laud the man who served it to him. "That was a great speech," said the colonel in a crackling voice, congratulatory hand extended. "And you know, Jack McManus always says if you want to know what's really goin' on in politics, you've got to see who's writin' the checks. And who's writin' the checks is the Federal Reserve!"

A tall, good-humored, round-faced fellow, Stormer laughed nervously. He seemed slightly embarrassed. "Well, yes. That's part of it," he proffered. Stormer shook the old man's hand and sent him on his way.

I was sitting near Stormer, watching him converse with a parade of hand shakers and back slappers. All very routine, but that particular exchange surprised me for its mundanity. I'd expected a more ardent affirmation of this admirer's antifed outburst.

That the Federal Reserve occupies the nucleus of a conspiracy to siphon America's wealth from the working man to the wealthy few is an article of faith among denizens of the conservative milieu to whom Stormer is a demigod. His rivet-hard right-wing rhetoric is crystallized in lectures titled with ominous queries: "Why Are Our Leaders Betraying Us?" "How Do They Plan to Get Us?" and "What Can We Do to Return America to Its Heritage as a Nation under God?"

Yet in those speeches, Stormer breezes by such conspiratorial superstars as the Council on Foreign Relations (CFR) and the Rockefeller family as if they were incidental players in the game of world power. He was almost embarrassed to mention them at all.

The quick and otherwise forgettable exchange between John Stormer and the colonel, I thought, was a succinct demonstration of a division in conservatism. There are hard-core conspiratorialists, the Birch Society most famously. They are "fringe groups." But their conspiracy theory in a sort of acid-washed form has become mainstream political currency. The softer version of the Birch/nativist theory has become a staple of Republican administration propaganda. The proponents of the more palat-

able version of the theory get themselves taken more seriously than the Birchers. They get the message out.
Televangelists such as Pat Robertson, who ran for president in 1988, and the now-discredited Jimmy Swaggart
had a ready audience of millions. Most of their viewers
were, I would guess, honestly religious people. Their sincere Christian beliefs were easily exploited by the likes of
Robertson and Swaggart, and more lately Larry Lea, who
calls for an "army" of believers to combat, physically if
necessary, homosexuals and other heathen. The preachers
raised, if not an army, then at least a vast coterie of voters
to prop up the conservative agenda.

Stormer is another proponent. So are Jesse Helms, Pat
Buchanan, Phyllis Schlafly, and Howard Philips, to name
a few. And let's not forget the best known conservative of
all, Ronald Reagan.

The Birchers and their ilk are "fanatics," scorned by
all who've been admitted within the boundaries of acceptable political discourse. The "conservatives," on the
other hand, are not only accepted within those bounds in
America, they've accrued an impressive measure of political power. Helms, of course, is a veteran of the U.S. Senate. Philips and Buchanan have held administration positions in the federal government and continue to hold
sway with their opinions for hire in newspapers and on
television. Stormer's profile is lower these days, but the
author of *None Dare Call It Treason* and his "Understanding the Times" road show are sought after by conservative klatches around the nation.

The conservative conspiracy theory enjoyed its peak
of power in the early 1980s. Now it is, at least partially, in
remission. Witness the 1988 presidential campaign in
which George Bush got considerable mileage from his
repeated indictments of the American Civil Liberties
Union (ACLU). Pat Buchanan, who is not only one of
the most conservative but, due to his televised ubiquity,
one of the most influential political commentators in the

country, called the ACLU an "anti-Christian organization" on national television.

The nerve Bush struck was the fear of conspiracy, the fear that "outsiders" or "special interests" will take over American institutions. The ACLU was part of the conspiracy to undermine what Bush called "mainstream" American values. It was the skillful use of conspiracy theory as propaganda that allowed Ronald Reagan, a man backed from the start by the defense-corporate Establishment, to run for president as an antigovernment candidate, lambasting "Washington" as the enemy with the same vitriol he spewed at the Soviets.

The difference between "right-wing fanatics" and "conservatives" is more packaging than product. Birchers see an active, organized network of Insiders working purposefully to overthrow the American government from within. The conservatives see our society becoming imbued with beliefs, attitudes, and opinions that can only lead to America's downfall. The "fringe" right-wing conspiracy theory holds that communism is being forcibly injected into the American mainstream. The acceptable-propaganda theory warns that subversion is quietly percolating through the American membrane.

Conservatives such as Stormer express discomfort with their brethren in the Birch Society. Ted Temple, a leading conservative activist in the heart of supposedly "liberal" Massachusetts, is hasty to add, when declaring his opposition to "One World Government," "I'm not a conspiracy theorist, a John Bircher." Temple prefers a more positive definition of his political faith: "I'd say conservative as defined now is one believing in less government, equal opportunity, a strong defense, and traditional family values."

Americans have been conditioned to reject "conspiracy theories," unless they're disguised as something else, but a French observer saw the essence of American conservatism immediately. Guy Sorman distilled it thusly: "The growth of big government was neither accidental nor necessary, but functionally organized as a project of a society strongly influenced by European socialism. . . . The groundwork for this outburst of leftist ideology was carefully prepared by the media and the universities. . . ."

What the Birchers believe is what conservative propagandists want the country to believe. Communism could never take hold in a country on its own merits. Communism, they both believe, is a prima facie evil needing billions of dollars worth of overt and covert coercion to establish itself as a national form of government—as if the same couldn't be said for any ideology.

Mainstream conservatives pay less attention to the machinations of the Rockefellers, the CFR, and that clique. They save their suspicions for more amorphous entities. The conspiracy to subvert America is "much broader" than the influence of a few think tanks for the rich and shadowy. Stormer focuses instead on a "conspiracy of shared values," as he calls it.

"If you teach people something, then you don't have to control them," he tells a rapt Thursday afternoon audience in New England. "We have millions of Americans who think they're good, loyal Americans who, in their fundamental beliefs, are Marxists."

How did they get that way? What is the mysterious "conspiracy of shared values" that can turn a red-blooded son of Uncle Sam into a pawn of Mother Russia? As foggy as the "shared values" notion sounds, there are tangible villains in the conservative conspiracy theory.

More dastardly than the ACLU is the American educational system, embodied by the National Education Association (NEA). No less an influential conservative than Ronald Reagan has accused the NEA of plotting to install a "federal school system with everything from curriculum to textbooks dictated by Washington." It was his fear of NEA domination that led Reagan during his presidency to all but cripple the U.S. Department of Education. The only purpose of the agency was "federal regulation of our schools under the domination of the National Education Association," he believed.

The mission of the NEA is to "completely destroy" the "dying laissez-faire," and to subject "all of us" to "a large degree of social control." The words are not Reagan's, or John Stormer's, though Stormer quotes them eagerly in *None Dare Call It Treason*. They belong to Dr. Willard Givens, who was executive secretary of the NEA from 1935 until 1952.

Even the California State Legislature, much to Stormer's delight, once excoriated the NEA for publishing social science textbooks by "Communist front organizations" and authors.

That was more than fifty years ago. But conservative antipathy toward the NEA hasn't subsided with the passage of the century. And understandably not. The "propaganda front of the radical left," participated in a 1982 "Peace Day" demonstration that received public endorsement from Gus Hall, America's most venerable Communist. If the NEA wasn't in step with Hall's radical agenda, asks conservative writer Sally D. Reed, why was the NEA's president marching in the Peace Day parade? "My own suspicion," speculates Reed, "is that the NEA is so friendly toward Soviet totalitarianism because it sees that any opposition to the Soviet Union would stand in the way of its goal of a collectivized world government." In other words, the NEA's design is to indoctrinate American youngsters with "one worldism," what Reed calls "global education."

"Its intended purposes sound harmless enough," writes Reed, "sensitizing students to the interdependency of the world's people, emphasizing human rights for everyone, and enhancing the student's appreciation for cultural diversity and philosophical pluralism." In fact, she continues, "globalism is aimed at inculcating young minds with political attitudes that are conducive to the creation of a socialist world order—you know, a United Nations, where every nation has one vote and we all share the wealth no matter what our contribution is."

How different is that from Jack McManus's statement in his pamphlet *The Insiders*? "The real goal . . . is to make the United States into a carbon copy of a Communist state, and then merge all nations into a one-world system ruled by a powerful few."

This exact viewpoint finds its way into the *Congressional Record*, courtesy of Jesse Helms. He delivered an anti-*glasnost* rant on the floor of the Senate in 1987, in which he warned that "the influence of establishment insiders over our foreign policy has become a fact of life in our time. . . . The viewpoint of the establishment today is called globalism. Not so long ago this viewpoint was called the 'one world' view by its critics. The phrase is no longer fashionable among sophisticates; yet the phrase 'one world' is still apt because nothing has changed in the minds and actions of those promoting policies consistent with its fundamental tenets."

The most durable and beloved spokesman for the conspiracy theory was Ronald Reagan. He began preaching its tenets when he was hired as a corporate shill by defense-contracting General Electric in the early 1960s, and subsequently turned into one of Barry Goldwater's most visible supporters, which in turn opened Reagan's own portal into electoral politics.

Backed by GE's corporate dollars, Reagan traversed the country giving slightly modified versions of one basic speech, a speech that drew on the thinking of Robert Welch and Phyllis Schlafly, who were in concordance on the thesis that Eisenhower had sold out America. Come

1964, when *None Dare Call It Treason* began to rack up paperback sales that would have put it high on the best-seller list had paperbacks been so included, Reagan drew on John Stormer as well. While still on GE's payroll, he gave his speech to an assembly of the Christian Anti-Communist Crusade, a right-wing group whose infamy rivaled that of the John Birch Society.

Reagan continued to sound the conspiratorial themes, couched in his comforting storybook imagery, while president. The more receptive his audience, the freer he felt to let loose, so when he spoke to a convention of evangelicals in 1983, he unleashed what became his most notable piece of conspiratorial rhetoric. He suggested that the nuclear freeze movement, very much in favor at the time, was nothing but a means for the Communists to achieve their "objectives," their "global desires." As if for good measure, he declared the Communists to be "the focus of evil in the modern world" and cautioned against ignoring "the aggressive impulses of an evil empire."

When the conspiracy propaganda diminished in usefulness to Reagan, the conservative believers from whom he drew his material began to turn on him. The propaganda was never aimed at them. They were its inspiration and when Reagan left that form of propaganda behind, they were disenfranchised. Reagan himself, through negligence or ignorance they believed, was becoming part of the very conspiracy he was elected to destroy. Portly Howard Philips, a man with the face of a German shepherd and the voice of an FM disc jockey, is a former Nixon aide who founded the Conservative Caucus (one of the right-wing lobbying groups that leapt to power in the early 1980s). He believes that it was really the Rockefellers' boy George Bush running the show all along.

"Bush got a lot of praise for being loyal to Reagan," he says. "In fact, Reagan was loyal to Bush. . . . I would say Bush probably had more input over policy from 1981 to 1988 than Reagan did, certainly with personnel."

Bush, then, probably had something to do with picking George Schultz as secretary of state. "Schultz was the worst secretary of state from the conservative anti-Communist perspective that we ever had," Philips proclaims. "He was simply an errand boy for the commercial establishment."

Philips also made news, when Reagan and Gorbachev were indulging in one of their summit meetings, by calling Reagan "a useful idiot for Soviet propaganda." The old anti-Communist warrior, as far as conservatives were concerned, had turned into a dupe for the Reds.

"If you really want to know what's going on in politics, follow the money," says Howard Philips. "And that is the great untold story. I'm sure there are large elements of treason. . . . I'm sure we've had our share of spies and traitors, but worse than the traitors are people who for reasons of greed rather than betrayal advance policies that are detrimental to the cause of liberty in our country."

Such market-driven traitors, according to Philips, include David Rockefeller, Armand Hammer, and grain tycoon Dwayne Andreas—the same Establishment "One Worlders" condemned in far sharper terms by the Birchers.

Besides the education establishment and the commercial establishment, the third big player in both the hard-core and soft-core versions of conservative conspiracy theory is the media establishment. The leading conservative media assassin is Reed Irvine, whose group Accuracy in Media, founded in 1969, organizes boycotts of sponsors for programming it considers too left wing. While the AIM program sounds like a throwback to the "Red Channels" era of 1950s TV, Irvine maintains that "our media are still being manipulated by time-worn Marxist tricks."

Recent issues of AIM's twice-monthly bulletin "AIM Report" contain headlines such as "Has Walter Cronkite Been Bought?" and "CBS Is Bankrupt—Morally."

As a supposed investigator of "left-wing propaganda," Irvine is a loudmouthed example of how conservative conspiracy theory is itself propaganda, kind of an official government conspiracy theory. Irvine himself belongs to the American Council for World Freedom, an offshoot of the World Anti-Communist League. That group is tied to an international web of right-wing terrorism and propaganda, and sometimes looks like a worldwide fascist conspiracy tied in with elements of the CIA, Central American death squads, and other unsavory elements.

Irvine often targets programming that advocates conspiracy theories, if they are conspiracy theories that challenge the status quo. AIM went after the 1988 NBC television movie "Shootdown," which had as its theme the possibility that KAL-007 (the commercial 747 that in 1983 strayed into Soviet airspace and was shot down) was actually on a spy mission for the CIA. That exact thesis was argued in the book *Shootdown* by British writer R. W. Johnson. Because NBC didn't insure that the movie had "a balanced script giving sufficient weight to the nonconspiratorial side," AIM directed one of its letter-writing campaigns at the show's prime sponsor, the Johnson and Johnson corporation. Johnson and Johnson responded with what amounted to an apology.

AIM spends most of its energy battling the major television networks, which, Irvine says, are "ill-equipped to screen out Communist or other propaganda inimical to our country's interests."

With piquant frequency, conservatives such as Irvine are linked to organizations that seem to be the support system for the very "Establishment" they accuse of Commie treason. The CIA for instance. Who these days

is more closely identified with the CIA than "conservative" ACLU-basher George Bush? It has also been said
that the Rockefellers' Exxon, in some countries at least, is
indistinguishable from the CIA. While it's true that conservatives often pain the CIA as a left-leaning organization, more objective observers see palpable links between
the agency and right-wing causes.

When the whole picture comes into view, right and left
start to look meaningless. Conspiracy theory can be used
as propaganda by the powerful, or it can be the result of
independent inquiry into the roots of power. The conservative conspiracy theory is the most public and popular, but it doesn't call itself conspiracy theory. There is a
legal definition of conspiracy in this country, however,
and that, too, has come under attack from conservatives
(and by civil libertarians). It has been used to put mobsters behind bars, as well as Wall Street wheeler-dealers.
One can understand why certain elements of the right
and the "Establishment" wouldn't enjoy having the concept of conspiracy entrenched in law.

The legal definition of conspiracy first came into discredit in 1967, when New Orleans District Attorney Jim
Garrison put it to work against an accused plotter in the
assassination of President Kennedy. All Garrison really
did was put into official legal documents the work of a
number of researchers before him and since, for whom
the Kennedy assassination was the event inspiring all
contemporary conspiracy theories. Of those amateur investigators, none was more unrelenting than one housewife in the seaside resort town of Carmel, California.

7

THERE IS NO WORD FOR RATIONAL FEAR

*The better the state is established the fainter is humanity. To make the individual **uncomfortable**, that is my task.*

FRIEDRICH NIETZSCHE,
Twilight of the Idols

Mae Brussell, sixty-six years old, died on October 3, 1988, of cancer. At her gravesite, David Emory, one of many who look on Brussell as a hero of the twentieth century, delivered a vengeful eulogy laden with vows to track down her murderers. Can cancer be induced? U.S. intelligence agents have likely considered using cancer and other "natural causes" as untraceable forms of killing. But was Mae Brussell a victim of oncological assassination? Two years after her death, Emory remained convinced that her cancer was "no accident."

In the spring of 1988, after seventeen years of broadcasting a weekly program of news, theories, and conspiratorial commentary called "World Watchers International," Brussell suddenly dropped off the air. She had received a death threat, she explained. That in itself was nothing remarkable. In her career of conspiracy research, she named so many politicians, business leaders, distinguished citizens, and American institutions as complicitous in the ongoing coup d'état that death threats were almost as routine as ridicule.

In 1988, for the first time, she was really scared. A man who is said to have identified himself as "a fascist and proud of it" threatened to visit her at home to "blow your head off." Something about him gave the threat sickening authenticity. Brussell immediately quit broadcasting.

Around the same time, surreal incidents began to haunt Brussell: break-ins at her home with nothing stolen, but furniture moved around; a jigsaw puzzle piece taped to the wall and a handwritten note, "We were here." She felt the onset of the sickness that would later kill her, already convinced that she was being monitored from a house on her street in Carmel, California. The day she died, a house on her street burned down. Was it the same house?

If in fact some mysterious power paid Brussell close attention, she worked hard to earn it. Her legend—and since her death it has become as much folklore as fact—begins on November 23, 1963. Brussell was at that time "just a housewife interested in tennis courts and dance lessons and orthodontia for my children." She had little reason for any other worries. Her great-grandfather started the I. Magnin department store chain, and her father was Hollywood Rabbi-to-the-stars Edgar Magnin.

The assassination of President Kennedy put all normal functions on hold for housewives and husbands throughout the nation, but it was the sight of Lee Harvey Oswald that would alter Brussell's life.

The television was on, with the arrested Oswald parading before the Brussell family. Brussell's daughter Bonnie, though she was a small child, could see that Oswald had been beaten. The little girl wrapped up a teddy bear to send to the abused, accused assassin. Two days later, Brussell watched horrified as Oswald was murdered on national television. The horror did not fade, and she needed to salve it. As soon as the Warren Commission published its evidence, she wrote a check for eighty-six dollars and ordered all twenty-six volumes.

The evidence, it turned out, was so voluminous as to be almost useless, because the commission, for reasons of its own, published it without an index. Rather than write off her investment to experience and return to the universe of tennis courts and braces, Mae compiled her own index. She not only indexed the twenty-six volumes, she cross-referenced them. Still not satisfied, she began annotating the volumes as well. The process produced twenty-seven thousand typed pages of notes and took nine years. By then, Mae Brussell's worldview was altered beyond all previous recognition.

In ferreting out every morsel from the Warren Report, supplementing her research with untold amounts of reading from the *New York Times* to *Soldier of Fortune*, Brussell discovered not merely a conspiracy of a few renegade CIA agents, Mafiosi, and Castro haters behind Kennedy's death, but a vast, invisible institutional structure layered into the very fabric of the U.S. political system.

Comprising the government within a government were not just spies, gangsters, and Cubans, but Nazis. Mae found that many of the commission witnesses—whose testimony established Oswald as a "lone nut"—had never even spoken to Oswald, or knew him only slightly. The bulk of them were White Russian émigrés living in Dallas. Extreme in their anti-Communism, they were often affiliated with groups set up by the SS in World War II—Eastern European ethnic armies used by the Nazis to carry out their dirtiest work.

Brussell also discovered an episode from history rarely reported in the media, and not often taught in universities. Those same collaborationist groups were absorbed after the war by United States intelligence agencies. They hooked up with the spy net of German General Reinhard Gehlen, Hitler's Eastern Front espionage chief. Gehlen made a secret deal with the U.S. government after the war, thus avoiding capture and possible prosecution. Far from facing trial, Gehlen and his entire espionage agency traded bosses—from Hitler to Uncle Sam.

"This is a story of how key Nazis . . . anticipated military disaster and laid plans to transplant nazism, intact but disguised, in havens in the West," wrote Mae Brussell in 1983. She didn't author too many articles, but this one, "The Nazi Connection to the John F. Kennedy Assassination" (in *The Rebel*, a short-lived political magazine published by *Hustler* impresario Larry Flynt), was definitive, albeit convoluted.

"It is a story that climaxes in Dallas on November 22, 1963, when John Kennedy was struck down," Brussell's article continued. "And it is a story with an aftermath—America's slide to the brink of fascism."

Many of Brussell's findings have been corroborated by recent books: *Blowback*, about the Gehlen organization, and *The Belarus Secret*, chronicling U.S. importation of Eastern European fascists, as well as a handful of others. The Cold War was manipulated, to some extent manufactured, by front-line Nazis and their henchmen.

When Brussell was forced off the air, beginning to feel sick, and dying, Nazis and JFK were old news. Her latest project, the one that her devotees feel induced her fatal traumas, was a study of Satanic cults—within the U.S. military. The hidden fascist oligarchy had progressed far beyond the need for patsies like Oswald. They were now able, Brussell asserted, to hypnotically program assassins.

Satanic cults are the state of the art in brainwashing. With drugs, sex, and violence, they strip any semblance of moral thought. They are perfect for use in creating killers. The United States military, Brussell found, was using them. Perhaps that discovery was too much for the conspirators to endure.

Despite corroboration of her premise—the Nazi link to the U.S. government—Brussell remains alone, long after her death, in connecting the Nazi network to the Kennedy assassination and its calamitous consequences. Her theories are supported only by former colleagues such as Dave Emory. For ten years, he has been broadcasting his own "Radio Free America" series, ferreting out all things fascist.

"Along with George Seldes," Emory proclaims, "Mae was the most brilliant political intellect of the twentieth century. Period. And I'll state that for the record. One of the problems Mae encountered was she used an unconventional format broadcast-wise. A lot of the criticism Mae endured was really criticism of *how* she said what she said. Her style, rather than what she had to say."

Emory enjoys describing his own conspiracy research as "pedantic." Brussell's was, if anything, dithyrambic. Her programs were not for the uninitiated, and even the initiated could have a hard time following along at home. She baked clippings, speculations, little-known facts, and occasionally unsupported assertions into an informational pudding so rich and thick it was difficult to stomach. She could be confusing and esoteric about her facts. Reading her writing is even more befuddling than listening to her tapes. But her message can't be missed, and her restless intellect was always at the fore. Listening to Mae Brussell, you knew that you were hearing the workings of an engaged mind. Synchronizing your own with hers was a task of a higher level.

Mae Brussell was a deeply busy person—not the superficial overscheduling that passes for a busy life in our society, but, rather, her mind required constant input and she never had trouble finding it. She subscribed to, and friends swear she read, twelve daily newspapers and more than 150 magazines. She clipped them, never tiring, running off photocopies for cross-referencing. She treated the vast amounts of information flowing daily through the media the same way she treated the Warren Report. By the time of her death, she had amassed thirty-nine file cabinets of clippings in her home.

"She led a remarkable life," says Emory. "In addition to doing all of her work—and she was remarkably productive—she was an avid photographer, a collector of art. She led the most complete existence of anyone I've ever known and she was a tremendously strong human being. And that helps create a cult of personality.

"I think a lot of people literally worshipped Mae for her strength. I admired her for her strength, but she was worshipped by a lot of people."

Emory's eyes, when he takes off his secret-service style mirrored shades, are close-set eyes that dart nervously from corner to corner, then fix and pierce. These are not the eyes of a man on a mission, the eyes of a man on the lookout. Emory has none of the look of a spy, with his ungainly lemon yellow baseball cap pulled down to cover his ears, a toothpick protruding from between his lips ("surrogate cigarette," says the former smoker), and the paunch of a working man over forty. "Style is not my strong suit," Emory announces in his signature sardonic baritone. "Information is." "What the show is about is not Dave Emory," he repeats. "It's about the information."

Information is Emory's favorite word. He always pronounces it *inforMAY-shun. "InforMAY-shun."* The breath must roll up from the diaphragm to deliver it correctly, with the proper reverence.

"We're going to take a short musical break," Emory will tell his listeners, before spinning some avant jazz or folk-protest record. "Then we'll be back with more *inforMAY-shun."*

Across the San Francisco Bay Area, his listeners absorb the *inforMAY-shun:* This is the truth we've never

been told, and it may be too late to learn. The U.S. is
spiraling into fascism, and fast. The government is corrupt, compromised. The military, the intelligence community, and the law enforcement system are overrun by
Nazis and quislings. Get in the way of the juggernaut,
and you die. More than a scandal, the "outlaw national
security establishment" has become a health hazard.

Knotted with contradictions, Emory can be ogling
some California beauty in jogging shorts one minute, and
the next announcing his intention to "head for the hills in
New Mexico or Vermont" to escape the imminent drop
of fascism's iron fist. Supporting himself as a short-order
chef, supplemented by a small inheritance from his
mother, he'll state that he plans to spend the next decade
in pursuit of some real money, then reconsider, noting
the futility of self-betterment "with this country going
fascist."

The country is going fascist. Emory offers that observation as casually as one might comment, "Prices are going up." From his two decades of digging, the trend toward fascism—no, not a trend; the country is being
deliberately driven that way—has assumed *a priori* standing.

"During the 1970s, as I began reading about the various materials that I feature on my program, I came to the
conclusion that *if* people were reading not enough of
them were reading," says Emory, between sips of wine in
the Sizzler restaurant where he works part-time. Despite
a degree from Amherst College in 1971, Emory has
worked nothing but blue-collar jobs since graduating. He
double majored in psychology and English, and his literary bent permeates his radio program; he reads extended
passages on the air from political books and relevant
newspaper articles.

"Where I learned about the stuff was from reading,
and it became apparent to me that most people simply
were not reading or the public's perceptions could not

remain as they are. My feeling is that the printed medium is the final arbiter of truth, and that's why what I do could be thought of as a sort of a hybrid operation. It is radio, yet printed material is featured. I don't hold myself up as the ultimate exemplar of truth. The ultimate verification is to come from the printed medium."

Unlikely as the wooded, college campus radio station setting seems, through this secluded sluice flows the information. Emory commences each broadcast with a caveat that "the information presented" will be unlike the type most news consumers are accustomed to receiving. As their tap into this subterranean spring, listeners are eager to extract all the wisdom they can from Emory. Pity the caller who questions him critically—the word arrogant has been applied to Dave Emory more than once. But for those honest knowledge seekers who phone in during his time slot, he'll willingly oblige.

His listeners' numbers are unknown. KFJC, which airs Emory's weekly "One Step Beyond" talkathon, is a ragged, noncommercial station with no access to ratings or listener surveys. But they are out there, the audience, enough to jam the phone lines every Sunday night.

"Yeah, hi, Dave. Just heard you talking about the guns . . ."

Even Emory's offhand remarks snare the imagination of his audience. He'd made a crack about gun control; a Bay Area man had been murdered at a party by a skinhead with a knife. If the victim had been carrying a gun, Emory suggested, he might still be alive. "Are you suggesting bringing guns to parties?" the caller inquires.

"Well, I'm not saying bring them to parties, but ask yourself this: If somebody comes to stab you, would you rather have a gun on you or not? It's a question you have to decide for yourself."

"I completely agree," the caller chimes. "I think that clearly the powers that be are trying to take our weapons away."

"I'll give you a couple of anecdotes, one from my experience and one from the late Mae Brussell's," intones Emory. "After Mae was receiving her death threats and after she was driven off the air, and before she was overtaken by cancer, she went out and had signed up for shooting lessons and she was going to buy a gun, and she was going to carry it with her at all times."

"No kidding," says the caller with evident surprise. Mae Brussell, the compassionate housewife, self-described airwave existentialist, dithyrambic mistress of monologue, often called the queen of conspiracy theories —she contrived to carry a gun? Mae planned to pack a piece?

"No kidding at all," Emory assures. "And last year, at the same time Mae was being threatened, I was receiving a number of interesting activities. A couple of times there were indications that people had entered my apartment. There was some blood smeared on my front door. A lot of weird phone calls, people would call and hang up and the usual sort of low level harassment. At that time I borrowed a gun from a friend of mine in law enforcement, and a box of shells and a speed loader so that I could put six extra rounds in.

"This goes back to my observation at the top of the broadcast. People are not really aware of the forces around them that threaten their existence at any given time, and as an activist, in a sense someone who is out front, I'm running into them perhaps a little earlier or to a somewhat greater extent at this stage of the game than you are. But ultimately what goes around comes around. You could be pursuing your software company, but then if the federal government or people in it want to take it away you may not have recourse. I'm not saying you're going to have to shoot 'em. But ultimately you're going to have to make a stand.

"In a normal civilized society, there shouldn't be a need for something like that, but this isn't a normal, civilized society. When you're facing organized political terrorism, well, you make up your own mind. I think you're going to want access to a gun when the time comes."

"Both the left and rightists are trying to take my guns away from me," complains another telephone voice, distant and shrill as radio phone-ins always sound. "What hope do we have as individuals?"

"Well, I would say keep your powder dry," advises Emory.

By now, Emory's employment history has become a point of political pride. He feels he knows how the working class thinks and feels, because he *is* a blue-collar guy, despite his Amherst College education. His working-class outlook is one he has had to grow into. For a time, he thought of himself as nothing more than "a failed scholar," living in the low-rent district of Allston-Brighton, Massachusetts, a working neighborhood of Boston heavily inhabited by college students.

Consistent with his affinity for hard-hat polity, Emory's mistrust of traditional left-wing political activists, particularly 1960s' pranksters like Abbie Hoffman and their 1990s' counterparts on the fringes of the environmental and gay rights movements, can lapse into outright hatred. The American left, he'll assert waving a fearsome fist, is purely elitist, with no regard for the working people. Worse than that, the tactics and attitude of the traditional left are so certain to drive the working class rightward, leftists couldn't serve the right wing better if they were covert agents.

Emory believes that some of them are. He's aired suspicions about Abbie Hoffman and Gloria Steinem. The Reverend William Sloane Coffin, longtime activist and now president of the antinuke group SANE/Freeze, was in the CIA, and Emory suspects that revered left-wing journalist I. F. Stone might have been. Earth First!, the once-obscure environmental direct-action group that got headlines in 1990 when two of its leaders were injured by a car bomb, is loaded, Emory fears, with agents provocateurs.

The correct form of political activism as far as Emory is concerned is "communication" and making people aware of *inforMAY-shun*—which not coincidentally is the means of activism he has chosen. The term "conspiracy theorist" is anathema to Emory; it's "stigmatized," or "a term of derision," like "calling a woman a 'sweet chick.'"

"It makes people who are interested in this material look like a bunch of 'Get Smart' fanatics sitting around watching reruns, playing with their propeller beanies," Emory sniffs. He is a "political researcher," even a "scholar," who takes a certain satisfaction in being labeled "pedantic."

When Watergate hit, Emory began his studies, consuming whatever he could find regarding the hidden inner workings of the government. The first connections were obvious. The Watergate burglars were anti-Castro Cubans and CIA agents whose history in intelligence dated back to the Bay of Pigs. Why were these specialists soiling themselves with a third-rate burglary? As the scandal unfurled and Emory read on, more connections emerged. E. Howard Hunt, the CIA executive who apparently engineered the break-in, was also a coordinator of the Bay of Pigs. More revelations came as the 1970s—which ironically have been dismissed as the decade when "nothing happened"—rolled on.

Numerous journalists and finally the House Select Committee on Assassinations tied the Bay of Pigs, anti-Castro/CIA cadre to the assassination of President Kennedy. The House committee concluded that there was "probably" a conspiracy behind the Kennedy assassination and, though it declined to name any conspirators, investigated several CIA, Cuban, and organized crime figures as possible suspects.

All of these revelations took months or years to come

out. Even then, they saw little attention from the above-ground media. But in August, 1972, a scant two months after the Watergate break-in, Mae Brussell published an article in a magazine called *The Realist.* Normally a journal of political satire edited by yippie humorist Paul Krassner, *The Realist* on three occasions took time out for Brussell's surreal revelations. Her first article was called "Why Was Martha Mitchell Kidnapped?" In it, Brussell spelled out the entire scenario behind Watergate.

Emory moved to California in the late 1970s, and in 1980 he met Mae Brussell. As a scholar, he felt "failed" no longer.

"I'm an existentialist," Mae Brussell, a former Stanford philosophy major, once said. "I believe that each of us in the last analysis is on our own. The newspapers I read—you can read them, too. These men can't kill all of you. You've got to get smart because if you don't, you'll all be at the end of that gun yourselves."

For every Dave Emory Brussell inspired, every independent researcher, she had a gaggle of slavish devotees. These were disciples, some straight from the bug-eyed and stringy-haired school that also seems to spawn Lyndon LaRouche's lower-level foot-soldiers. To encourage a healthier legacy, on her deathbed she authorized that a research center be created in her name, donating her overstuffed files and plenary political library.

Emory donated money to starting up the center, but the curatorship went to John Judge, with whom Emory has been embroiled in a simmering feud since 1984.

Judge also managed to get himself some lecture bookings and onto radio talk shows. According to Tom Davis, a longtime friend of Brussell's whose mail-order book service is one of the best sources for political books, Judge and Emory had been "competing for radio kudos" since at least 1984, when they were interviewed jointly on

Los Angeles station KPFA and ended up in a vocal shoving match, won by the indomitable larynx of Dave Emory.

Emory swears that his differences with Judge are no mere "personality conflict." He makes a series of charges against Judge, which, frankly, sound like flights of fancy and in any case are unconfirmable and therefore unprintable (Judge is, after all, unlike the subjects of most conspiracy theories, a private individual). Emory has not been shy about publicizing his opinion that the center was infiltrated by the intelligence community, and has said so on the air. Not as wild an allegation as it sounds, given the government's addiction to monitoring and harassing activists of all stripes. True or not, Emory's charges are a measure of how shattered Mae Brussell's death left him. Not only does he stick by his contention that Brussell was murdered by a cancer potion, he once told me, "I think I know who slipped her the mickey."

The Mae Brussell Research Center was set up in Santa Cruz, California. Judge, a Washington, D.C., native (in the conspiracy milieu, he's a suspect on that basis alone), moved cross-country in 1988 to set it up and begin fundraising.

He collected thousands, somewhere in the mid-five figures, then a series of personal conflicts and health problems drove him back to the East Coast. The center collapsed and Brussell's formidable collection of books and papers is now in her family's possession.

There was a string of problems with the center, one of them Judge's refusal to open it to the public. According to Davis, the new library will be open. But, says Davis, "one of the problems was Dave Emory."

Davis says he personally implored Emory, to whom the Mae Brussell Research Center will always be "so-called," not to attack the center on his show. In the fall of 1989, Emory burst. Restraining himself for a year, he could no longer hold it in and went on the air accusing

Judge of financial improprieties and other sordid acts. In private, Emory is even more vitriolic.

In early 1992, Judge flatly denied Emory's allegations to a Santa Cruz newspaper, saying he was "hounded out of [the center] by this kind of nonsense."

The same article quoted one center volunteer calling Judge's management skills "dysfunctional." But center board member Dave Ratcliffe was quoted scoffing at the idea of a sinister government plot underlying the project's failure. "The mind control thing is more Dave Emory loving to spin very detailed, wonderful sounding scenarios that are of his own invention," he said.

Whatever the objective reality of the Mae Brussell Research Center controversy, the version that navigates the canals of Dave Emory's brain is another of his many traumas.

John Judge does not appear to be a very traumatizing person. Bushy of beard, scraggly of ponytail and hefty of weight, he resembles nothing more than a leftover hippie. Standing on stage at a Berkeley nightclub, there to celebrate a tribute to the late Abbie Hoffman, Judge launches into his theory of Hoffman's murder. The coroner said suicide. Judge says the autopsy is inconsistent with that conclusion and, besides, why would happy-go-lucky Abbie off himself?

"He was depressed!" comes an angry woman's voice through the smoky haze. Judge stammers, but continues. The coroner who did Abbie's autopsy was the same one who covered up the murder—disguised as a car accident —of television journalist Jessica Savitch.

"She was a coke head!" the same voice shrieks. Judge, normally somewhat jaded, becomes impassioned. He gestures emphatically at the audience, which is rustling uneasily, unsure whether to cheer the heckler on and boo this conspiracy nut off the stage—or do exactly the reverse.

"No, I don't have the name of the person who killed Abbie Hoffman," Judge declares. "But if you don't think that kind of thing happens here, you don't know where you're living!"

The audience makes up its mind. It applauds Judge heartily as he stomps off. "I don't know if she was a plant or just an idiot," he says afterward. "But that's what they're going to say about everyone whom they kill in this decade. He was a coke head."

A precocious, somewhat maladjusted child of civilian Defense Department employees, Judge's career as a conspiracy researcher began at the age of ten, when his folks would drop him off in the Pentagon library.

"I didn't have a lot of friends and made friends out of books," he recalls. "I was growing up with neighbors from the CIA, NASA, Defense, understanding that there was a covert or sub-rosa reality to the government. And liking to do research . . . I had a twelfth-grade reading level by sixth grade. They wanted to boost me up in grades, but my mother wouldn't do it. She didn't want me to lose my social milieu."

Emory has one word for Judge's research: "garbage." Yet there are few factual points where they disagree except perhaps that Judge speaks at Abbie Hoffman memorial benefits, while Emory considers Hoffman a CIA provocateur. The difference as far as I can determine is a matter of personalities and of style. Emory makes it a point of honor to read his printed sources on the air. Judge is averse even to using footnotes, feeling they're all part of the corrupt academic game.

Emory grants scant room for hope, with his melodramatic threats to pitch civilization and head for the hills, his ideology teetering on the brink of survivalism. Judge believes that the ultimate purpose of the fascist conspiracy is to "camouflage" the surplus of material goods created by industrialization. Without the swinging fist of capitalist-fascism, the world's wealth would be equitably distributed and we'd be living in something akin to paradise.

"To concentrate the wealth and maintain power, it's necessary to create a commoditized consumer society that wastes the material," Judge explains. "Also, to highlight war and war production, which is the ultimate capitalist product because it destroys other products, can only be used once and it brings in tremendous profit."

Emory veritably sneers at the appellation, "conspiracy theory." Judge embraces it. He runs a mail-order service for his articles and related literature. The name of the service is "Conspiracy!"

"Big deal," he shrugs. "Conspiracy. You don't think human history operates that way. How do you think the class carries out its will? All Adam Smith's magic hand, or do they have some schleppers to do their dirty work? And if they do, don't they have names, don't they have addresses and histories? Eventually you unearth a net of people who do certain things, who have interests aligned to money.

"I operate on that level. I don't operate on the level of looking around and saying all of history is a secret plot in a boardroom. But history is a concentration of power and wealth in certain hands, an aggregation of wealth from quite a while ago. And that concentration is going to do certain things to protect itself."

Emory and Judge have one common denominator— Mae Brussell. With her, they share a nightmarish vision of how far the "concentration of wealth" will go, and has gone—what "certain things" it will do.

From the Kennedy assassination to the Jonestown massacre to the bombing of Pan Am 103. Assassinations by induced cancer, hypnoprogrammed gunmen roaming suburban schoolyards, biological warfare weapons (AIDS, for one). Not even the crust of the earth is safe from manipulation. Invoking his signature slogan, "food for thought and grounds for further research" (his catch-all for pure speculation), Emory noted that the 7.1 San Francisco earthquake of 1989, a 5.4 earthquake in the same area just two months earlier, and the rapacious Armenian earthquake of December 1988 had one thing in common. During each quake, the U.S. space shuttle was in orbit.

Earthquakes coinciding with shuttle flights could be chalked up to happenstance, Emory is well aware. Yet there remains the nagging problem that, according to Emory, some military weapons experts have predicted that seismic manipulation would render nuclear warheads obsolete in the twenty-first century. And Judge alleges that spy master general Reinhard Gehlen advocated weather warfare as a cleaner means of genocide, replacing the inefficient and unpopular extermination camps.

In the early 1970s, Mae Brussell predicted that the intention of the subterranean ruling class was to install Ronald Reagan in the White House. She said she was "laughed out of auditoriums" for publicizing this prediction. Reagan, then governor of California, was thought of much the way Dan Quayle is today, as a brainless boob beloved of right-wing extremists, but with no real national possibilities.

"The candidate is selected twenty years in advance," she said in early 1988, "and there is no stopping him." She pointed out that the predetermined ascendant to Reagan's seat would be George Bush.

Under Reagan and his successor, the country has been transformed from a creditor nation to a debtor, and the world's largest debtor at that. The national deficit is larger than ever and making matters worse, the Defense contracting, HUD, and Savings and Loan scandals amount to a large-scale, unprecedented looting of the national treasury. In Ian Fleming's *Goldfinger,* James Bond stops a criminal conspiracy from looting Fort Knox. That was fiction. Under Reagan and Bush, it really happened and there was no James Bond. In his place were David Emory, John Judge, and, for a while, Mae Brussell, howling at the moon.

"During the Great Depression, there were all sorts of Keynesian options that were open to us," says Emory. "They are not open to us anymore. Given the fact that America operates under the law of supply and demand, given an economic crunch, the comfort and perceived well-being of the American middle class is going to depend on their continued access to a sufficient number of goodies to preserve that illusion.

"I think what's going to happen is the number of goodies will be kept accessible by reducing the number of people competing for those goodies. I expect in this country to see large-scale eliminations of population." The extermination option has already been exercised he says, and the American people are blissfully unaware. The general public never questioned the "utterly preposterous" cover story of the Jonestown massacre, for example, despite the fact that many friends and relatives of the dead believed that Jonestown was some kind of government experiment. An aide to gunned-down congressman Leo Ryan found evidence that the CIA was involved. No coverage. No outrage.

"Granted that was down in Guyana, so people aren't going to investigate it, but are people going to investigate it if it's up in the Sierras?" says Emory. "Or how many people will go to Montana?

"It would in my opinion be very possible to round people up, put them in concentration camps, and *gas* them without having the public aware of it."

"If other people come up with stuff, it's called history," complains John Judge. "If we come up with it, it's called conspiracy theory. Then the model they tend to discount or lump you with is that you're personally paranoid. There isn't even a *word* in the English language for realistic or rational fear."

If Emory's hopes for Mae Brussell's place in history come true, such a word will exist someday. I don't know what it would be, and I'm not optimistic that she will ever be recognized as, in Emory's words, "the Albert Einstein of political science." Then again, there was a time when you could say something similar about Albert Einstein.

"Intellectual culture," notes Dave Emory, the ominous voice in the night, "is by its very nature reactionary, and what Mae had to say went against the grain." The same is true for Emory's own research, and John Judge's. Mae Brussell may never find the mass acceptance that Emory says she deserves. If she does, she will do for the rest of us what she's already done for him. She not merely, as he puts it, "redefined the proper channels of inquiry in political science," she redefined reality.

Reality may never be the same.

8

SHADOW PLAY IN NEW ORLEANS

It's exactly like a chess problem. The Warren Commission moved the same pieces back and forth and got nowhere. I made a new move and solved the problem.

JIM GARRISON

There were more than forty reporters by the pool at New Orleans' Fontainebleu Motel. They were waiting for the district attorney, a six-foot-six, pipe-puffing, pistol-packing politician, worthy to shoulder the tradition of high-living Louisiana politics. Often sighted lounging at the city's Playboy Club, he was also the scourge of Bourbon Street. A fighter pilot in World War II, he was discharged for psychological reasons during a tour of duty in Korea. When he ran for district attorney, he defeated a criminal court judge who had been the legal community's 3:1 favorite—by a 2:1 margin.

As renowned as the D.A. had become, his notoriety did not traverse the boundaries of New Orleans, where populism is as potent as voodoo. He knew that was about to change when he saw the swarm of reporters. Under his breath he whispered, "My God." It was February 20, 1967.

Garrison called the press conference to elaborate on

his statements of two days earlier, statements he had made in aggravation after the *New Orleans States-Item* revealed the secret of Garrison's most sensational and daring stunt yet. He'd raided strip joints, unseated judges, and faced down the mayor. But in late 1966 and early 1967, his office had been forebodingly silent.

Checking public records, where Garrison's expenditures were recorded, a couple of *States-Item* reporters found some unusual travel vouchers totaling eight thousand dollars. Where were Garrison's men going? Piecing together facts and rumors, they came out with a startling story. Three years after the Warren Commission concluded that Lee Harvey Oswald acted alone, the New Orleans district attorney was conducting his own investigation into the assassination of President John F. Kennedy.

The paper followed up its story with an editorial demanding an explanation from Garrison, implying unsubtly that he was gearing up not a solid case, but a grab at national media coverage.

Garrison shrugged off the revelations about his investigation as inevitable. The editorial's personal tone, on the other hand, infuriated him. He blasted back. Yes, he was conducting an investigation into a New Orleans-based conspiracy behind the president's murder and more than that, he proclaimed. "There will be arrests."

Arrests. The assassination of President Kennedy was less than four years into history. His successor was still in the White House, a constant reminder that a U.S. president had been murdered, and no one had ever been tried for the crime. There were no answers. The Warren Commission had satisfied some, at least in government circles, but it left much of the public with a queasy feeling. In 1966, an attorney named Mark Lane came out with a book that took a long ride on the best-seller list. Titled *Rush to Judgement,* it found enough holes, inconsistencies, and errors in the Warren Commission findings to set off a nationwide debate.

Tagged as a "Warren Report critic," Lane obviously believed there was a conspiracy in the assassination. Yet he never specified what the conspiracy might consist of. While he helped sharpen that vague uneasiness about the Warren Commission report, he created as much confusion as he quelled. And then came the district attorney of New Orleans: "There will be arrests."

Either the mystery would finally be solved, or this man was the most brazen opportunist in political history. Whichever, it made an irresistible story. When Garrison called a press conference at a private motel (where he'd be safe in barring the "irresponsible" States-Item), the national media was there. His switchboard was deluged with calls from as far away as Moscow. Six years before, Garrison was a nobody city attorney with no political backing and an irrational urge to run for D.A. Over the next two years, he would become one of the country's most controversial public figures.

Twenty years after Garrison held his poolside press conference, Daniel P. Sheehan filed an affidavit with a federal court in Florida. Chief attorney for a nonprofit law firm called the Christic Institute, Sheehan was at least as obscure as Garrison, and the case he proposed to try—in civil court, not criminal—was an assassination case, but a little-known one. The allegations made by Sheehan, the result of a private investigation, were nonetheless as nerve-racking as anything envisioned by Garrison.

The assassination cabal fingered by Garrison is the same underground empire unearthed in the Sheehan affidavit. It had not disbanded with Kennedy's assassination. According to Sheehan's narrative, the conspiracy was still in business. He found it hard at work in Central America, where, in the 1980s, the contra war was still hot.

From Garrison to Sheehan, New Orleans to Nicaragua, the more things remain the same, the more they've changed. If I understand what Garrison and Sheehan say —each in his own inimicable idiom—there has been one small group of men in charge of not only the American government but the American psyche. The shots to Kennedy's brain were the first wounds to our collective mind. The crossfire continued through the morally murky and bloody events of the three decades since. These days, sometimes it seems, our own brains have been blown away.

Jim Garrison sprang from nowhere to national infamy on that February day in 1967, but his entrance into New Orleans politics was equally confounding. As suited as he seems to that city, he was born seventy years ago in Denison, Iowa. His name was Earling Carothers Garrison. He didn't do much growing up in the corn country. When he was three, his parents split and his mother hustled the future conspiracy theorist to Chicago. After a while, his father snatched him and took him back to Iowa. A legal battle ended with the boy in his mother's custody, back in the Windy City.

He served his tour in World War II, then went to Tulane University, where he earned his law degree. At Tulane, he insisted that people call him, simply, "Jim." He later changed his name legally to "Jim Garrison."

Garrison went to work as an assistant prosecutor in the New Orleans D.A.'s office, but his real sights were set on his boss's job. In 1961, after a couple of failed attempts at lesser offices, Garrison performed a political miracle. With no significant political support and just as little name recognition, Garrison drew on his considerable abilities as a political thespian. Vigorous, confident, and youthful, Garrison offered himself as a clear choice against the entrenched incumbent, Richard Dowling. He chided Dowling as "The Great Emancipator," for what

Garrison said was Dowling's disposition to let felons go free.

Dowling did his own cause no good. A democratic patrician whiling away his latter years in what appeared to be secure public office, he wallowed in a stereotype of his own making. When Garrison blasted him for retaining his private practice with a prominent firm while in office, Dowling replied that he could not maintain a lifestyle befitting his stature on his paltry fifteen thousand dollar public salary. If the voters didn't like this comfy arrangement, Dowling declared, they could go right ahead and elect themselves a "new boy."

Jim Garrison was that new boy.

Grand flourishes continued once Garrison took office. He began "cleaning up" Bourbon Street, arresting homosexuals, prostitutes, and B-girls, putting the sleazier joints out of business, pressuring the more classy to further refine their ambience.

When the city's criminal court judges, a panel of eight, tried to bring Garrison under their control by cutting off his vice-busting cash flow, Garrison refused to be chastened. He challenged the judges' integrity, suggesting that there may have been "racketeer influence" in their decision. He also ridiculed the judges' work ethic, or lack thereof, needling them for taking over two hundred holidays in a year. The judges sued him for defamation. Garrison held his ground right through to the Supreme Court, where he won a landmark decision upholding the right to criticize public officials.

He announced his candidacy for state attorney general, but let the filing deadline pass without doing anything. He insinuated that he might run for mayor against Victor Schiro, whom he'd crossed during the D.A.'s race. Schiro responded by investigating Garrison for corruption. Garrison parried with an investigation of the mayor.

When the state legislature failed to pass one of Garrison's pet bills, he wondered aloud if the legislators had been bribed. The legislature censured Garrison, and he responded with characteristic *cojones* calling the censure "an honor."

In 1965, he won a second term, crushing his opponent, who just happened to be one of the allegedly goldbricking judges Garrison had previously humiliated. Returned to office, he turned his public-relations bazooka on the New Orleans police, who he felt were not adequately supportive of his crackdown on Bourbon Street vice. The cops returned serve, arresting Linda Brigette, a stripper who danced in a club owned by a Garrison ally. Garrison prosecuted her but she never served any time, and soon he was lobbying the new governor (who was elected with Garrison's help) for her unconditional pardon.

Such was the turbulent tenure of Jim Garrison, district attorney, man about town. Until November 1966. Then the grandstanding ceased, the pyrotechnics fizzled. The towering figure clad in white dinner jacket barhopping the French Quarter was gone. Garrison vanished from public view, even changing his unlisted phone number.

He broke his silence three months later. "There will be arrests."

The secret investigation in 1966, the one that led Garrison to announce in May 1967 that he and his staff "solved the assassination weeks ago . . . we know the key individuals, cities involved, and how it was done," was not the first time Garrison had peeked into the assassination mystery. On November 23, 1963, one short day after J.F.K. died, Garrison decided to check out whether Lee Harvey Oswald had any associates in New Orleans. Oswald, as we detailed earlier, spent the summer of 1963 in New Orleans, his hometown.

A couple of stories whetted Garrison's suspicions. He had heard that an acquaintance of his, a normally level-headed if extremely right-wing private investigator named Guy Bannister, had spontaneously pistol-whipped a drinking buddy the day of the assassination. The buddy was Jack Martin, another P.I. Martin, the story went, triggered the assault by taunting Bannister. There had been certain people frequenting Bannister's office that summer, Martin chided. He told Bannister he would remember who they were. Bannister responded by trying to pound the memory out of Martin's head with a gun butt.

Bannister's office was at 544 Camp Street in New Orleans, the address made famous by Oswald, who stamped it on his Fair Play for Cuba handouts. Putting the two facts together, Garrison—along with a lot of other people—figured that Bannister was running Oswald as a front. Bannister, it would turn out, had CIA connections. The theory expanded: Oswald was being set up as a fake Marxist, giving him a prefabricated motive for the assassination.

Those musings would all come much later. In 1963, Garrison was intrigued by Jack Martin's tales, and Martin was well known to spin them. A New Orleans *States-Item* reporter once termed Martin "as full of that well-known waste material as a yule hen." The same reporter also noted, however, that Martin did have "the friendship and confidence of reputable, well-placed individuals . . . he must be taken with a grain of salt leavened by a grain of confidence."

Martin told of another Bannister operative, a flying ace named David Ferrie, who, on the evening of November 22, drove all night through the rain to Houston, Texas. According to Martin, Ferrie was to fly the J.F.K. assassins over the Mexican border. Presumably his flight would be the second leg of the shooters' getaway. When Ferrie got back to New Orleans a couple of days later, Garrison had him arrested and turned over to the FBI. Ferrie was quickly released.

In 1967, after Ferrie died suddenly, Garrison beatified

him as "one of history's most important individuals." Perhaps. Perhaps not. One thing is certain; Ferrie was one of New Orleans' most bizarre individuals. His reputation as an aerobatic adventurer was local legend. Much of his derring-do was performed under contract to the CIA. Ferrie was both a fanatical anti-Communist and a well-known night crawler on the New Orleans homosexual party circuit. When some of Ferrie's exploits with teenage males became public in 1962, he lost his job at Eastern Airlines.

In all likelihood, Ferrie knew Oswald since the accused assassin was a teenager. Oswald served in a Civil Air Patrol unit commanded by Ferrie, who was said to have the boys under his command mesmerized.

The most strikingly strange trait Ferrie flaunted was his face. Somehow, he had lost all his hair, all over his body. He once said it was burned off in a plane crash. He once said he lost it due to a rare tropical disease. Ferrie's macabre attempt to compensate for this deficiency consisted of dressing for Halloween every day. He wore a badly fitting scarlet toupee and scribbled on Groucho Marxian eyebrows with greasepaint. To match his Dadaesque visage, he adopted the fashion sensibilities of a circus clown.

A true nut case, Ferrie took up cancer research as one of his hobbies. His apartment was filled with caged mice, on which he carried out a regimen of unusual experiments, the nature of which is not quite clear.

The FBI cleared Ferrie. Garrison saw no reason to dispute the findings of the largest law enforcement agency in the land. He forgot all about it.

At least, he says he forgot all about it. When the news of his 1966 investigation broke, Ferrie surfaced again. Panicking, he went to the local media and announced that he was Garrison's suspect and that he was completely innocent. Two days after Garrison's press conference at the Fontainebleau Motel, David Ferrie was found naked under a sheet in bed at home, dead.

Ferrie's curiously timed demise was the one event that turned the Garrison investigation from a sideshow to serious business. The coroner ruled that death came from a cerebral aneurism, noting that Ferrie had actually suffered one before, with no apparent ill effects—a medical rarity.

Garrison announced that Ferrie's death was suicide—Ferrie figured the game was up, and snuffed himself. Proponents of the "strange deaths" hypothesis find it more likely that Ferrie was murdered by an insidious method that could disguise the death as natural.

Within hours after Ferrie's body was found, his close friend Aladio del Valle, a Cuban exile, was discovered shot through the heart in Miami.

Most of the press expected that Garrison, whom they took for a grandstander anyway, would now claim victory as verified by the "suicide" of his star witness and suspect, and get back to the business of busting burlesque houses and aggravating local politicians.

Jim Garrison double-crossed his detractors again. Less than two weeks after "one of history's most important individuals" was discovered cold and unclothed, Garrison made good on his promise that "there will be arrests."

Clay Shaw was a pillar of the New Orleans business community. Garrison pilloried him. The case against Shaw began on May 1, 1967, with his arrest on charges of conspiracy in the murder of President John F. Kennedy, and ended exactly two years later, with his acquittal.

"I continued to believe that Shaw had participated in the conspiracy to kill the president," writes Garrison in his autobiography, "his role having been essentially to set up Lee Oswald as the patsy." But he had an impossible time establishing Shaw's motivations. Garrison attempted to tie him in with Ferrie, Oswald, the New Orleans homosexual underground, and, of course, the CIA. Publicly, the businessman was known as a moderate liberal who felt favorably toward Kennedy. To make the case tougher, Shaw appears to have committed perjury by denying on the stand that he had known David Ferrie.

Garrison's failure to pin even a small part of the postulated J.F.K. conspiracy on Shaw was widely read as a repudiation of conspiracy theories. It was not. Much of the evidence Garrison gathered goes far toward supporting a conspiracy.

Nonetheless, damage was done. It wasn't simply that Garrison lost his case. It was the way he lost it. His best witness, Perry Russo, claimed he'd been in a meeting at which Shaw, Oswald, and Ferrie discussed assassinating the president. Russo was caught in contradictory statements, and Garrison tried to sculpt his testimony with hypnotism and drugs. Another witness who testified he'd seen Shaw and Oswald together admitted he was on heroin at the time. Garrison also relied heavily on a notation in Shaw's address book, a post office box number for someone called "Lee Odom" in Dallas, Texas. Garrison said he found the same P.O. number, sans identification, in Oswald's little black book and, furthermore, he contended, the number was actually a coded version of Jack Ruby's phone number.

Pretty flimsy stuff on which to base the criminal case of the century. All the while, Garrison marched on with shoulders back, chest out, chin up, without a qualm that his conduct was bringing down not only his whole prosecution, but justifiably or not, an entire movement.

The taint of Jim Garrison sticks to assassination conspiracy theories. Things did not have to turn out that way.

Whether Garrison had the goods on Shaw for sure can never be known. Shaw died in 1974. Witnesses saw ambulance attendants carrying a covered body on a stretcher *into* Shaw's house before he was found, and no autopsy was ever performed. Ferrie died; Bannister died of a heart attack; and another of his associates was thrown out—or fell out—of a Panama hotel room in 1964. That was Maurice Gatlin, Sr., who was also connected with the CIA and its anti-Communist activities in Latin America. Even with the lead players six feet under, and Garrison stereotyped in the media as a man eloping with his own ambition, there are still suggestive remnants from the Jim Garrison investigation.

In 1979, Richard Helms, zipper-lipped former CIA director, finally admitted that Clay Shaw had in fact been what he called a "part-time contact" of the agency. Shaw's CIA connections had been confirmed four years earlier when whistle-blower Victor Marchetti, Helms' one-time deputy, described how Helms fretted throughout Garrison's probe, worried that Shaw's cover would be blown. That doesn't necessarily mean Shaw had anything to do with the Kennedy assassination. It does mean that he wasn't telling his whole story, and neither was the CIA.

One of Garrison's earliest and harshest detractors, Warren Report skeptic Edward Jay Epstein, accuses Garrison of numerous "self-fulfilling prophecies." Garrison's major theme, once he became a national media personage replete with an appearance on Johnny Carson's "Tonight Show" and a lengthy interview in *Playboy* magazine, was CIA "news suppression." In Epstein's view, Garrison was using this charge as a convenient out whenever he was devoid of evidence to support an allegation. That is, Garrison would make unsubstantiated allegations, claiming that supporting evidence was in the hands of the CIA. When the CIA didn't cough it up, that proved that the CIA was covering it up. The cover-up, or "second conspiracy," allowed Garrison to cite nonexistent evidence to support virtually any charge.

That's how Epstein saw it. He was right to take Garrison to task for this clever twist of sophistry. Even so, there was more to the story than Garrisonian demagoguery.

Garrison asserted perhaps somewhat recklessly that Oswald worked for U.S. intelligence agencies. True, he did base this conclusion on, as Epstein wrote, "[his] own private interpretation of 'missing' or classified documents he had never seen."

Tom Bethell was the man who brought those secret documents to Garrison's attention. Bethell, a British schoolteacher and jazz buff, was in New Orleans to study the city's musical heritage. He got sidetracked by a strange fascination with Garrison's theory (Bethell is now an editor of the conservative political magazine *The American Spectator*). At Garrison's behest, Bethell went to Washington and dug through the National Archives. He turned up over 350 Warren Commission documents that were still classified. Of those, he noted twenty-nine that, based upon their headings, appeared to be of particular interest.

The CIA, according to Bethell's list, had a secret document containing information on Oswald's knowledge of the U-2 spy plane program, begging the question, why would a ne'er-do-well private have any knowledge of the U-2 plane? Also in the classified files was a document recording "statements of George DeMohrenschildt re: assassination." DeMohrenschildt was the White Russian émigré who became Oswald's friend and mentor after Oswald returned from his odd "defection" to the Soviet Union. He was also CIA connected. Why would the CIA keep secret his comments regarding the assassination?

One of the nonclassified documents Bethell found contained a notarized statement by a state department official who said he had received information on Oswald from the CIA a month prior to the assassination. While the mere fact that the Oswald file was classified does not "prove" any of Garrison's claims, why the CIA would be interested in this supposedly alienated loser with a failing marriage and few friends seems a fair question.

Nor is it unreasonable to infer that the CIA would take such an interest because the agency is interested in keeping track of its agents—or the agents of other intelligence agencies. There's often speculation that Oswald worked for some branch of military intelligence, possibly Naval Intelligence, since he was a marine. Guy Bannister, reportedly Oswald's controller, was a Naval Intelligence vet in addition to his work for the CIA and his employment by the FBI.

More than a decade after Garrison first made news, the House Select Committee on Assassinations interviewed a former CIA employee who said he was "convinced" that Oswald "had been recruited by the agency to infiltrate the Soviet Union." The committee questioned Richard Helms, who acknowledged that the CIA had a file on Oswald, but that it was a "dummy file," just a folder, nothing in it. He was not asked if the folder had ever contained anything, or why the CIA would keep even an empty file on a disaffected loner like Oswald.

Again, Garrison's public motor mouthing obscured and discredited an aspect of the case that deserved serious investigation. He chose to make his case in the papers, rather than the courtroom.

Garrison had more curious evidence. In the three weeks before the assassination, Ferrie (the alleged would-be getaway pilot for the J.F.K. killers) deposited seven thousand dollars in the bank, Garrison discovered. Jack Ruby, Oswald's killer, had a similar financial windfall around the same time. Garrison was also right in his allegation that the wealthy Shaw and Ferrie knew each other. In Robert Groden's book *High Treason*, there are photos of the pair at what the author says is a gay party.

David Ferrie, in addition to being a CIA operative, worked for New Orleans mob boss Carlos Marcello. On the morning of the assassination, before he jumped in his car and took off for Houston, Ferrie was in a courtroom watching Marcello fight off another of Attorney General Robert Kennedy's deportation attempts. Marcello had previously made what at least one of his associates considered a serious threat against President Kennedy's life, as had Marcello's mob associate Santos Trafficante—one of the CIA's contacts in its Castro hit plots. The FBI learned of Marcello's threat and dismissed it. In 1979, when the Select Committee on Assassinations heard about this incident, it characterized the FBI's reaction as "deficient."

Garrison for some reason never displayed any interest in Ferrie's mob ties, only in his homosexual and intelligence contacts. For that and other reasons, Garrison himself has been suspected of taking more than a prosecutorial interest in organized crime.

John Roselli was one of the CIA's main connections to the mob. He was strangled and dismembered shortly before he was to testify to the Assassinations Committee. When the committee came out in 1979 with its report, it noted that Garrison and Roselli met within the month after Ferrie's fortuitously timed death. The "secret meeting" took place in a Las Vegas hotel.

Garrison dismisses the committee's notation as "absolutely false," the work of the "disinformation machinery of the government's main clandestine operation." Being targeted by this formidable opponent, remarks Garrison in his autobiography, is "no small honor."

Not surprisingly, Garrison labels all attempts to link him with organized crime as "canards." Both *Look* and *Life* magazines ran articles during his investigation, insinuating that Garrison owes favors to Carlos Marcello, who, according to the allegations, gave Garrison some meaty perks.

Not only does Garrison deny any ties to organized crime, he has come forth with Hooveresque denials that organized crime exists in New Orleans. In his autobiography, Garrison says he never found "any evidence that [Marcello] was the Mafia kingpin the Justice Department says he is."

On the other hand, as Garrison himself points out, it was not much of a friendly overture to the underworld when he stamped out numbers running and flattened the brothel business in New Orleans. Author William Turner has reported that Garrison once refused a sizable Mafia bribe.

Through the mob allegations, through his many confrontations with powerful politicians, through his battles with the national media, Jim Garrison never fell too far out of favor with the New Orleans voters. He won three terms as D.A., finally losing a race in 1973. His constituents didn't let him stay down for long. He was elected to the appellate bench in 1977, and after serving a ten-year term, was elected to another one. Today, he is a judge on the Louisiana Court of Appeals.

None of that has quelled the skepticism of Garrison's doubters, who ask if Garrison's blasé approach to David Ferrie in 1963 had less to do with his faith in the FBI's omniscience than with Ferrie's underworld connections.

An even darker suspicion sprung from the Left. As Garrison's case frayed, the notion appeared that despite Garrison's vituperative tirades against the Warren Commission, his investigation and theirs may have more than a little in common. Could Jim Garrison, the new skeptics asked, be part of a second-level cover-up designed to discredit legitimate inquiries into an assassination conspiracy? Intended or not, Garrison produced that unfortunate effect.

To diehards, Garrison is still a hero, a man against the system who fought courageously in pursuit of truth against a Big Brother federal government determined to uphold its own destructive fiction. To his credit, Garrison was the only law enforcement official to attempt a prosecution of any kind in the most important American murder case of the century. To his shame, he blew it.

For most people, even for serious researchers into the Kennedy assassination of whom there remain plenty, Garrison is an historical curiosity. In many ways, he is as complex and confused a character as Lee Harvey Oswald, a blight of contradictions, not completely cognizant of his own mission. Maybe, just maybe, he had cracked one of history's most cryptic cases. At this point, it doesn't matter. There is another lawyer crusading on the conspiracy trail who has tracked the plot from New Orleans to Nicaragua.

9

SUING THE SECRET TEAM

*Nothing could hurt us! We'd become a
corporation an' unner business law corporations are defined as immortal beings! HA HA! We're IMMORTAL!
WE NEVER DIE!*

> Speech by a drunken American
> Eagle from *Brought to Light* by
> Alan Moore and Bill Sienkiewicz

Daniel Sheehan, who studied at Harvard Divinity
School, has his spiritual side, but since 1986 he has been
chasing spooks. The forty-five page affidavit he filed in a
Florida federal court is now the eye in a pyramid of a
conspiracy theory called the "Secret Team." But the "Secret Team" is more than a theory. It is a corporeal group
of men with names and addresses. Names that can be
listed on a civil lawsuit under "defendants." Addresses
where they can be served subpoenas.

Sheehan is chief counsel for the Christic Institute, a
Washington, D.C.-based shoestring-budget, public-inter-
est law firm and self-described "interfaith public policy
center" that takes up cases, and causes, with some socially
conscious tilt. Before the founding of the Christics,
Sheehan always leaned in that direction. He was fired
from his first job, a plum that most law school grads
would kill for, at a big-time Wall Street litigation firm.
They said he was doing too much *pro bono.* He was de-

fending rioting prison inmates and Black Panthers. Not
Wall Street style. He spent a year working for headline-
hounding trial lawyer F. Lee Bailey, but that experience
fell short of his ideals as well. Sheehan was lost in the law
in 1973.

Almost two decades later, Sheehan looks like he never
drifted away from that era. I saw him in late 1989 at one
of his many fund-raising lecture stops. He had the bushy
hair and sideburns of a legal aide to the Watergate Committee. A tan sportcoat and a sunny yellow wide tie
topped off the anachronism. Politically, he lives in the
early 1970s.

The 1970s are a decade much ridiculed—the "nothing
happened" decade. Actually, it was an era of American
soul-searching and gut spilling, of intense self-examination, something that vanished in the cash-fixated 1980s.
This was not the narcissistic personal self-examination
memorialized as the "Me Decade"; that came later. The
last years of Vietnam and the Nixon-Ford days brought
on a national, political self-scrutiny that this country
could use today. The aversion to meaningful introspection in the 1980s and 1990s is Sheehan's frustration.

Watergate opened a crack into the nocturnal world of
clandestine politics and allowed a splinter of light to shine
through. The crack threatened to widen into a chasm
with the Church Committee's probe of the CIA, the
Rockefeller Commission, and House Select Committee
on Assassinations.

The secret government was being seductively stripped,
and Sheehan was aroused. He was on the five-lawyer
team that defended the *New York Times* in the Pentagon
Papers case. After dropping out of divinity school, he
worked for the American Civil Liberties Union and defended Native Americans from Wounded Knee, the radi-
cal-Catholic Berrigan brothers, and Dick Gregory.

In 1976, Sheehan took over a civil lawsuit brought by
the parents of a young woman who had been killed in a

car accident—Karen Silkwood. She died en route to give
evidence to the Atomic Energy Commission about dangerous practices at the nuclear power plant where she was
employed. Silkwood, apparently, was contaminated by
radiation. The government never heard her evidence. Her
friends and family believed she was not an accident victim, but that she had been murdered. Sheehan agreed. His
opponent in the case was Kerr-McGee, a gigantic energy
company.

Sheehan shoved the corporate monolith and dislodged
it, winning a civil suit and vindicating Silkwood. Although the lawsuit did not prove that Silkwood was murdered, it was another foray for Sheehan into the demonic
inner workings of the corporate-government establishment. His latest adventure, the "Secret Team" suit, bores
right to the black heart of that monster.

Sheehan now alleges that he has identified the shadow
government, the group of ruthless men who really run
the country, and who have been in that position at least
since the assassination of President Kennedy. Watergate
allowed a peek behind the veil of secrecy. The Christic
Institute lawsuit paints a portrait—nude. But outside of
Danny Sheehan and his devotees, the nation is averting its
eyes.

Sheehan's clients are two American journalists. In 1984,
Tony Avrigan and Martha Honey were in Honduras covering a press conference. The speaker was Eden Pastora, a
contra, but not a typical one. Fed up with CIA manipulation of the contra cause, he wanted to break away and
start his own movement. At the press conference called to
announce his intentions, a bomb went off. One American
reporter was killed. Avrigan was badly injured.

The husband-and-wife reporters began to investigate
the bombing, an investigation joined by the Christic Institute when it took them on as plaintiffs. They discov-

ered that the attempt on Pastora's life was not, as it had
originally been portrayed, Sandinista sponsored. The cul-
prits were Pastora's rival contras, or, more precisely, the
invisible institution behind the contras. That nameless entity was a chimera of CIA agents and Colombian cocaine
kingpins, soulless mercenaries and fanatical ideologues,
multinational businessmen and guttersnipe thugs.
Sheehan labeled this chthonic enterprise "The Secret
Team."

The Avrigan-Honey/Sheehan-Christic lawsuit names
twenty-nine men as participants in the Secret Team. The
term itself was the title of a book by Col. L. Fletcher
Prouty, former liaison officer connecting the CIA and the
Pentagon. In a position to know, Prouty wrote that the
government is actually operated by just such a "team."
The twenty-nine individuals listed in the lawsuit are not
Sheehan's true targets. The reeking maw of a system that
disgorged them is what he really aims to shut down.

Included on the list of defendants are names well
known to trackers of the Iran-Contra trail: Richard Secord, the retired general who was the Iran-Contra congressional committee's leadoff witness; John Hull, CIA
operative whose Costa Rican ranch was allegedly a drug
and gun runners' airport; and Albert Hakim, the elusive
arms dealer who helped pull the Iranian arms deals together. Also on the list were such masterminds as Ted
"The Blond Ghost" Shackley, former CIA covert operations chief often credited with setting up the agency's
Laotian opium smuggling connections, and General John
Singlaub, leader of the fascistically tinged World Anti-
Communist League.

The allegations in Sheehan's affidavit come from a private investigation with close to seventy sources, many
deep inside the CIA and the defense establishment,
Sheehan says. One of the few sources he names is Edwin
Wilson, the supposedly "renegade" CIA man now in jail
for selling arms to Libya. Sheehan has assembled asser-

tions, information, and innuendo, and he has written a
story. Like Jim Garrison, Sheehan is struggling to reify
his theory in the firm ground of law. He has a tool unavailable to Garrison. The federal Racketeer-Influenced
and Corrupt Organizations Act (RICO) allows Sheehan
to accuse the Secret Team of "a pattern of racketeering"
that includes every transgression against man and nature
from drug smuggling to murder to coup d'état. They
trade not only in narcotics, missiles, and money, but in
nations and lives, hearts and minds.

"By any definition," says Sheehan's affidavit, "these
defendants, alleged merchants of heroin and terrorism,
are organized criminals on a scale larger than life."

A florid, torrid rhetorician, Sheehan's sweeping proclamations have been both the greatest risk to his credibility and his most powerful means of winning support—
support the Christic Institute urgently needs. The case
cost something like forty thousand dollars per week to
maintain, even with Sheehan and Sara Nelson—his wife
and the institute's director—taking salaries under twenty
thousand dollars per year.

On February 3, 1989, a U.S. District Court judge
tossed the lawsuit out of court and ordered the institute
to pay one million dollars in attorney's fees to the defendants. Whether or not that total included the sixty thousand dollars Richard Secord reportedly spent on propaganda to discredit the institute is not clear. But the case
continued. At this writing, it is still awaiting its day in
court, before a panel of three appellate judges in Atlanta.
Like the horizon, that day never seems to get any closer,
no matter how far forward Dan Sheehan moves.

Sheehan insists that fear among the Secret Teamsters is
peaking as his chance of getting the Christic case heard
increases. He has been successful in provoking outrage
from the defendants. John Singlaub's animosity toward

the Christics is not something he hides. He once said that, if he could, he'd "ask for an air strike to blow the bastards away." Ted Shackley has called the institute "malevolent" in an article he wrote for *Defense and Diplomacy*. John Hull rants that the Christics are nothing but a Commie front.

Their power is threatened by public exposure, Sheehan says. His affidavit makes only a brief mention of the J.F.K. assassination, but in his public appearances Sheehan is unequivocal. Once the Secret Team is exposed, so, too, will the conspiracy behind the deaths of John Kennedy, Robert Kennedy, and Martin Luther King, Jr. —as well as the drug epidemic and the vast stupefying of America produced by disillusionment combined with deliberate policies that strengthen the forces of violence while ignoring basic human needs.

Jim Garrison and Daniel Sheehan were never after a single group of criminals. The Secret Team theory is not merely a gangster novel; it is a biblical epic. The conspirators are not simply greedy or power mad; they are the agents of an almost alchemical social, political, and psychological transformation. They created a world of twilight, torture, and mendacity. Their world is now our world.

Whether the conspiracy theories derive from faith, fact, or a mixture thereof, the world we live in is unavoidably real, and it seems to get less livable all the time. If only we could understand it, we might be able to find our way through. But in a society where the obfuscation of elitist "experts" passes for understanding, the relative clarity of even the most convoluted conspiracy theories— and the Secret Team theory is not exactly crystalline in its simplicity—will always be thrown out of court.

Part Two of this book looks at the flip side of popular reality. What follows is as exhaustive a compendium of

American conspiracy theories as I could compile. Rather than list every theory, and attribute it to a particular theorist—an impossible task, with the endless overlap among them—I've let the conspiracy theorists guide me to the "evidence" itself. Most of the material in the following chapters comes from mainstream or slightly off-center sources.

Journalists like to think of themselves as a skeptical lot. This is a flawed self-image. The thickest pack of American journalists are all too credulous when dealing with government officials, technical experts, and other official sources. They save their vaunted "skepticism" for ideas that feel unfamiliar to them. Conspiracy theories are treated with the most rigorous skepticism.

Conspiracy theories should be approached skeptically. But there's no fairness. Skepticism should apply equally to official and unofficial information. To explain American conspiracy theories, over the next eight chapters, I've had to rectify this imbalance. I've opened myself to conspiracy theories, and applied total skepticism to official stories.

Dan Sheehan has been trying in court to prove how this nation has been corrupted by a conspiracy. He is using the system as it was designed, to change what the system has become. Before the system can be changed from within, I believe, there has to be a change in the way we think about our country. The second part of this book is the result of an experiment in making that change: within myself, because, for each of us, that's where it all must begin.

Part Two

THE
CONSPIRACY

10

COUP D'ÉTAT IN THE U.S.A.

> *There is no doubt now there was a conspiracy, yet most of us are not very angry about it. The conspiracy to kill the president of the United States was also a conspiracy against the democratic system—and thus a conspiracy against you. I think you should get very angry about that.*
>
> GAETON FONZI
> Investigator, House Select
> Committee on Assassinations

Assassination is a special kind of killing. Not murder for money, not murder for revenge. Assassins kill for political control. One bullet and a whole nation—government policies, economy, zeitgeist, and all—can be altered.

History is speckled with assassinations—from Julius Caesar to the shooting of Austrian archduke Francis Ferdinand, which set off the First World War. In other countries, assassination is part of the political process.

Not in America. In America, our assassins are like our serial killers—roving lunatics who crisscross the country stalking their prey. They cause politicians a few nervous hours, but they're no threat to the American way of life. They have no motives. Therefore their actions, traumatic as an earthquake or a tornado, are just as meaningless.

The consequences of their senseless violence is mere historical chance. Or so we'd like to think.

Assassination conspiracies, of all conspiracy theory genres, drill into America's rawest nerve. They shatter the foundation of our national ego, the firm American faith in our moral superiority. We like to think of ourselves as the world's original, and most stable, democracy. It is a comforting notion: Because we're always in the right, nothing can ever go wrong. Other countries change their political system through murder; ours is immune to its influence. Political murder is impractical, not to mention uncouth.

But American chauvinism is only one reason assassination conspiracy theories cut so deep. Another is more paradoxical. The very plausibility of assassination conspiracies is what makes them so hard to swallow. The more real our fears, the greater our psychological defenses. Assassination theories are terrifying because they could be true.

As difficult as it would be to maintain a massive conspiracy to rule the world, a limited conspiracy against one person is easy to assemble. Yet eliminating one person can be a most powerful means of controlling a whole society of people. If President John F. Kennedy was killed by a conspiracy, this doesn't necessarily mean that there is a permanent, global conspiracy. But killing Kennedy was a good step toward ruling America, which rules a large part of the world.

The United States Congress, in the form of the House Select Committee on Assassinations, took the official position that J.F.K. was "probably" assassinated by a conspiracy. The committee reluctantly acknowledged the most limited kind of conspiracy—a conspiracy of two people, Lee Harvey Oswald and an unknown accomplice. But the committee investigated any number of Mafia and intelligence community characters on its road to that conclusion. The congressmen clearly suspected something bigger, although they lacked the will to specify what.

Even a larger conspiracy involving criminals and intelligence agents does not mean that there is an all-consuming, illuminati conspiracy. It doesn't mean there isn't one either. Researchers such as Mae Brussell and Dave Emory place the Mafia-CIA brotherhood into a sprawling network of Nazis and fascists who gained their grip on the U.S. government after World War II, when the U.S. collaborated with thousands of Nazis to set up the then-burgeoning Cold War national security establishment.

That's the problem with admitting even the tiniest conspiracy. Once you step into the forest, there's no telling where the trails will lead. Perhaps our government can be controlled by a shrewd group of killers. There have been more than a few political assassinations in recent decades, including one of an American president. Perhaps the coup d'état has already been carried out.

The official mythology of American politics prefers a combination of two different theories of history. For lack of better labels, let's call them the "process" theory and the "accident" theory.

The "accident" theory gave us the "lone nut" political assassin. If all assassinations are merely the work of crazies acting on their own, then there is no such thing as a coup d'état. When lone nuts appear, it's the fault of psychology, not politics. Such random occurrences may cause a few policies to shift, but they don't affect the American system.

One noteworthy policy change: President Kennedy was, as one of his top State Department officials recently put it, "determined not to let Vietnam become an American war." He made a major symbolic move by ordering 1,000 of the 16,500 "advisers" in Vietnam home by Christmas 1963, and Kennedy adamantly opposed sending American combat troops over there under any circumstances—despite the nefarious efforts of top military brass and even his own vice president to cajole, coerce, or deceive him into doing so. Lyndon Johnson had his own intelligence link to the military in Vietnam, which told him that the civil war was such a mess that American troops would most certainly get trapped in the proverbial quagmire. Johnson didn't share his private info with Kennedy, instead letting the president rely on doctored information. Military brass tailored intelligence for J.F.K., designed to persuade him that the war against communism there was winnable with a quick injection of U.S. man power.

Kennedy still didn't fall for it. Says military historian John Newman, "There seems little doubt that Kennedy was headed for a total withdrawal—come what may—when he left for Texas."

Two days after J.F.K. returned from Texas in a coffin, November 24, 1963, President Johnson—the same L.B.J. who knew that American boys couldn't win the war quickly—signed National Security Action Memorandum Number 273 which tossed out Kennedy's withdrawal plans and, in Newman's words, "opened the door to direct U.S. attacks against North Vietnam . . . a significant escalation of the war." Everyone knows the rest of that story.

The "lone nut" doctrine is dogma, and assassination conspiracy theories heresy, because homicidal kooks have no political motives. When film director Oliver Stone, armed with Newman's research, proposed in his 1991 *JFK* that escalation of the war and the assassination of President Kennedy may have been more than coincidental, reaction in the national media was ridicule. Yet the suggestion, though not necessarily verifiable, is wholly plausible. But even to acknowledge the link is to give the assassination political meaning. It suggests not only a motive for and therefore the possibility of a high-level assassination conspiracy, but it also makes plain a truth ever more troubling for America in the long run: violence *can* change the American system.

Typical of academics is the psychoanalysis of assassination conspiracy theories offered by G. William Domhoff: "We all have a tremendous tendency to want to get caught up in believing that there's some secret evil cause for all of the obvious ills of the world." Conspiracy theories "encourage a belief that if we get rid of a few bad people, everything would be well in the world," he muses.

This school of thought sees conspiracy theories as some sort of psychological defense mechanism, but, armchair analysis aside, the personality quirks of conspiracy theorists hardly serve as refutation of the odd facts they uncover. How they string those facts together is more a matter of the way they see the world—a different viewpoint, not a mental defect.

If the J.F.K. assassination was the work of lone nut Lee Harvey Oswald, acting out of some personal sense of disgruntlement and alienation, then the whole Vietnam War was an accident. But what if the assassination was carried out by a conspiracy? Could escalating the war, for reasons of ideology and corporate profiteering, have been one of the conspirators' motivations? Then wouldn't the Vietnam War be an event planned by individuals outside the American system of electoral politics, of check and balance? The American system, it would appear, could have been altered by that cross fire in Dallas. And, more importantly, by the people who planned it.

The history of American assassination conspiracy theories starts on November 22, 1963. The killing of John F. Kennedy was not the first time an American president was assassinated. Nor was it the first time that the possibility of conspiracy was mentioned in connection with a presidential assassination. Eight people besides John

Wilkes Booth were convicted of conspiring to assassinate Abraham Lincoln. Four were hanged.

The Kennedy assassination was different. More modern.

There is a whole generation of students in college now who were born after the 1960s were over, born in a world in which the Beatles had already broken up. A world in which Richard Nixon had already been president and, rather than carrying out his promise to end the Vietnam War, was dropping bombs on Cambodia instead. The love-in at Woodstock had already happened; peace marches and civil disobedience had been replaced by orgies of hatred and burning cities.

Something new and malignant had surfaced in America. It first appeared when Kennedy's head was blown open as he rode in an uncovered limousine through a grimy section of Dallas, on a route, incidentally, that he had never planned to take.

Political scientist Bradley Klein gave a concise description of the American metamorphosis when I interviewed him for a story I wrote on the assassination's twenty-fifth anniversary in 1988. "It was a different world," he said, of the days before Dallas. "It was a world in which people still had savings and you got by with a family of four on one income. There was a sense of America's place in the world. Now things have become vicious and ugly and nasty."

Doesn't it feel like there's a direct path from Dallas to the brutal state of society today?

The path leads from the assassination through Vietnam, the assassination of Martin Luther King, Jr., which led to several years of rioting, and the slaying of Robert Kennedy—without which Richard Nixon would almost certainly never have been president. The calamities continue, through Watergate, another national trauma. The same year, conservative Democratic presidential contender George Wallace was shot and paralyzed. Together with the Watergate dirty tricks campaign, the Wallace shooting insured that Nixon would be president for a second term.

Watergate was followed by all sorts of sordid revelations about the CIA—including its plethora of attempts in cahoots with the Mafia to knock off Fidel Castro. There was conflict in the Middle East, which led to a false "gas shortage." Oil companies were able to jack up prices several hundred percent. They enriched themselves, consolidated power, and unleashed oppressive inflation.

In a later chapter, we'll see links between oil companies and the CIA. As early as the 1950s, the National Security Council had authored a secret directive designating multinational oil companies "instruments" of U.S. foreign policy. Big oil companies were put beyond the reach of U.S. law.

The overthrow of American-backed Shah Reza Pahlavi of Iran by a radical Islamic uprising came next. The Iranian revolutionaries seized an embassy full of American hostages and destroyed the administration of President Jimmy Carter. Carter's "Desert One" attempted rescue mission only made matters worse. The rescue copters crashed in the Iranian desert. One of the players in the Desert One scenario was General Richard Secord, who would become a public figure a few years later, as one of the Iran-Contra conspirators.

Mixed into this parade of perdition were assorted terrorist killings, hijackings, and kidnappings in the U.S. and abroad, which reinforced American feelings of national irrelevance, individual impotence, and governmental iniquity.

It is a logical fallacy to assume that outcome and motive are necessarily the same. Nonetheless, after the Kennedy killing, the United States petrified into a permanent war economy. The Vietnam War segued quickly into the renewed Cold War. Even when our Eastern Bloc "enemies" loosened up, President Bush warned that there would be no "peace dividend" from reduced military spending. Of every America federal tax dollar, more than twenty-five cents goes to the defense budget. Huge defense contracting companies siphon trillions from the economy. The money goes to no productive use, crippling the capacity for individual enterprise and, with it, the American spirit. Draw your own conclusions.

The harvest of these sad seeds was the cynical and shallow Reagan 1980s. Political involvement dropped to record lows, while power grew ever more centralized in a shrinking number of gigantic corporations. Freed from public oversight, the corporations acted almost as nations unto themselves. The weak ones died while the strong merged. The corporate takeover of America concentrated economic power in the hands of a few, but showed its most anti-democratic effects in the media business. Not only money, but information—the air, water, and food of democracy—came under the control of elite interests.

Americans turned inward. Our spirit crushed and hope for a better world so remote it became unfashionable, we substituted consumerism for meaningful political liberty. "Greed is good," became the credo, but more sensible citizens wondered if they weren't living in a nation turned inside out.

Logically, it is rather a reductio ad absurdum to blame the whole bleak panorama of the past thirty years on the assassination of President Kennedy. Nor could it all be the preplanned result of a conspiracy. Is anyone really that forward-looking to plan such a string of events? Still, it is only natural to ask how it all happened. If there was a conspiracy behind the Kennedy assassination, it must have had a motive. If that motive was more than a vendetta, if it was control of the country, would the conspirators stop with one murder to maintain that control?

Is America in the pocket of its own killer cabal, one much cleaner and quieter than the gangs who rule the "banana republics" we hold in contempt? Are we a nation in the grip of kinder, gentler death squads?

The Kennedy assassination happened almost three decades ago, which is not a very long time when you think about the breadth of history. But I can't think of any other single event that has been the subject of such voluminous writing, research, and contemplation in the first thirty years after it occurred. There are probably hundreds of books about the Kennedy assassination. New ones are published every year. Combine these books with shorter articles, television programs, and radio talk shows, and I would guess that there are thousands of pieces of work from scholarly to speculative to fictional devoted to the J.F.K. assassination.

Most are dedicated to the proposition that there was a conspiracy involved. To summarize all the evidence and arguments, obviously, is beyond the reach of this short space. Suffice to say that suspicion has been stirring since the moment Kennedy's head snapped backward from the impact of a bullet that hit him from in front.

On the famous Zapruder film, an eight-millimeter home movie of the assassination taken by a Dallas businessman, you quite clearly see Kennedy's head lurch violently backward at the precise instant that a geyser of blood and brains erupts from the right side of his head.

The Warren Commission insisted that Kennedy had been struck only from behind. The anomaly fascinated UCLA graduate engineering student David Lifton. Laws of physics require that an object struck from in front be propelled backward. Lifton couldn't accept that these laws of physics were suspended at the moment a bullet struck Kennedy's head.

That single observation altered Lifton's life. He devoted the next fifteen years to scraping through the assassination's medical evidence. By the time he was finished,

and his work culminated in the best-seller *Best Evidence,*
the backward head snap was the least of the peculiarities
Lifton had uncovered. His conclusion that Kennedy's
body was shanghaied once it arrived from Dallas at
Bethesda Naval Hospital, then medically altered to eliminate evidence of shots from in front, is still one of the
most debated hypotheses of the J.F.K. conspiracy. But no
one has yet been able to refute fully Lifton's findings.

Who was on the Warren Commission, the government
body that scripted the tale of Lee Harvey Oswald, "lone
nut"? Lyndon Johnson appointed the Warren Commission to quell national trepidation. "Out of the nation's
need for facts, the Warren Commission was born," Johnson earnestly stated. The commission was headed by
United States chief justice Earl Warren. It also included
former CIA director Allen Dulles. Dulles had been removed from his CIA fiefdom in 1961—by Kennedy.

Gerald Ford was also on the commission. Ford later
became an unelected president of the United States when
Richard Nixon resigned and handed him the job. Nixon
had appointed Ford vice president to fill the slot vacated
by the disgraced Spiro Agnew.

Ford pardoned Nixon unconditionally for any crimes
he had committed in connection with Watergate, even
though Nixon had never been charged with any crimes.
The pardon insured that he never would be. Nixon, who
had been narrowly defeated by Kennedy in the 1960
presidential election, was in Dallas the day before Kennedy arrived, as corporate lawyer for Pepsi at a bottlers'
convention. While in town, he garnered much ink after a
few death threats, but, in true macho Republican style, he
refused to add any new bodyguards to his entourage.

One researcher I've interviewed, Trowbridge Ford, believes Nixon's bravado was a setup, goading the self-con-
sciously virile Kennedy into eschewing simple security
measures while riding through Dallas. The ploy also di-
verted the attention of the secret service.

"I think he knew the president was going to be assassinated," says Trowbridge Ford. He also believes that Nixon's worried references to "the Bay of Pigs thing," sprinkled throughout the Watergate tapes and White House correspondence, are euphemistic references to Dallas. "You can't say 'Dallas' because if you say 'Dallas,' people are going to say 'My God! Dallas!' So you say, 'The Bay of Pigs thing—that's a consequence of the Bay of Pigs thing' "

Did Gerald Ford become president as a political payback for keeping "the Bay of Pigs thing" under wraps?

Trowbridge Ford (no relation to the president—that is, none that I know of) is far from the only researcher to draw a line from the Bay of Pigs fiasco in 1961, to the Kennedy assassination in 1963, to Watergate nine years later. In November 1973, while Nixon was still president, University of California at Berkeley professor Peter Dale Scott published an article "From Dallas to Watergate: The Longest Cover-Up," in muckraking *Ramparts* magazine. "I believe that a full exposure of the Watergate conspiracy will help us to understand what happened in Dallas, and also to understand the covert forces which later mired America in a criminal war in Southeast Asia," Scott wrote. "[W]hat links the scandal of Watergate to the assassination in Dallas is the increasingly ominous symbiosis between U.S. intelligence networks and the forces of organized crime."

It is, Scott wrote, "no coincidence" that most of Watergate's shadow players dwell in the same "conspiratorial world" that led to the Bay of Pigs, the Castro assassination plots involving CIA-mob teamwork, the gun- and drug-running syndicates formed in pre-revolutionary Cuba (later transplanted to Miami), and the Kennedy assassination cover-up.

Richard Nixon, topping that roster, instigated the Bay of Pigs plan in the Eisenhower administration. Through his friend Bebe Rebozo, who laundered illegal contributions to Nixon from (among others) Howard Hughes, Nixon is linked to international narcotics and gambling operations. Rebozo's business associate "Big Al" Polizzi, named in 1964 congressional hearings as "one of the most influential figures of the underworld in the United States," is one link. Miami's Keyes Realty Company, which bought land for mob bosses, Cuban government officials, and Nixon, is another. Nixon's curious cooperation with the mob-infested Teamsters Union and his pardon of Teamster boss Jimmy Hoffa are other crime connections.

While Nixon was in Dallas working for Pepsi, he may have met with right-wing oilman Clint Murchison. The Texan oil magnate was part of an elite Texas circle of power that included H. L. Hunt—who once tried to finance a death squad to assassinate leftist activists and who paid for publication of the book *Krushchev Killed Kennedy*. Lyndon Johnson and John Connally can also be counted among the Texas power brokers of the time.

Murchison was a close political and personal friend of J. Edgar Hoover. The legendary lawman made regular visits to Murchison's estate. Murchison was also tied to the Teamsters, into whose pension fund he was allowed to dip, and to underworld financial kingpin Meyer Lansky. Murchison's direct tie to the Kennedy assassination cover-up is his company, Great Southwest. The company's lawyers took on a curious client following the assassination: Marina Oswald, Soviet wife of Lee Harvey Oswald. They even housed her in a hotel owned by Great Southwest. The House Select Committee on Assassinations found it probable that Marina's Murchison-connected lawyer told her exactly what to say in her testimony to the Warren Commission.

One of Marina's most important pieces of testimony was her allegation that Oswald was the unknown gunman in an attempted shooting of General Edwin A.

Walker in Dallas a few months before the assassination. The Warren Commission used her revelation as key evidence to establish Oswald's deranged motives.

Remember Walker, the general relieved of his command for indoctrinating his troops with John Birch Society literature? He was another widget in the Dallas machinery of right-wing extremism.

What the commission could not explain was how Oswald's guilt in the Walker near miss, supposedly Marina's secret, was reported in a German neo-Nazi rag, *Deutsche National-Zeitung und Soldaten-Zeitung,* just one week after the assassination. The paper had phoned Walker the day after Kennedy was killed. From him, or from other sources, the German "journalists" heard not only that Oswald fired the shot, but that he was arrested for it—get this—along with Jack Ruby!

Unable to fathom that twisted tale, the Warren Commission wrote it off as "fabrication."

Odd as it may seem for a German ultraright propaganda sheet to phone an American retired general right after the assassination of the U.S. president, for that paper there was nothing unusual about it. Its editor, Gerhard Frey, was a friend of Walker's through circles of the American and international right. They even shared the status of "journalist." Walker was military editor of the *American Mercury,* a Birchesque paper, in 1963.

H. L. Hunt, a big Nixon bankroller, tried persuading Nixon to pick Gerald Ford as his running mate in 1968. Earl Cabell, the mayor of Dallas when Kennedy was killed, was another element in this Texas oligarchy. Cabell's brother Charles was deputy director of the CIA—until he was fired, by President Kennedy.

CIA adventurers E. Howard Hunt (no relation to H. L.), Frank Sturgis, and others—the "Cubans" of Watergate break-in fame—had proven connections to both the Bay of Pigs and Watergate. Oddly enough, one of the Cubans was a vice president of Keyes Realty. Not by coincidence, these creatures also lurk around the Kennedy assassination.

Sturgis, a member of the CIA-Mafia kill-Castro clique, fed disinformation to a Miami journalist right after the assassination. His false tip led to news stories that Fidel Castro had ordered the Kennedy hit. Hunt recruited Cubans for the Bay of Pigs invasion. He was a CIA agent in Mexico City, according to findings of reporter Tad Szulc, when Lee Harvey Oswald or someone calling himself that name made a scene at the Cuban embassy there (described in Chapter 1). Hunt may also have been in Dallas on November 22, 1963. One of three distinguished-looking "tramps" photographed "under arrest" after the assassination looks uncannily like Hunt. But Hunt strongly denies being in Dallas or Mexico.

The tramps were never booked. Their names remain unknown. Despite being arrested, photographs show they were not handcuffed nor did the arresting officers restrain them in any way.

As for assassination theorist Trowbridge Ford, he was forced into "early retirement" from Holy Cross. The school saw him, he says, as "that Kennedy nut, the asshole of the faculty." He believes that his retirement came at the behest of Holy Cross trustee Edward Bennet Williams. A well-placed (to say the least) Washington lawyer, Williams, now deceased, represented clients as diverse as the *Washington Post* when it broke the Watergate story, and CIA chief Richard Helms, one of Watergate's cover-up artists.

Ford developed most of his theories combing through "the public record." For observers closer to the crime, forced retirement is a fate they would have welcomed.

Since the mid 1960s, researchers have been enthralled by the "suspicious deaths" theory. More than one hundred witnesses to, alleged participants in, or investigators of the assassination supposedly died "suspiciously." Some are more "suspicious" than others, but here's a sampling:

The majority of eyewitnesses that day heard shots from in front of the president (the "grassy knoll"). Some saw possible assassins—none matching Oswald's description. Lee Bowers, Jr., was in a railroad control tower overlooking Dealy Plaza, where Kennedy was shot. He saw two men standing behind the fence on the grassy knoll before and immediately after the shooting. He saw a car driving around back there, its driver speaking on what looked like a two-way radio. Bowers died in a one-car accident three years later.

James Worrell told the Warren Commission he heard "the fourth shot" (Oswald was supposed to have fired just three) and saw a man in a dark coat run from the Texas School Book Depository. Worrell was killed by a car while riding a motorcycle in 1966. Richard Carr corroborated Worrell's testimony. He didn't die, but survived a stabbing and an attempted car bombing (three sticks of dynamite didn't explode).

The list goes on and on. Not all of the people on the list were eyewitnesses. Some were suspected of involvement in a higher level of the conspiracy—George DeMohrenschildt, for example. He was a White Russian émigré with intelligence connections who took Lee Harvey Oswald as his protégé. It was an odd relationship, considering that Oswald was supposed to be a Marxist who had returned from defection to the Soviet Union. DeMohrenschildt died of a gunshot wound, presumably self-inflicted, the same day a congressional investigator located him, and the same day he was to be interviewed by longtime Warren Commission skeptic Edward Jay Epstein.

Congressman Hale Boggs was a member of the Warren Commission. He had his doubts about elements of the commission's conclusions, the "single-bullet theory" especially. He also had information on the FBI's surveillance of Warren Report critics, which prompted him to accuse the bureau of "Gestapo tactics." Flying over Alaska, he was on a plane that simply vanished.

Mobsters Sam Giancana and John Roselli were murdered shortly after getting slapped with congressional subpoenas. Both were key to the CIA-Mafia liaison. Clay Shaw, the only person ever tried for conspiracy in the J.F.K. killing (by Jim Garrison, who failed to get a conviction partly because his star witness, David Ferrie, was dead), was found dead in his home. No cause of death could be determined; Shaw's body was embalmed too quickly.

The witness most conspicuously dead is Lee Harvey Oswald himself, shot by low-level mobster Jack Ruby. A prodigious hustler, Ruby had his own busload of bizarre connections in crime and government. During a break in his trial, Ruby sighed, "The world will never know the true facts of what occurred."

He did offer to tell his story to the Warren Commission if the government would transfer him to Washington, D.C., out of harm's way. The commission refused. Instead, Gerald Ford traveled to Ruby's Dallas jail, and heard nothing but babble.

Ruby died of cancer in 1967. The cancer, he contended, had been administered to him by injection.

For months leading up to his assassination, oil companies and other big corporate interests had been lobbying Kennedy to step up, not cut back, the Vietnam effort. In May, Socony Mobil lobbyist William Henderson presented a paper at a conference sponsored in part by the Asia Society. The president of the Asia Society was John D. Rockefeller, III. The Rockefeller family is the leading oil family in America, and owned much of the stock in Socony Mobil. Henderson's paper called for a "final commitment" to Vietnam. Socony Mobil made over half of its profits from operations in the Far East.

None of this should be a revelation. The oil companies and big banks (Rockefeller-run Chase Manhattan for one) were unabashed in their desire to protect investments in the region. Adopting publicly expressed wishes of the country's most powerful corporations as United States foreign policy was nothing new. Kennedy posed a threat to that system. He was easily disposed of.

Any number of astute analysts have scrutinized the fearsome power of the corporate state. Professor Bertram Gross's book *Friendly Fascism* is an outstanding example of power-structure scholarship. Like most in his field, and in academia generally, Gross rejects the idea of a "a single central conspiracy."

If the Kennedy assassination was a conspiracy, however, it suggests that the various factions of the power structure are capable of coalescing into a "central conspiracy" if the need arises. Once that possibility is granted, the difference between a faceless corporate machine and a conspiracy to run the country becomes merely semantic.

According to Jim Garrison, the oil-banking-military cabal creates dreadfully real structures to enforce its will. He noted that Clay Shaw was a director of Permindex (short for Permanent Industrial Exhibits), an enigmatic Swedish company set up, it claimed, for the promotion of international industrial exchange. Garrison saw a darker purpose.

Nomenclature of an Assassination Cabal, a manuscript that circulates among conspiracy researchers, takes Garrison's scenario to its extremes, combining Garrison's findings with underpublicized Warren Commission evidence and all kinds of corporate documentation from Switzerland, codifying the Permindex conspiracy legend.

Permindex, the book argues, is actually a private assassination bureau. It works in cooperation with a top secret department of the FBI called Division Five. Among the numerous and illustrious financiers of Permindex are Clint Murchison and H. L. Hunt.

Regardless of Garrison's credence (even his critics acknowledge that he turned up salient facts), or the scholarly standards of underground xeroxes such as *Nomenclature*, there are too many facts that don't add up. Too much weirdness engulfs the Kennedy assassination—and evident attempts to cover up who really did it. To coldly dismiss the conspiracy angle is pure dogmatism. There is as much evidence for conspiracy as for the "lone nut" theory.

There are motives galore. CIA cold warriors and anti-Castro Cubans had a grudge against Kennedy for backstabbing them on the Nixon-sponsored Bay of Pigs invasion. The CIA had an extra beef: Kennedy had become appalled at its outrageous conduct. He vowed to smash the CIA's power and started by firing Allen Dulles.

The Mafia had its own vendetta against Kennedy for letting his brother carry out the vigorous, almost fanatical prosecutions that J. Edgar Hoover had shunned. In fact, Hoover had prominent friends with underworld ties, though he publicly denied that the Mafia was real. Chicago boss Giancana had reason to feel sharply betrayed. His vote-rigging probably meant Kennedy's margin of victory in the razor-close 1960 election.

Oilmen such as Murchison and H. L. Hunt had a grievance of their own with Kennedy. They were ultraright ideologues who despised the president, but they had an even more compelling motive. The oil depletion allowance let them multiply their wealth to unthinkable dimensions. Kennedy had promised to strip that allowance.

J. Edgar Hoover bore a disdain for the Kennedys that is well known. Their unwillingness to control their sexual escapades provided Hoover with copious stuffing for his file cabinets. According to one book, rather tenuous in its credibility, Hoover hired a hit squad. "Mr. Hoover had decided that the courts of the United States did not properly administer justice the way he thought they should," an alleged member of the squad claims. "Mr. Hoover had a way to deal with that. He found ways to make the guilty parties disappear."

At the same time, Hoover maintained an alliance with Interpol, the international police organization commandeered by Nazis in 1938 and according to some investigators, still infiltrated by the remnants of the Third Reich.

The Nazi network extends to the upper rim of the American defense establishment. In Chapter 17, we'll discuss "Operation Paperclip," the government's program to recruit top Nazi scientists and engineers. The Germans supercharged the U.S. defense industry and many assumed high-level positions with defense contracting corporations.

We've discussed what the military-industrial complex gained from Kennedy's death. The Vietnam War, Lyndon Johnson's and Richard Nixon's gift to history, was a bounty the defense industry never would have enjoyed had Kennedy lived.

Johnson and Nixon received a modest little perk of their own from the assassination: the presidency of the United States. Johnson plunged into the presidency as soon as Kennedy was certified dead. Nixon had to wait. Things didn't come as easily for him.

Nixon was big oil's candidate, the CIA's liaison with congress, a friend of the FBI, and a fellow traveler with organized crime. For those forces to keep their grip on America, one assassination could never be enough.

In the words of L.B.J.'s former press secretary Bill Moyers, commenting on the CIA's affair with the Mafia, "Once we decide that anything goes, anything can come home to haunt us."

11

KINDER, GENTLER
DEATH SQUADS

*These men should be equipped with
weapons and should march slightly behind the innocent and gullible participants.*

Instructions for assassins in a CIA
guerrilla warfare manual

Robert F. Kennedy died on June 6, 1968, from a bullet
fired into his head. The bullet came from two inches behind his right ear. Sirhan Bishara Sirhan, convicted of
firing that shot, stood in front of Kennedy when he
pulled the trigger. No witness saw him come closer than a
few feet.

The young senator was celebrating his victory in the
California Democratic presidential primary at the Ambassador Hotel in Los Angeles when he was gunned
down. With California secure, Kennedy would have won
the Democratic nomination for president.

His prospective Republican opponent, Richard Nixon,
had already been cheated out of the presidency once by a
Kennedy boy. He would not be deprived again. Nixon
tiptoed to a whisper-width victory over Hubert Humphrey that November. It's hard to imagine that he would
have beaten Bobby Kennedy.

Humphrey was the weakest candidate the Democrats

could run, with is wishy-washy platform on the war. How many opponents of the Vietnam War, who would have voted without reservation for Kennedy, simply stayed away from the polls?

For the second time in five years, the American electoral system was altered by violence.

Sirhan was written off as another solitary wacko. How he could have fired at Kennedy from a spot where he never stood went unexplained. The coroner who located the fatal wound, Thomas Noguchi, was fired from his job. After a hearing, misconduct charges against him were found baseless, and Noguchi got his job back.

Someone in the pantry of the Ambassador Hotel *was* standing to Kennedy's immediate right rear when Sirhan attacked. That person had a gun, and admitted drawing it. His name is Thane Eugene Cesar. In June 1968, he was a twenty-six-year-old plumber employed by the Lockheed corporation. He was moonlighting as a security guard, and it was in that capacity that he carried a gun to within inches of the likely next president of the United States.

Though he admits drawing the gun, Cesar has always denied firing it. Almost always. In *The Second Gun*, a documentary by journalist Ted Charac, a friend of Cesar's says the security guard told him he did fire, and was concerned that his action would have "repercussions." Cesar's clip-on tie was found lying next to the senator's bleeding body.

There has been speculation, most recently from investigative reporter Dan Moldea, that Cesar shot Kennedy accidentally. That's possible, of course. Nonetheless, Cesar was no fan of Kennedy. He was one of thousands of rightists who loathed Kennedy. He had ties to right-wing groups. The exact nature of his work for Lockheed, the nation's largest defense contractor, is also cloudy. The same friend who heard Cesar say he fired has also said that Cesar worked in an "off-limits" area of Lockheed, open only to "special people."

Cesar, according to crime reporter David Scheim, had connections to the mob. If that's true, it dovetails with the fact that Sirhan's chief attorney once represented gangster Johnny Roselli—the same bigwig who worked with the CIA to kill Castro—who told Kerry Thornley that the CIA "killed their own president," and who was hacked to pieces and stuffed in a floating drum just before he was scheduled to testify before the House Select Committee on Assassinations.

There were other creepy characters in the pantry, which was stuffed with more than seventy-five people. There was a Pakistani named Ali Ahmand, who was seen standing right behind Kennedy. Former CIA contractor Robert Morrow thinks Ahmand may have fired the head shot from a gun disguised as a Nikon camera. Morrow remembers seeing such weapons while working for the CIA.

Most infamous on the roster of accomplices is the ethereal "woman in the polka-dot dress." A number of people saw this woman, and more than one heard her say, "We shot him," as Kennedy lay on the floor. The polka-dot lady fled the pantry immediately. On her way, she passed Sandra Serrano, then twenty years old and chairperson of Youth for Kennedy in Pasadena. Serrano recognized the woman. She had seen her just moments earlier walking toward the pantry with a slim young man. Serrano identified the man as Sirhan.

As the polka-dot lady rushed by Serrano, she uttered her infamous, "We shot him." Serrano, who said the woman appeared "pleased," asked who had been shot.

"Senator Kennedy," the polka-dot lady replied, then disappeared.

Serrano was the only witness who clung to the polka-dot lady story. For her determination, she was rewarded with weeks of intensive, often abusive questioning by the

Los Angeles Police Department, culminating in a lie detector test that had more in common with a tribunal of the Spanish Inquisition. The "tester," Enrique "Hank" Hernandez, badgered her relentlessly. At one point he pleaded with her not to "shame [R.F.K.'s] death by keeping this thing up," and accused her of having no sympathy for Kennedy's family.

Hernandez warned Serrano to recant her "lie," lest it become "a deep wound that will grow with you like a disease, like cancer." Practically in tears, Serrano stuck by her memory. But when Hernandez, like some kind of shaman, implored Serrano to "let this thing that is going to grow with you and is going to make you an old woman before your time come out of you," she finally cracked.

"It's too messed up," Serrano cried. "Even I can't remember what happened anymore."

Shortly thereafter, Hernandez triumphantly announced that Serrano had admitted her polka-dot lady story to be "pure fabrication."

Treating Serrano like a medieval heretic was only one in a series of strange procedures the LAPD took in the R.F.K. investigation. Declaring from the outset that they wouldn't allow "another Dallas," investigators ignored or dismissed several damning dollops of evidence, the impossible angle of the fatal shot not least among those. They also ignored extra bullets found in the pantry. There were more bullets in there than Sirhan's gun contained.

The LAPD may well have been linked to the CIA, which infiltrated numerous police departments in the 1960s, and is thought to have trained LAPD officers in clandestine methods. Manuel Pena, head of the department's "Special Unit Senator," which conducted the assassination investigation, worked for an "international development" unit of the LAPD. Congressional investi-

gators later exposed that unit as a cover for CIA activities
in Southeast Asia and Latin America.

Hank Hernandez, Sandra Serrano's inquisitor, worked
for the same unit. He bragged to Serrano that he had
administered tests in "South America, Vietnam, and Europe." He claimed to have lie tested "the dictator in Ca-
racas, Venezuela," Marcos Perez Jiminez.

Why those far reaches of the globe fall under the jurisdiction of the Los Angeles Police Department is, shall we
say, uncertain. If Hernandez was telling the truth about
his far-flung assignments, he must have been working for
someone else.

And what about Sirhan Sirhan? Didn't he confess to
the killing? He leapt to his feet in the courtroom and
shouted, "I killed Robert Kennedy with twenty years
malice aforethought!" (Quite a claim, considering he was
only twenty-four.) Isn't that self-incriminating enough?

Actually, Sirhan never remembered shooting Kennedy. He confessed, he said, because "all the evidence has
proved" that he was the assassin. He failed as well to
recall keeping the bizarre notebooks found in his apartment, even though he agrees he must have written them.
They contain scribblings like "R.F.K. must die," "R.F.K.
must be assassinated," and "My determination to eliminate R.F.K. is becoming more the more of an unshakable
obsession." He also wrote the unexplained phrase "please
pay to the order of" again and again.

The writings were ranting and incoherent. Sirhan,
some researchers believe, was under hypnosis at the time
of the assassination. That would account for his lapses of
memory. It would also make him the perfect patsy, one
who actually fired a gun in front of a roomful of witnesses. Much easier to make a frame-up stick when
you've got twenty-five or fifty people who saw your fall
guy do the crime.

To work such a plot, the conspirators must have control of their agent in both body and mind.

The idea of a mind-controlled assassin, a human robot who'll kill on command, goes back much further than Richard Condon's 1959 novel, *The Manchurian Candidate* (and the classic film of the same title). As early as the thirteenth century, a Persian secret society known as the Hashishim—Assassins—perfected techniques to turn ordinary young men into killers. It is fitting that history appropriated the sect's name for both assassination and hashish. They used drugs to gain control of the minds of their unsuspecting hit men. The bedazzled dupes were the original "lone assassins."

The Assassins unleashed a skein of violence aimed mainly at political leaders, which gave them control over large portions of the Middle East, and brought the sect incredible wealth. In the thirteenth century, nobody was baffled by the wave of lone assassins. Everyone knew who was behind them and why.

In the twentieth century, an equally strange cult, the intelligence community of the United States government, has also experimented with remolding the human mind. The umbrella for these efforts was a program called MKULTRA (pronounced M. K. ULTRA), approved in 1953 by CIA director Allen Dulles at the urging of Richard Helms, who would later become director of the Central Intelligence Agency himself.

MKULTRA was an ultrasensitive program of experiments in search of a drug that could alter human behavior. The program was not publicized at the time. It didn't come to light until more than twenty years later, when congressional investigators revealed it, and a set of exhaustive Freedom of Information Act requests led to several books on the macabre operation.

MKULTRA gained its notoriety for introducing LSD into America, giving birth to the 1960s counterculture. Its darker purpose was to create the perfect agent, the Manchurian candidate: an agent who would take any order without question, who would be absolutely trustworthy, an agent with no free will.

MKULTRA was just one part of the government's ongoing mind-control effort. Both the CIA and the Army were involved. The Army was more public about it, selling its program as a national security measure, to keep ahead of the Communists, who were known to have developed brainwashing techniques.

The sales pitch for mind control was based on half-truths. Various Communist countries had come up with mind-control methods, but they relied on the tried-and-true formula of indoctrination and propaganda, not on psychopharmacology. Either way, the U.S. was ahead. Going back to the days of "Wild Bill" Donovan and the Office of Strategic Services (OSS) (precursor to the CIA), the government was exploring methods of mind control. Always, one of the program's aims was to create human robots—unsuspecting citizens who would act without their knowledge, against their will, as couriers, spies. Assassins?

There are only suggestions that they succeeded in these sinister endeavors. Donald Bain's 1976 book, *The Control of Candy Jones,* details how a former USO pin-up girl was hypnotically transformed into a CIA courier. Her "controller" may have been—according to journalist Walter Bowart—a doctor named William Jennings Bryan, a psychiatrist who had been technical consultant to the film version of *The Manchurian Candidate.* Bryan died in 1977 at the age of fifty, "allegedly," writes Bowart, of a heart attack.

Among assassins, there are three good candidates for Manchurian status. One is Sirhan. The repetitive writing in his notebooks bears the mark of what his defense psychiatrist Dr. Bernard Diamond called "automatic writing." When Diamond interviewed Sirhan under hypnosis, the alleged Kennedy killer would often write his rambling answers. At one point, Diamond asked him why he was "writing crazy."

Sirhan's scribbled answer: "MIND CONTROL MIND CONTROL MIND CONTROL."

A former U.S. intelligence officer who gave Sirhan a psychological stress evaluation (more sophisticated than an old-fashioned polygraph test) seven years after the R.F.K. assassination is quoted as saying, "Everything in the PSE charts tells me that someone else was involved in the assassination—and that Sirhan was programmed through hypnosis to kill R.F.K."

The Jodie Foster-obsessed John Hinckley, Jr., appears to be another suspect for brainwashing. He was copiously dosed with mood-altering drugs, prescribed by a hometown psychiatrist, and was on Valium when he shot President Reagan on March 30, 1981. His father, John Hinckley, Sr., is a friend of George Bush. Another of the senior Hinckley's sons had a dinner date with Bush's son Neil on March 30. It had to be changed due to extenuating circumstances.

The other assassin who could have been mind controlled is Mark David Chapman. On December 8, 1980, Chapman pumped a revolver full of hollow-tipped bullets into the back of ex-Beatle, cultural icon, and peacenik John Lennon.

The first reaction of an arresting detective, Arthur O'Connor, who scrutinized Chapman, was that "he looked as if he could have been programmed." Chapman's behavior was described as "dazed."

British lawyer Fenton Bressler unfolds the entire scenario in his book *Who Killed John Lennon?* Bressler contends that Chapman came into contact with the CIA through the international auspices of the YMCA. That would explain why, when Chapman was able to choose any foreign city to do YMCA work abroad, he chose Beirut—a cesspool of spies, terrorists, and killers. Bressler wonders if Chapman was trained to kill in Beirut. Or at least "blooded," that is, desensitized to violence there. Mae Brussell insisted that the CIA maintained a training camp for assassins in Beirut. There's no hard evidence, but if you had to pick a place to train assassins, Beirut is as good as you'll get.

The official version of Chapman's motive is that he was a "deranged fan," that he harbored a paranoid obsession with John Lennon. Bressler establishes that Chapman was not a fan of John Lennon. Suddenly, a few months before the murder, he began to identify with Lennon, even signing his own name "John Lennon" on at least one occasion. Could an image of John Lennon, one wonders, have been deliberately stamped into his puttylike brain?

Could Hinckley—whose travels took him through a number of strange interludes, including membership in a neo-Nazi group—have been a similar victim? His identification with the Travis Bickle character in the film *Taxi Driver* suggests that Hinckley, like Travis, was an alienated loner. Could the Jodie Foster gimmick have been the clever plan of someone who shaped Hinckley's mind, opening him to suggestion with drugs, then programming him with a movie, like Alex in *A Clockwork Orange*?

Before drawing his gun to shoot at Reagan, Hinckley has said that he had hoped someone would stop him. As he drew his gun, he felt, "Now I have no choice." He said he felt "relieved" once the shooting was over. Like Chapman and Sirhan, he squeezed out bullet after bullet, then became preternaturally calm, as if his predetermined function was now complete.

There are also a couple of parallels between Hinckley and Patrick Purdy, the commando-geared gunman who slaughtered seven Vietnamese children in a Stockton, California, school yard in 1989. Both had flirtations with neo-Nazi groups. And both were heavily dosed with psychiatric drugs—mind-control drugs, by definition. Purdy strode coolly into that playground, pumping away at his

AK-47, with the same glaze-eyed robotic demeanor characteristic of one-day spree killers. Many of those killers are dosed with mood-altering drugs, a fact little publicized when such tragedies occur.

Perhaps Hinckley and Purdy were the victims of psychiatry gone berserk, monsters manufactured by accident. Or perhaps they were deliberately programmed. Mind control is all very nebulous. Nonetheless, mind control is real, and no one seriously disputes that it is. Nor does anyone argue that under mind control, human beings can be made to do virtually anything, even take their own lives. No one argues these facts, because everyone knows that they happened, on November 18, 1978, in Jonestown, Guyana.

The United States government has worked on perfecting mind control for a long time. The CIA says it cut off its program in 1973, without having succeeded. If the sleazy "Messiah from Ukiah," Jim Jones, could master the art of mind control, is it crazy to believe that the government, with its vast resources, would also succeed?

Many survivors of the Jim Jones experience believe it. And, what's more, they believe Jonestown is *where* the government succeeded.

Jonestown bloomed in the moral and spiritual abyss of the 1970s. Like countless cults cropping up in that decade of soul-searching in the dark, its members were said to be brainwashed—living proof that human beings were just so much wire and circuitry. Cult members were often kidnapped back by their families. The hired kidnappers were called "deprogrammers." They might better have been called "reprogrammers."

Jim Jones transplanted his cult from its church in downtown San Francisco to the jungles of Guyana. There he set up his own utopia, and christened it in honor of himself. His followers were mostly black, mostly women, almost all poor. Some were homeless until they found the People's Temple and its prophet/king, clad in shades that made him look like a Secret Service agent. Even Jones's adopted home base, Ukiah, in California's unspoiled north country, suggested paradise on Earth.

The paradise of Jonestown was really hell. Jones abused and degraded his followers. He forced them into slave labor with minimal rations of food. When Congressman Leo Ryan made a trip to Jonestown, investigating allegations of Jones's brutality, he and several reporters were murdered.

One of the most ghoulish horrors in American history followed. On Jones's command, his brainwashed followers killed themselves, more than nine hundred of them, by the particularly gruesome method of drinking cyanide.

Those are the events as recorded by most chroniclers of the Jonestown massacre—the facts as most Americans believe them. As we often find with grisly murders, assassinations, and prominent suicides, there are unanswered, upsetting questions.

On audiotapes of the Jonestown massacre, Jim Jones's voice is audible. At one point, he is heard shouting, "Get Dwyer out of here!" This "Dwyer" was Richard Dwyer. And who was Richard Dwyer? He was a twenty-year veteran of the U.S. Central Intelligence Agency.

After the killing of Congressman Ryan and four others at the airstrip outside Jonestown, an eyewitness saw Dwyer "methodically" washing his hands.

"I've been stripping the dead," Dwyer explained. "It's not a nice job." Then the CIA agent, under cover as an embassy official, produced the wallets and other effects of the five killed there. Dwyer had been shot in the leg during the attack, but he said his wound was "fine." He stayed behind, apparently returning to Jonestown.

When Joseph Holsinger read, one year after the massacre, about the CIA man's presence at Jonestown, he was mortified. Holsinger was an aide to Leo Ryan, who was his best friend and mentor. The shadow of the CIA over Jonestown stirred grim suspicions in Holsinger. He began to contemplate the same possibility a number of People's Temple defectors had feared ever since the massacre.

Jim Jones was already a Mansonlike icon of evil to the American public. Holsinger and the others suspected that the reality of Jonestown was a far darker, more terrible evil.

Contrary to the television-movie Jonestown scenario, which spawned innumerable "Kool Aid" jokes, many of the Jonestown dead received their cyanide by injection into their upper arms, an unlikely spot for a suicide shot. The first coroner on the scene, Guyana's top pathologist C. Leslie Mootoo, stated that only two hundred of the victims actually died by their own hands. All 260 children who died at Jonestown were murdered, he said. Mootoo found one seven-year-old who died when cyanide was forcibly squirted into the back of his mouth.

The death toll jumped from initial reports of about four hundred to the final 913 total a couple of days later. The official explanation of the discrepancy is that bodies were stacked on top of each other. The skeptics' version is that hundreds of escapees were hunted down and slaughtered.

There were large quantities of psychotherapeutic drugs, including John Hinckley's favorite, Valium, found at the massacre site. The assassins of Leo Ryan were described as glassy eyed and methodical. The man charged with killing Ryan, Larry Layton, was said by his relatives to have lapsed into a "posthypnotic trance" as he became ever more absorbed by temple affairs. Layton's own father called him "a robot."

A CIA agent accompanying Jones. Murders, not suicides. Indications of a government cover-up. For Leo Ryan's aide Joseph Holsinger, the pieces were assembling to a shattering conclusion.

"[The] possibility is that Jonestown was a mass mind-control experiment by the CIA as part of its MKULTRA program," Holsinger said in 1980. An essay he'd received in the mail from a U.C. Berkeley psychologist, entitled "The Penal Colony," provided the final piece in the puzzle. "The Berkeley author of the article . . . believes that rather than terminating MKULTRA, the CIA shifted its programs from public institutions to private cult groups, including the People's Temple," Holsinger said.

Joyce Shaw, who spent six years in the temple but broke away before the move to Guyana, wondered if the mass suicide story was a cover for "some kind of horrible government experiments, or some sort of sick, racist thing . . . a plan like the Germans to exterminate blacks." Soon after Shaw quit the temple, her husband was killed in a strange railroad accident. Her father-in-law happened to be a friend of Leo Ryan, and that's how Ryan's investigation began.

There are eerie footnotes to the Jonestown conspiracy theory. They suggest that the conspiracy did not end with the slaughter in Guyana.

Far from a relic of 1960s' utopian naivete, Jones was for six years a Republican. He raised money for Richard Nixon. He was a Republican when he announced himself the reincarnation of both Jesus and Lenin, and led anti-war protests. His rightist ties extended to one of his closest advisers—a mercenary for UNITA, the CIA-supported Angolan rebel army.

In the early 1960s, Jones spent eleven months in Brazil, where, according to his next-door neighbor at the time, he "lived like a rich man." Why he was in Brazil—who knows? According to that same neighbor, "Some people here believed he was an agent for the American CIA."

The temple's lawyer was Mark Lane, who always seems to be around when events take a strange turn. Lane first became famous as the author of *Rush to Judgement*, a best-seller that spurred early doubts about the Warren

Commission. He has since represented several unusual clients, including the conspiracy-stalking Liberty Lobby, publishers of *Spotlight*, and sponsors of the neo-nativist (if not neo-Nazi) "Populist Party."

Lane is also coauthor of a book explaining a conspiracy behind the assassination of Martin Luther King, Jr. He is the longtime lawyer for James Earl Ray, King's accused assassin (like Mark David Chapman, Ray pleaded guilty and was never tried; he claims he was tricked into pleading the case by his pre-Lane legal team).

A memo recovered from Jonestown files showed that Jones and Lane considered smuggling a star King assassination witness to Jonestown (when the memo was discovered, Lane denied discussing the possibility). There are other bits of weirdness about Lane. Did he know about the danger to Leo Ryan, yet fail to warn the congressman? How did Lane escape the massacre?

Another bizarre footnote: There have been attempts to repopulate Jonestown. Not with blacks this time, but with Dominican and Indochinese refugees. Billy Graham's evangelical group was behind the repopulation program.

Jonestown was not the only "Jonestown." In Guyana, at the same time Jim Jones presided over what was either a cult or a government experiment, self-styled "Rabbi" David Hill lorded over "Hilltown." His eight thousand-member Nation of Israel cult made the People's Temple look puny. Hill had power outside his own domain. Some people in Guyana's capital called him the "vice prime minister."

The spookiest Jonestown doppelgänger was Chile's Colonia Dignidad. The 7,500-acre camp was home to a cult founded by German Paul Schaefer, and to the torture chambers of DINA, the Nazi-trained Chilean secret police. In fact, Colonia Dignidad, a slave-labor enterprise, was the concentration camp of Chile's fascist regime.

The American government running its own concentration camp at Jonestown—a brainwashing laboratory whose specimens spilled into public view. Unthinkable. No more unthinkable, though, than 913 people swallowing cyanide at the command of a lone madman.

One theory of Jonestown is that it was part of a "black genocide operation," intended to be one of many such programs to entrap, enslave, and eventually kill off black people.

In the game of American power, blacks are consistent losers. Many of those black political leaders with the most potential to alter that situation have been cut down. No conspiracy theories required: Effective black politics has been decapitated by violence.

Malcolm X was assassinated just as he was beginning to moderate his views on separatism, just as he was coming in from the political fringe. Martin Luther King, Jr., who never ran for office, was capable of changing the American system, and he did. He bridged society's gaps. When he was assassinated, he was beginning to preach about economic democracy that would unify the underprivileged of all races.

Civil rights leader Medgar Evars was also assassinated. King's mother was shot to death just days after King's widow stated that she believed a conspiracy killed her husband.

Huey Newton founded the Black Panther Party. Their violent public image to the contrary, the Black Panthers' most important achievements were in promoting community self-determination. Their free breakfast program for black schoolchildren was a model, and they started a private school that offered the quality education unavailable to inner city blacks in public schools. Newton was shot in an altercation with police and jailed for allegedly killing a police officer (long since passé, Newton was murdered on an Oakland street in 1989). Another Panther leader, Fred Hampton of Chicago, was gunned down by a gang of police who burst into his apartment at four in the morning.

The most recent death of an effective black leader came in August 1989. Mickey Leland, the Texas congressman who was the leading congressional advocate of African hunger relief, was killed on a mission to an Ethiopian refugee camp. The small plane carrying Leland and fifteen others—and which had been scheduled to have on board another outspoken black congressman, Ron Dellums—apparently crashed into the side of a mountain near Addis Ababa. The search for Leland in Marxist-ruled Ethiopia was the largest of its kind ever conducted. The intelligence community was openly involved, sending U-2 spy planes to survey the country.

A couple of the killings on the preceding list were obvious conspiracies. Others are more doubtful. The question is, if any were conspiracies, why?

There seem to be government connections to the assassination of Martin Luther King, Jr. Accused killer Ray was not arrested until nearly a month after the fact, in England, of all places. Where a nickel-and-dime crook like Ray got the funds for his extensive trans- and intercontinental travels piques the interest of all conspiracy researchers.

The government's unusual behavior in prosecuting (and some would say, defending) Ray was also cause for concern. Only one witness, a chronic drunkard and self-avowed racist named Charles Q. Stephens, gave a positive make on Ray as the gunman. But he didn't "recall" that Ray was the man he'd seen until six weeks later. On the night of the assassination, when interviewed by a newspaper reporter, Stephens described the man he'd seen fleeing from the alleged sniper's nest as "a nigger."

Stephens' live-in girlfriend, Grace Walden, has said that he was nearly unconscious from booze that night and couldn't have observed much of anything. Walden

had her own story. She had seen a white man—*not* fitting
Ray's description—running from the scene.

Walden was committed to a mental institution the
same day her boyfriend was taken into FBI protective
custody. A court later found that she was committed ille-
gally. Grace Walden was the witness Mark Lane and Jim
Jones discussed smuggling to Jonestown, according to the
memo found in Jonestown files.

Is there a systematic conspiracy to eliminate black
leaders, to disable and discredit black activist groups?
There are conspiratorial cadres, the Ku Klux Klan and
others, who wouldn't be averse to that aim. The FBI
formed its own conspiracy, COINTELPRO (short for
counterintelligence program), which planted provocateurs in black activist groups, crippling them.

When Hoover ordered a COINTELPRO against
white hate groups, it had a very different effect. Former
G-man Wesley Swearingen says Hoover "just didn't like
black people." The FBI actually formed its own chapter
of the KKK and recruited two hundred members. The
spectacle at one point featured an FBI agent promising
"peace and order in America if we have to kill every
Negro." Instead of weakening the racist movement, the
FBI strengthened it.

In addition to wrecking black activist movements from
within, the government has exercised official plans to
squash civil disturbances with force. The Nixon White
House "Operation Garden Plot" was originally aimed at
racial uprisings. After the 1970 invasion of Cambodia,
demonstrations erupted throughout the country. The
government activated Garden Plot against college students. Following the Kent State killings and numerous
clashes in California (where Governor Ronald Reagan
lustily cheered the operation on) the antiwar uprising was
critically maimed. Operation Garden Plot was still in effect as late as 1985.

Rex 84, a collaboration between the Defense Department and the Federal Emergency Management Agency, had a similar purpose. It provided for the president to declare martial law and round up Central American refugees into detention camps together with, presumably, domestic dissidents. One of Rex 84's authors was reportedly Oliver North.

Suffice to say, official conspiracies exist against minority groups, protesters, radicals, and activists. Whether they have secretly involved the systematic assassination of black leaders, whether they have entailed large-scale experiments in detention, mind control, and extermination, is the subject of conspiracy theory. The hypothetical purpose of such a large-scale conspiracy is a fact of social life in America: Blacks and other minorities remain the bulk of a massive economic underclass, a source of cheap labor, and a scapegoat for social ills like crime and drugs.

Traditional liberal analysis has it that the vicissitudes of economics and an amorphous "institutionalized racism" are the real roots of black economic subjugation. But the effort to find something more specific to blame is understandable. And in light of the public record, wholly justified.

Effective black leaders are a threat to the status quo, and that is motive enough for conspiracies to knock them off. Likewise, conspiracy theories surround the death of virtually anyone who poses a threat to the power structure. Often with good cause. The official explanations for many assassinations have more of a fairy-tale ambience than conspiracy theories. Conversely, many suspicious deaths give the appearance of not being suspicious at all.

The death of Pope John Paul I, for example, was attributed to a heart attack. Author David Yallop's bestseller *In God's Name* argues that John Paul I's papacy was truncated at thirty-three days by poisoning, not natural causes. The pope's plan to eradicate the Vatican's

global financial empire and expose the Masonic membership of high-ranking clergymen, Yallop says, aroused the
wrath of the Masonic-fascist Propaganda Due (P2)
Lodge.

As early as 1952, the CIA was discussing how to
"knock off key guys" and make it look like natural
causes, declassified CIA memos have revealed. Heart attacks and cancer are preferred methods. CIA director
William Casey developed a brain tumor just as he was
supposed to make public his knowledge of the Iran-Contra affair. Nelson Rockefeller suffered a heart attack *in
flagrante delecto* with his secretary. Two assassination
plots against Gerald Ford would have made Rockefeller
president, but they both failed. Once Rocky was no
longer useful, he turned up dead.

Suicides are also popular, as are one-car accidents.
Kennedy haters have no trouble envisioning a heavy-
handed Kennedy-engineered conspiracy behind Chappaquidick and the death of Mary Jo Kopechne. Other theorists take the same anomalous facts—unusual dents in the
car, time lapses in Ted Kennedy's memory—to mean that
Kennedy and Kopechne were victims: he drugged, she
murdered. Chappaquidick was final insurance that a Kennedy brother would not be president.

Some researchers have told me that even journalist Jessica Savitch was the victim of a conspiracy. She was coming back as an investigative reporter, after cocaine-
burnout, when she perished in a Chappaquidick-style
plunge.

The argot of conspiracy theory has given us the word
"suicide" as a verb, as in "He got too close, so they sui-
cided him." Was Joseph Daniel "Danny" Casolaro "sui-
cided" on August 10, 1991? He was found dead with
slashed wrists in a hotel bathtub. He had been investigating, in some weird way, an entity he called "the Octo-
pus," supposedly the brains behind a slew of scandals and
alleged conspiracies in the Reagan administration. Those

two facts alone were enough to start a maelstrom of speculation.

There were other facts, too. His missing notes and papers. The death threats that had been phoned to his home. The strangely quick embalming. The mysterious "source" he was supposed to meet that night. Casolaro's brother suspected "suiciding." So did Eliot Richardson, a former attorney general of the United States whose credibility has never been questioned. At this writing, the Casolaro case is still foggy. One thing is certain. In places like Colombia and other countries where conspiracies really do happen, journalists get whacked all the time, though police ruled Casolaro's death self-inflicted.

The most reliable method, at least for big jobs, is still the lone nut. Not one but two lone nuts took separate shots (or tried to—neither was very competent with a handgun) at Gerald Ford, who stood in the way of intelligence and oil overlord Nelson Rockefeller's ascendance to the Oval Office. One of the "nuts," Sarah Jane Moore, worked for the FBI and three other police agencies. The other, Lynette Fromme, was a member of the Manson Family, conspiracy theories about which are the subject of a later chapter.

Michael Milan, who claims he was a hit man for Hoover, says that he was offered a contract on Ford, but declined it as "suicide."

Then there is the long list of dead people connected with the Iran-Contra affair. Many of them may have had knowledge of an "October Surprise" deal between the 1980 Reagan for President campaign and the Islamic Iranian government. The deal is said to have delayed the release of American hostages until after Reagan's inauguration in exchange for arms shipments and other covert collaboration.

The list of Iran-Contra/October Surprise casualties should be taken in the spirit as the hit parade following the J.F.K. assassination. Topping the charts is the aforementioned William Casey, who was Reagan's campaign manager in 1980. Amaram Nir, an Israeli officer who was his country's Oliver North, went down in a possibly sabotaged plane late in 1988. Fund-raiser Carl "Spitz" Channel died in a hit-and-run accident.

Arms dealer Cyrus Hashemi met his maker a surprisingly short two days after finding out he had cancer. Iranian foreign minister Sadegh Ghotbzadeh may have been the person who talked Khomeini into holding the hostages until Reagan was safely in office. A year later, he was tortured and executed on Khomeini's orders after plotting a coup. William Buckley, CIA Beirut station chief, was killed by Islamic fundamentalist kidnappers in 1985. There are reports that Buckley, too, knew firsthand of the Reagan-Iran deal in 1980.

My reaction, when I first began researching assassination conspiracy theories, was probably a typical one: "Doesn't anybody just die?" I've heard conspiracy theories for every dead person from J. Edgar Hoover to Lenny Bruce. My instinctive reaction was always if not to scoff, then at least to look askance. But far be it from me to dismiss any theory out of hand. I've only been able to study a few, and most in less than the detail I would have liked. Inevitably, when I do a little digging, I find enough strange circumstances to make me dizzy.

The average human mind can handle a few conspiracies; the concept of conspiracies by the hundreds is harder to accept. Still there are premises: People are killed, and their deaths lead to political changes. These political changes benefit a few people at the expense of the great many. There are murky circumstances around many such deaths. The conclusions one can draw from those premises often cross the threshold of belief.

Assassination conspiracy theories are easy to write off as fantasy conceived in trauma—the desperate imagination of disappointed idealists grasping for reasons why their dreams are as dead as their heroes. But there is an upsetting logic to those theories. The dyspepsia is worsened by the unreal quality "official versions" usually exude. Violence, murder, war, and terror have restructured America's social and political order over the past three decades.

Something is terribly wrong. No one can be blamed for asking what it is. We can blame only ourselves when we expect the answer to comfort us, and it does not.

12

THIS IS YOUR GOVERNMENT
ON DRUGS

This is your brain on drugs.

> Voice-over from an anti-drug
> public service announcement
> on television, read while an
> egg is shown frying.

In 1931, Aldous Huxley published *Brave New World,* the story of a totalitarian government satiating citizens with drugs, to maintain their complacency. The novel, now familiar to tenth-grade English students everywhere, was set in the future. Suppose Huxley's future is now.

"I think it is no mistake that a majority of the drugs in this country is being deposited in black and Hispanic and lower-income neighborhoods across the country," film-maker Spike Lee said, on an ABC "Nightline" show.

"The epidemic of drugs and violence in the black community stems from a calculated attempt by whites to foster black self-destruction," echoes Louis Farrakhan, head of the Nation of Islam.

"The theory is that the white establishment pushed heroin into the black community to divert young people from political action," explains Andrew Cooper, publisher of Brooklyn weekly newspaper *The City Sun,* "so they'd be zonked out and wouldn't be a threat."

The drug conspiracy theory is not peculiar to the African-American community. In varying permutations and degrees of intensity, it is widely discussed. Senator John Kerry of Massachusetts would hardly endorse the rather rash pronouncements of Spike Lee or Louis Farrakhan. But he did "see a larger conspiracy here than met the eye." His committee's investigation concluded that CIA agents and U.S. government officials knew about and participated in cocaine smuggling by Nicaraguan contras in league with Colombia's cocaine barons. In the 1980s, when the contra war was flaring, cocaine suddenly became cheap and plentiful. Previously a status drug of decadent neo-sophisticates, cocaine emerged in smokable "crack" form, permeating inner cities as well as suburbs.

On the other end of the spectrum from Kerry is Lyndon LaRouche, who ascribes the international drug trade to British masterminds, secretly perpetuating the empire, with the full knowledge of the queen.

The truth is in there somewhere. Individual drug problems may be the fault of individuals, but despite current enthusiasm for persecuting "the casual user," America's drug problem appears to have been inflicted upon it.

At one level, most of us are vaguely aware of that fact. While not usually reported in the news media, the entertainment media—which speaks to far more Americans—have occasionally taken up the theme. I won't go through a filmography here. But one movie scene that said more than it probably intended cropped up in *The Godfather.* At a meeting of Mafia chieftains trying to plan how to handle the previously taboo heroin business, they agree to confine sales to black neighborhoods. "They're animals anyway," says one of the celluloid dons. "Let them lose their souls."

That was only a movie, of course. But it is hardly unthinkable that a real-life version of that conversation took place. It is only half true that the Mafia had a code of honor prohibiting it from trafficking in narcotics. Salvatore C. Luciana, a.k.a. Charles "Lucky" Luciano, was first arrested for heroin possession in 1915, when his criminal "family" was still known quaintly as the "107th Street Gang."

But the heroin business did not begin booming for Luciano, who innovated and dominated it, until after World War II. Luciano organized Sicilian gangs into a nationwide structure, and aligned them with their Jewish counterparts controlled by the likes of Meyer Lansky and Bugsy Siegel. With this flourish of managerial élan, Luciano created the national organized crime syndicate—the Mafia, La Cosa Nostra, the Outfit, the Mob.

The immediate postwar period seems an ironic time for an increase in heroin traffic. At no other time since the drug was introduced did U.S. law enforcers have a better opportunity to wipe out the problem of heroin. Austerity inflicted by the war forced most junkies to go cold turkey, so demand was down. At the same time, supplies came up short. Shipping channels were impeded by the always inconvenient presence of torpedoes whistling through the water, and American customs security had been tightened. The intent was to stop spies and saboteurs from getting into the country, but heroin smugglers got caught in the net as well.

In China, opium operators found themselves face-to-face with Mao's rebel armies, which swept them away. In France, Corsican gangsters were the source of the heroin business, and many of them shortsightedly chose to collaborate with the occupying Nazis. Once the Allies liberated France, the Corsicans' wartime selection of associates did not sit well with their countrymen. They had a hard time reopening for business. In Italy, Mussolini carried out a personal vendetta against the Sicilian Mafia, which left that heroin stronghold in sorry straits.

After World War II, there were a scant twenty thousand addicts in the whole U.S.A., down from ten times that twenty years earlier. A mild tightening of the thumbscrews and heroin could have been, for all practical purposes, banished from the country.

Instead, the exact opposite happened. This entrepreneurial coup owed much to the amazing ingenuity of Luciano and his fellow mobsters. But he couldn't have done it without the help of his dear, dear friends in the United States government.

The military first bonded with organized crime in 1942. Unable to control sabotage of Allied ships on the New York waterfront, the Office of Naval Intelligence had what Oliver North might call "a neat idea." Gangsters already had their hooks into the New York docks. The naval spies decided to get them to help out. "Operation Underworld," as the Navy called this little adventure, led them directly to Lucky Luciano. Doing business from prison, Luciano agreed to cooperate, and the government's first show of good faith was to have the underworld overlord transferred to a cushier jail, near Albany, New York. There he received military intelligence officers as visitors, and also met with colleagues like Lansky.

The military-Mafiosi joint venture extended overseas. General George S. Patton, the legendary blood-'n'-guts commander of the Seventh Army, sliced through Sicily like scissors through silk. Patton was a general of extraordinary martial dexterity, but the sixty thousand troops and countless booby traps in his path should have given him at least a few problems. His way had been cleared by Sicily's Mafia boss Calogero Vizzini, at the request of Luciano.

The mob and the U.S. military nuzzled closer once Allied forces secured Sicily and installed an occupational government. Needing to maintain law and order, but also needing as many of its own troops as possible for the remaining campaign through Italy, the occupying Ameri-

can Army appointed Mafia bosses—including Vizzini—
mayors of many Sicilian townships. Gangsters became an
American-backed quasi-police force.

The Americans used the gangsters to bust the burgeoning antifascist resistance in Italy. This seems paradoxical, because the Americans were fighting the Italian
fascists and one would think they'd welcome a strong,
indigenous resistance movement. The problem was, the
resistance was loaded with leftists. Italian Communist
Party membership swelled. These developments were far
more alarming to the American occupiers than any fascists they might have to fight. The Mafia became willing
warriors in the anti-Communist struggle, which seemed
to supplant the not-yet-complete effort against the fascists who still ruled Italy.

The military literally let their Mafia henchmen get
away with murder. Vizzini killed the police chief in Vil-
laba, where, thanks to the Americans, he was mayor. In
American-occupation headquarters, one of the best employees was Vito Genovese, who eventually inherited Luciano's New York operation. The Genovese crime family
is one of New York's five families, among the most formidable mob syndicates in the country.

After the war, military intelligence sprang Luciano
from prison and had him deported along with a legion of
his organized crime associates. From abroad, Luciano and
Co. founded what might as well be called Heroin, Inc., an
illegal multinational corporation.

Havana, Cuba, became Luciano's hub of operations.
When Luciano himself was forced out of Cuba, he turned
management chores over to Santos Trafficante, the Miami
boss. Trafficante grew into one of the most powerful—
maybe *the* most powerful—godfather in the country.
When the CIA wanted to assassinate Fidel Castro, Trafficante was one of the mobsters it turned to. In 1979, the
House Select Committee on Assassinations recommended Trafficante as one of the "certain individuals" in

organized crime bearing investigation in connection with the John F. Kennedy assassination.

Between 1946, when Luciano set up his heroin shop, and 1952, the addict total in the U.S. tripled, then jumped to 150,000 by 1965, due primarily to the efforts of Luciano's new operation.

Six years later, that number had doubled and nearly doubled again, the addict population topping half a million. The epidemic is often attributed to the Woodstock generation and the proliferation of hedonistic hippies, but the CIA's partnership with opium-growing Laotian warlords probably has as much to do with it. The CIA's covert operation in Laos during the Vietnam War remains the largest it has ever staged.

The "Golden Triangle," Laos, northern Thailand, and Burma, is where seventy percent of the world's opium comes from. Much of the raw opium goes to Marseilles and Sicily, where Corsican and Mafia gangs have laboratories to turn it into heroin for sale by the Luciano-founded crime syndicate.

The CIA's own thinly disguised cover airline, Air America, flew raw opium in and out of Laos, as a way of financing the illegal Laotian war without going to Congress. Much of the heroin manufactured from the CIA-couriered base was sold to American servicemen in Southeast Asia, who developed a widespread heroin problem.

In the fall of 1990, a book called *Kiss the Boys Goodbye,* coauthored by intelligence expert William Stevenson and his wife Monica (a former "60 Minutes" reporter), documented how the CIA and the military quashed investigations into POWs left in Vietnam after the war. Many of the POWs, the book says, were involved in CIA drug operations, which is why the government is none too eager to get them home.

Conservative billionaire H. Ross Perot was charged by President Reagan with scouting out leftover POWs.

Frustrated, he told then vice president George Bush, "I go looking for prisoners, but I spend all my time discovering the government has been moving drugs around the world."

Those junkie GIs who did make it back stateside brought their jones to the home front, fostering the worst drug problem the country had, to that date, ever seen. The heroin plague led Richard Nixon to declare the first "War on Drugs." It was an interesting move for Nixon, because he was also responsible for the war on Laos.

These things always seem to come full circle.

A little more than a decade later, the CIA staged its second largest covert operation—propping up Afghan *mujahedin* guerrillas against Soviet invaders. Like the Laotians before them, the Afghans used opium as a financing tool. And the Americans were there.

Author James Mills spent five years tracking international drug traffic for his book *The Underground Empire*. He came away with that same observation.

"You do not have to be a CIA hater," noted Mills, "to trek around the world viewing one major narcotics group after another and grow amazed at the frequency with which you encounter the still-fresh footprints of American intelligence agents."

Heroin was not made illegal in the United States until 1924. Invented in the nineteenth century as a "nonaddictive" pain reliever to replace morphine, it was in widespread medicinal use until the country noticed that not every heroin consumer was using the drug strictly according to doctor's orders. The drug's real name is diacetylmorphine. "Heroin" is a brand name invented by its first distributor, the Bayer corporation.

In the early 1990s, heroin is back in fashion and appears more plentiful than ever. It's now used as a supplement to the drug that took the country by storm in the decade just past—cocaine.

Like heroin, cocaine started out as a legal drug. A popular pick-me-up, it was an ingredient in the soft drink that bears its name, Coca-Cola. Once outlawed, cocaine became the purview of gangsters. Heroin ran westerly, controlled by the Mafia, but cocaine filtered north, from Latin America. Once again, the United States government was there to help out. It was, as Yogi Berra might say, déjà vu all over again.

The CIA-contra-cocaine connection is a complicated conundrum. One of the biggest names in the business was Manuel Noriega, the former dictator of Panama, who was seized during the December 1989 U.S. invasion of Panama. At this writing, Noriega sits in a Florida jail after being found guilty of drug smuggling in April 1992.

To comprehend the government's role in cocaine traffic, Noriega is useful as a kind of focal point. He was on the payroll of the CIA at the same time he worked for the Medellín Cartel for four million dollars per month. The Medellín Cartel is the Colombian cocaine syndicate, responsible for most of the cocaine that enters the U.S.A.

Noriega was also connected to George Bush, and through Bush to Oliver North. They used Noriega as a conduit for getting arms to the contras.

Bush, North, and other government insiders at the CIA and the National Security Council (which under Reagan got heavily into covert operations) most likely knew about Noriega's involvement with drugs. Revelations about Noriega, and about direct contra and CIA involvement with cocaine smuggling, found their way into the public record via a subcommittee of the Senate Foreign Relations Committee, chaired by John Kerry.

In 1986, Senator Kerry received information that the Costa Rican branch of a Miami-based shrimp company Ocean Hunter, widely regarded as a drug-running front, had received checks for more than $200,000 dollars from the U.S. government. The money was part of the "humanitarian aid" allocated for the contras by Congress. Wondering why the cash was channeled to this shrimp-and-dope outfit, Kerry went to the FBI asking for an inquiry. Instead, the FBI investigated Kerry himself.

According to FBI reports, North asked the FBI to investigate Kerry, to find links between the Massachusetts senator and the Nicaraguan Sandinista government. The investigation was reportedly initiated by a crack FBI counterintelligence group usually employed to track foreign agents in the United States.

To North's distress, the agents did not find evidence to follow through with a full-scale investigation. North may have had reason to worry. The Drug Enforcement Administration had knowledge in the fall of 1986 that the flight crews making clandestine arms deliveries to the contras were flying cocaine into the U.S. on their return trips. When DEA agents confronted one of the pilots, he told them he had White House protection. He dropped North's name. The agents didn't pursue the North connection, dismissing the pilot's statement as "a bluff."

Accounts of secret testimony before Kerry's committee revealed that Felix Rodriguez, CIA agent and friend of George Bush, arranged a ten million dollar donation to the contras direct from the Medellín cartel. The cartel's chief accountant and money launderer (at least until he was arrested), Ramon Milian Rodriguez, testified to the donation. Milian Rodriguez is said to have conveyed $180,000 in campaign contributions from the cartel to Ronald Reagan's 1984 presidential campaign, and was invited to Reagan's inauguration as a gesture of thanks from the grateful candidate. It was Milian Rodriguez who made the monthly multimillion dollar payoffs to Noriega on the Medellín cartel's behalf.

The guns-for-drugs deals, many of which centered on the Costa Rican ranch of alleged CIA operative John Hull (who kept a private army of up to one hundred men) have been officially documented. Both Kerry's committee and the Costa Rican government uncovered the drugs-and-government conspiracy, yet the scandal has little resonance. In the middle of an inexorable flow of antidrug hysteria, the United States Senate found government officials smuggling drugs. The official House-Senate Iran-Contra investigating committee never touched the contra drug connection, and, therefore, the daily press ignored the story. The omission looks like nothing if not a deliberate cover-up. On the other hand, who knows if the cognitive dissonance induced by a government both fighting and favoring drug traffickers would have been too much for the American people?

The whole story might have emerged if the media had paid attention to an obscure case of dirty money and drug smuggling in California's Napa Valley, a plush area beloved for its vineyards and wineries. The story, which has enough intrigue to hook any audience, has been covered by no media outlet other than a free semi weekly called the *Napa Sentinel*, with a circulation of twenty thousand. Mixed in with stories about the local Oktoberfest and "Volunteer of the Year" were such headlines as "Drugs, CIA, Real Estate and Napa Connections" and "Former Napan Linked to CIA Arms-Drugs."

As with the Collier brothers and their Votescam series in the *Home News*, it takes an eccentric little local paper to touch such torrid topics. The only other play the Napa "Drug Tug" case gets is from David Emory, who has read all of the *Sentinel*'s articles on his Sunday night show and enriched them with his own uninhibited speculations.

The story began in 1988, when a tugboat packed with hashish, the "Drug Tug," was seized by federal agents in San Francisco Bay. Subsequent investigations found that the fees collected by the Drug Tug's captain were laun-

dered through a Napa real-estate investment firm called
"LendVest," which collapsed after the boat was seized
and Captain Calvin Robinson arrested.

"The Drug Tug—which made several trips before being seized—was a transportation instrument used to ferry
drugs from CIA-appointed sources to CIA-designated
drug brokers," wrote Harry V. Martin, the paper's editor
and author of the series. "The purpose was to gain a
source of clandestine financing to aid the *contra* movement."

The *Sentinel*'s stories disclosed a Möbius loop of links.
According to Martin's stories: Robinson was connected
to Thomas Smith, a drug trafficker with ties to the
Medellín cartel, and to the CIA through Air America.
The Drug Tug's up-front fifteen-million dollar fee came
from Panama, laundered through Costa Rica. The Costa
Rican laundry man was Kenneth Armitage, a wealthy En-
glishman on the lam for fraud charges. Armitage was later
returned to England, where he died in prison before coming to trial.

Armitage was also a business partner of Noriega. The
Brit owned an island off of Costa Rica used as a midway
point for El Norte-bound drug shipments. To keep the
island secure, Noriega funneled money into the 1982
Costa Rican elections. When the contra war started siz-
zling, the CIA touched down on the island, leaving weapons there which would later be funneled to the contras
via Hull's ranch.

The Costa Rican government, investigating the CIA-
arms-drugs operation, in 1989 reported that Hull and
Noriega were also working for Oliver North at the National Security Council. North testified to the U.S. Congress that the president approved of everything he did.
North was also working with George Bush, or so documents that have materialized through Freedom of Information Act releases indicate. North and Bush traveled
together in 1983 to a meeting with Noriega.

Part of the Drug Tug scam was a counterfeit passport operation that let smugglers travel freely to the "drug island," according to Harry Martin's reporting. In 1990, Christic Institute chief counsel Daniel Sheehan, unaware of the Drug Tug case, made a prediction; news of the Noriega case had dropped from the headlines, but Sheehan predicted that when the case finally came to trial Noriega would be charged with little more than passport forgery.

The *Napa Sentinel* series is full of surprises. It draws Colorado mob figures into the Drug Tug scenario, and the outre personage of Christopher Boyce. A cellmate of Calvin Robinson, Boyce spied for the Soviets and ended up with his exploits glossied and glorified in a movie, *The Falcon and the Snowman*, in which he was played by Timothy Hutton. Boyce, according to Martin's stories, tried to enlist Robinson in a bank-robbing spree. Boyce escaped prison less than a week after Robinson was released, and the Drug Tug skipper may have sheltered the CIA turncoat in Santa Cruz.

Martin included plenty of historical support for his Drug Tug revelations. He wrapped up his series with a fifty-six-name "Who's Who in the Drug Tug Series" inventory. On the list, alongside Oliver North, Manuel Noriega, and Dan Quayle, is Lucky Luciano.

For government insiders, collaboration with the drug trade appears to have been a matter of convenience rather than an organized conspiracy to somatize the population, or certain segments thereof. Still, it did and does have that numbing effect. America's thirst for instant gratification is quelled by drugs better than anything, with the possible exception of television.

Just as disseminating fire water to Native Americans insured the final victory of the white man, infusing American culture, particularly its economically lower branches, with heroin and cocaine has gone a long way toward keeping minorities and the poor out of the ball game.

Middle classes, too. Drug use, cocaine use especially, began as a middle-class diversion and infects placid suburbs, school yards, and executive boardrooms. As drug use in America has gone up, political involvement (measured by voter turnout) has dropped. Could be a coincidence. Nevertheless, drugs are an important element in the stupefaction of America.

The government officials who gave aid and comfort to drug traffickers were surely aware that the stuff was not cotton candy. I can see them justifying their involvement with the *Godfather* rationale: "They're animals anyway, let them lose their souls." Only this time, they're talking not only about blacks, but about everyone.

Opiates and coca derivatives are soul stealers, to be sure. The other popular strain of "illicit" drugs, hallucinogens, have had, at least ostensibly, the opposite effect. LSD and its fellow psychedelics politicized a generation.

LSD, which like heroin and cocaine was developed by corporate researchers (in the case of LSD, Sandoz Pharmaceuticals), was introduced to America largely by the CIA through its MKULTRA program (see the previous chapter). Like cocaine, it began as a luxury, a perk that came with membership in the ruling class. Henry Luce, *Time* magazine publisher and CIA mouthpiece, was among the first users, as was his wife, Clare Booth Luce. *Life* magazine, a Luce subsidiary, ran a lengthy piece by J. P. Morgan Company vice president R. Gordon Wasson, extolling the joys of psychedelics. In the early MKULTRA experiments, CIA agents ate LSD with enthusiasm, even if they often feigned detachment.

MKULTRA fed the drug to human subjects, both willing and unsuspecting, in prisons, hospitals, and university labs. The public record renders disingenuous the statement of former CIA director and MKULTRA father Richard Helms: "We do not target American citizens."

Could the MKULTRA-related LSD programs have extended beyond the appalling instances of human experimentation that are fully documented? We've mentioned the theory that MKULTRA was never terminated, only transferred to "cult" groups that use mind control to train assassins. Did the CIA go even further than that, inundating American streets with LSD in an attempt to bring about some kind of societal transformation?

The whole idea smacks of Lyndon LaRouche's "New Dark Ages" conspiracy theory. LaRouche pegs such psychedelic pioneers as Aldous Huxley as part of the British establishment still ruling the world through occult techniques, manipulation of the drug culture most notably. A more plausible motive (realizing that "plausible" is a relative term here) would be the establishment's need to rip apart the fabric of progressive politics. The CIA, FBI, and various other intelligence organs were trying to do just that throughout the 1960s and before, placing provocateurs and informers inside all significant left-leaning political groups. If there was a governmental LSD conspiracy, it could have been trying to accomplish the same thing on a massive scale.

The book *Acid Dreams: The CIA, LSD and the Sixties Rebellion*, by investigative journalists Martin A. Lee and Bruce Shlain, contains the curious tale of Ronald Stark, the most prolific manufacturer of LSD in the late 1960s. The largest percentage of LSD in circulation, more than fifty million doses, came from Stark's laboratories, in those years that the youth movement was spinning out of control. Ronald Stark, as Lee and Shlain report, may well have been a CIA agent. He was chummy with European terrorists as well as diplomats, and bragged that the CIA tipped him to shut down his French LSD lab.

"Was Stark a hired provocateur or a fanatical guerrilla capable of reconciling bombs and LSD?" wonder the authors of *Acid Dreams.* They note that when Stark, a fugitive from drug charges involving his 1960s LSD operation, was finally brought back to the U.S. in 1982, he was imprisoned only briefly and then the Justice Department dropped all charges against him. Two years later, Stark died of a heart attack. Or should that read "apparent" heart attack?

Acid Dreams also records that on Richard Helms's command, most of the official documents concerning the CIA's romance with LSD were shredded due to what one official called "a burgeoning paper problem." That explanation has the same ring as the Defense Intelligence Agency's claim that their shredding of files on Lee Harvey Oswald was "routine."

"The use of LSD among young people in the U.S. reached a peak in the late 1960s, shortly after the CIA initiated a series of covert operations designed to disrupt, discredit and neutralize the New Left," Lee and Shlain comment. "Was this merely historical coincidence, or did the Agency actually take steps to promote the illicit acid trade?"

The first effect of LSD on the radical, progressive movement was catalyzing, invigorating. Its final effect was dissipating, destructive. What doomed the movement —one of the many factors—was the "delusions of grandeur" that charged it, fueled by LSD, say Lee and Shlain. "They wanted to change the world *immediately*—or at least as fast as LSD could change a person's consciousness."

In the end, it was impatience that led the progressive movement into trying to change the world by fiat, rather than through the organization, education, and strategic action that leads to deep changes in the system. LSD began as a spark and ended as a short circuit. And LSD, at least to some extent, came from the CIA.

"LSD makes people less competent," notes drug culture paragon William S. Burroughs, who wondered if the

LSD craze was something other than what its adherents thought. "You can see their motivation for turning people on."

The irony of the LSD conspiracy, if it was real, is that while it wrecked the progressive movement, the social transformation it wrought was far larger than any narrow political goal. Whether on purpose or not, elements of American society were alchemically transformed.

Or is it so ironic? Perhaps that was the plan: like all conspiracies, a design of a few to induce a change in the masses—the secret agenda of a secret society.

13

CIA: THE DEPARTMENT
OF CONSPIRACY

There exists in our nation today a powerful and dangerous secret cult—the cult of intelligence.

VICTOR MARCHETTI and JOHN
D. MARKS, *The CIA and
the Cult of Intelligence*

The United States Central Intelligence Agency was created on September 18, 1947, when Harry S. Truman signed the National Security Act. Most of the debate over the act centered on its restructuring of the military. The Army and Navy were joined, the Air Force was created, and all three branches were placed under the secretary of defense, a new position. All but lost on the public, and Congress as well, was an equally unsettling concentration of power. The act brought the nation's numerous intelligence services under a single department. It seemed almost an afterthought.

Following the chaos of Pearl Harbor, the government was desperate to assemble some sort of clearinghouse for intelligence. Eisenhower himself bemoaned the "glaring deficiencies" of the manifold intelligence bureaus. Virtually every agency of the U.S. government has an intelligence wing. The Central Intelligence Agency was chartered to collect information from those diverse outfits, and pull it into a neat little package for the president. Hence the name, "Central" Intelligence Agency. The CIA was to be the central station through which all intelligence was routed.

The CIA was never meant to do its own spying. And it certainly wasn't meant to conduct clandestine operations. The original purpose of the CIA was to summarize and analyze the information turned up by other intelligence operations. It was a report-writing department.

Truman's intention appeared innocuous—to create a smoother running intelligence collation machine. But when he'd created the CIA's immediate predecessor, the Central Intelligence Group a year earlier, Truman celebrated by throwing a party at which guests were presented with cloaks, daggers, and black hats. Strange, for a bunch of supposed pencil pushers. Truman was a devoted Mason, and therefore accustomed to clandestine rituals and bizarre symbolism. Maybe he was just being funny.

Truman's possible true purpose notwithstanding, almost everything the CIA does today violates the terms of its creation.

The CIA's one loophole is a fuzzy phrase in the 1947 law. According to the bill signed by Truman, the Central Intelligence Agency would perform "other functions" at the discretion of the National Security Council. The language of the act is fairly specific. Those "other functions" relate only to intelligence. Nowhere does it mention clandestine operations. Even so, the "other functions" clause has been the rationale for what over the past more than forty years has become, in addition to a massive government bureaucracy, a fully functioning, government-sanctioned, secret society.

There is little doubt that Congress did not mean "other functions" to encompass all of the operations the CIA is known to have undertaken, and that it definitely was not intended to cover the things the CIA *may* have done (namely, the assassinations and dope dealing cov-

ered in the previous two chapters). When they were de-
bating the National Security Act, some congressmen
worried that a centralized intelligence operation could
turn into a United States "Gestapo." Because of those
fears, the agency has remained on the penumbra of government operations.

The CIA stays there for the same reason secret societies over the past few thousand years have kept their internal workings encrypted. Secret societies are secret because what they do offends popular morality.

There are many other American intelligence agencies
besides the CIA. Nor is the CIA directly responsible for
everything its agents do. The agency is known to contract
much of its touchier business out to semimoral mercenary types, who, even when their CIA obligations expire,
still feel free to claim CIA affiliation as license to do almost anything. The agency probably is inclined to cover
for them, lest past questionable endeavors be exposed.
Then again, these lone operators are so easily written off
as "renegades" that, when they do work for the CIA,
they lend convenient deniability to illegal operations. The
sophisticated use of covert agents is but one strategy the
CIA shares with the archetypical, conspiratorial secret
society.

The CIA keeps its very charter a mystery. No one on
the outside knows the real purpose of the CIA, as set out
in top-secret presidential directives, piled up over the
years, which constitute the "charter." In 1968, the deputy
director of the agency's "dirty tricks" department said (in
what he thought were confidential remarks) that the
CIA's charter "must remain secret . . . the problem of a
secret charter remains as a curse, but the need for secrecy
would appear to preclude a solution."

"We are not Boy Scouts," added one of the CIA's
most storied directors, Richard Helms. Helms put his un-
scouting morality to work as the originator of MKUL-

TRA, the CIA's mind-control project, which tested the brand new drug LSD on human subjects.

There is a long-standing regulation that any incident that might embarrass or expose the CIA is to be immediately reported to the agency's Office of Security, the CIA's internal police force meant to secure it from enemy infiltration. In reality, the Office of Security spends much time securing the agency from exposure to the public. That's what happened when a CIA employee, Frank Olsen, was slipped a dose of LSD without his knowledge. Olsen was a lab rat for a MKULTRA experiment. The bad trip drove him crazy and he leapt out of a New York hotel room window. The CIA denied for years that it had anything to do with his death.

Secret societies stay secret by draping their real affairs in myth. Some of the myth is beyond their control. Whenever something is secret, people are going to speculate about it. Some of the myth is deliberately concocted by the secret society itself, to mystify the uninitiated, or terrorize them. With all secret societies, it is difficult to demarcate where the myths end and truth begins. Often, the two are commingled.

The CIA is no different. The catchall myth the agency whips up to garb its true designs is "national security." Exposing CIA activities, we're told, would endanger this "security," which is your personal security, by implication. The myth, more than a little self-aggrandizing, creates a mystique, a godlike importance for all the secret practices of the CIA.

As a rationale for too many CIA endeavors, "national security" is about as real as the cloaking device used by alien spaceships on "Star Trek." And it serves the same purpose, just as effectively.

The CIA is a deft, effective manufacturer of myth about itself. When the CIA's station chief for Greece, Richard Welch, was gunned down on his doorstep on December 23, 1975, the agency wasted little time griev-

ing. Reflexively and with consummate cynicism, it turned
the assassination into the perfect case for tightening its
own security. The CIA's self-serving disinformation effort in the Welch affair was so sudden and smooth that
one wonders if the CIA itself didn't know about the killing in advance. Welch's murder couldn't have come at a
better time for the CIA. In the aftermath of Watergate, its
secrets were exploding in Congress and in the press with
the severity of an aneurysm. The agency needed to stop
the hemorrhage.

Welch's identity had been revealed in *CounterSpy,* a
magazine of investigative reporting on the CIA,
cofounded by CIA dissident Philip Agee. *CounterSpy*
made a practice of publishing the names of CIA officers,
ferreting out the data from public records. The CIA was
not pleased by this practice. What it didn't want the
American people to know is what any interested citizen
of a foreign country already knew: that the names of important CIA officers were readily available to anyone
with the mild determination needed to discover them.

The Greek revolutionary "November 17" group had
been planning Welch's "execution" long before his name
was published. The assassins staked him out for months.
But as soon as CIA headquarters got the news of Welch's
killing, the agency's press spokesman phoned reporters
(on "deep background" of course) to inform them of
both the murder, and the *CounterSpy* article naming
Welch. The national press needed little prodding to make
the link. Official hysteria was immediate. Eventually,
Congress passed the "Intelligence Identities Protection
Act," outlawing publication of CIA names.

It was all a myth. The CIA knew, in the summer of
1975, even before it shipped Welch to Greece, a nation in
loathing of the CIA, that he was in danger there. Headquarters warned him not to move into the same house
that several previous CIA station chiefs had occupied, but
he moved in anyway. After his name appeared, along

with his address and job description in the English-language *Athens News,* the CIA, if it were really worried, could have removed him from Greece, but it did not. Welch's killing had nothing to do with *CounterSpy* or any other publication.

But the CIA took the opportunity to rebuild the then-eroding fiction that public scrutiny of the CIA endangers not only national security, but the lives of individual men. Such propaganda only fuels more myth, of a type not as flattering to the CIA.

The conspiratorial demonology of the CIA, the myths that originate with ordinary people who feel the need to pierce the CIA's secrecy, are different from the propaganda myths authored by the CIA. Popular myths, seething from the zeitgeist, are not deliberate falsehoods. They grow to explain things that we can't understand. There is often far more truth to them, literal and figurative truth, than we'd like to suppose. The CIA myths explain evidence that is suggestive but not conclusive. Speculation—ranging from wholly reasonable, if startling, to utterly farfetched—must fill in the gaps. Hard facts have been spun into conspiracy theories about the CIA's still-secret machinations.

With good reason. Again, just because myths are myths doesn't mean they're lies. The CIA intersects again and again with other secret societies. Reagan's director of central intelligence William Casey belonged to the Knights of Malta, a Catholic order formed several hundred years ago along the lines of the Knights Templar, and other "holy" military fraternities (the Teutonic Knights were another).

John McCone, another of the CIA's most prominent directors, was a Knight. William F. Buckley, "patron saint of conservatives" and a former CIA man, is a Knight, too, and a member of Yale's quasi-Masonic, elitist Skull and Bones. The most famous Bonesman hanging around these days is CIA director turned United States president George Bush.

Through Licio Gelli, the CIA also comes into contact with both the Knights of Malta and the Masons. Gelli was the founder of Propaganda Due, aka P2, the shadowy Masonic lodge that became, under Gelli's guidance, a worldwide fascist conspiracy. A 1987 indictment of 20 P2 members called the group a "secret structure [that] had the incredible capacity to control a state's institutions to the point of virtually becoming a state-within-a-state."

P2 has tried to set up a fascist countergovernment in Italy and is known to be behind a 1980 terrorist bombing that killed eighty-five people in a Bologna railroad station. At the time, it was Europe's deadliest terror attack. P2 surfaced again in connection with the Vatican banking scandal, and the murders and "suicides" that went with it.

Gelli, a real "joiner," is a Knight of Malta, which brought him into contact with Casey and Al Haig (yet another Knight). Casey was Ronald Reagan's 1980 campaign manager before becoming CIA director, and Gelli helped secure good press for Reagan in Italy. As a show of appreciation, Gelli was awarded a ticket to Reagan's 1980 inauguration gala, in the good seats.

There is also some speculation that George Bush may be at least an "honorary" member of P2, or an affiliated lodge. It would hardly be out of character. One of Bush's 1988 presidential campaign advisers, Philip Guarino, is definitely *Piduisti* (as members of the lodge are called). Guarino also worked for Reagan in 1980.

Gelli's CIA contacts helped him get P2 off the ground in 1966 (Gelli first became a Mason in 1963. It took a few years to get his own lodge). The CIA, according to its lapsed contract agent Richard Brenneke (more about him later), has financed the P2 organization since 1970 through a corporation called Amitalia, itself an offshoot of something known as the "International Fund for Mergers and Acquisitions," based in Panama.

The Masonic Grand Lodge of Italy ultimately suspended P2 for refusing to reveal the names of its members. Through the P2 membership roster, Gelli also brings the CIA into contact with another, better known secret society, the Mafia.

But that's not a new relationship. The best-known snuggle-up between the CIA and La Cosa Nostra came when the two joined hands in an attempt to knock off Fidel Castro, whose regime put the mob out of business in Havana, a plot that may have twisted into the assassination of President Kennedy.

The Italian government has long suspected that P2 is not Gelli's baby (bear in mind, many members of the Italian government belong to P2). The lodge, it is widely believed, is controlled by some outside power, with headquarters beyond Italian borders. Maybe the Mafia, some feel. Maybe even the Prieure de Sion, the apparently gnostic, proto-Masonic group that became the subject of all kinds of theorizing after the 1983 publication of *Holy Blood, Holy Grail,* the book that exposed its existence to an international audience.

Journalist Mino Pecorelli, himself a P2 member, wrote an article in 1979 naming the outside power pulling P2's strings. He named the CIA. Pecorelli had tried to blackmail Gelli before writing the piece. Shortly after it was printed, Pecorelli was killed as he sat in his car outside the offices of his magazine. He was shot twice in the mouth, a Sicilian Mafia way of saying, "Shut up."

The list of CIA types on the rosters of powerful secret societies seems endless. The Knights of Malta contingent included, conspicuously, General Reinhard Gehlen. Gehlen was the Nazi spymaster who turned around after the war to become, in effect, a founder of the CIA. His anti-Soviet Nazi espionage network was transferred virtually undisturbed to American intelligence. "He's on our side," said CIA director Allen Dulles. "That's all that matters."

According this honor to Gehlen, and other top Nazis, exacerbated the Cold War immeasurably, almost triggering World War III. The very act of signing Gehlen and his entourage of war criminals and stormtroopers was "a substantial escalation of the cold war," author Christopher Simpson points out. More important, Gehlen's intelligence reports systematically exaggerated the Soviet "threat," fueling American paranoia about the Soviet Union's military intentions and about domestic communist "subversion."

"The only intelligence provided by the Gehlen net to the United States," asserts Carl Oglesby of the Institute for Continuing De-Nazification, "was intelligence selected specifically to worsen East-West relations and increase the possibility of military conflict between the U.S. and the Soviet Union." The effect of the decidedly undemocratic Gehlen "Org" on America's institutions of democracy, adds Oglesby, was to "weaken them incalculably."

Who knows how the influence of unrepentant Nazis shaped the philosophy and methods of the CIA? "Whatever the CIA was from the standpoint of law, it remained from the standpoint of practical intelligence collection a front for a house of Nazi spies," Oglesby says.

The CIA's involvement with Nazis didn't end with Gehlen, and led it into contact with another powerful secret society, the Order of the Death's Head, better known as the Schutzstaffel. The SS. The SS was more than the Nazi police force and terror unit. It was fashioned by its leader Heinrich Himmler to be an elite chivalric order. It had mystical rites, oaths, and internal rankings, or degrees—the trademarks of a secret society.

Hundreds, even thousands, of SS men became part of CIA operations after the war. Among the most notable was Otto Skorzeny, the hulking hero of numerous high-risk Nazi adventures, known in Germany as "Hitler's favorite commando." In the 1950s, Skorzeny worked for the CIA in Egypt. Skorzeny was sent ostensibly to train that country's security forces, to insure that Egypt would be safe from the Soviet threat.

Into the Egyptian "security forces" Skorzeny recruited about one hundred former SS men and neo-Nazis. Skorzeny's mucking about in Egypt eventually helped trigger the Suez crisis, one of the Middle East's bloodier wars. While the CIA was underwriting "Scarface" (Skorzeny's face bore a frightful duelling scar) Skorzeny's nazification project, it was also paying another former SS man to stave off the Soviets in the Middle East: Alois Brunner, Adolf Eichmann's gung-ho chief aide, said to be responsible for murdering 128,500 human beings.

It was Dulles who bestowed this congeniality upon Gehlen, Skorzeny, Brunner, and their Nazi ilk. Before World War II, Dulles's law firm did considerable work in Nazi Germany and showed a startling degree of indifference to Hitler's increasingly evident policies.

It was also Dulles, in all probability, who "rehabilitated" the pro-Nazi corporation International Telephone and Telegraph (ITT) into a South American host for CIA operatives in the early 1950s. In 1970, the CIA would secure Chile for ITT with a coup in which its elected president Salvador Allende was assassinated.

It was Dulles, after all, who once said, "An intelligence service is an ideal vehicle for a conspiracy."

Commies are bad, but, to committed Nazis like Skorzeny, Jews are worse. Once in Egypt, Skorzeny busied himself training the first Palestinian terrorist groups. Descendants of those groups still wreak havoc in the Middle East today.

The CIA also bumps into secret societies in the Far East. Through its Golden Triangle operations tied to international opium smugglers, the CIA also touches base with the "triads," an Asian secret-society equivalent of the Mafia.

Then there is the unlikeliest intersection of all.

The late Stephen Knight, a British investigative reporter who specialized in covering Freemasonry, believed Licio Gelli was working for the CIA's Soviet doppelgänger, the KGB. Although it is hard to believe a hardline fascist like Gelli would sell out to the Soviets, he is said to have made a number of Communist contacts after World War II. He was a survivor first, a fascist second. Knight says that the KGB made a practice of infiltrating Freemasonry in a number of countries, because of its convenient blend of access to influential people and good cover.

The truth, probably, is that all of these organizations—Knights of Malta, Prieure de Sion, Freemasons, SS Nazis, Asian triads, even the KGB—bond with the CIA somewhere in the twilight zone of international intrigue.

On a somewhat lighter note, even the initiation rite—that is, the entrance interview into the CIA—has something in common with secret society initiations. It is common in secret societies—and in cults, not coincidentally—for initiates to be put through an ego-stripping process that usually involves revealing the details of one's sex habits. Pledges into Skull and Bones must lie naked in a coffin and recite their entire sexual histories. The mind reels at the concept of George Bush or William F. Buckley stripping to their birthday suits, climbing into a coffin, and then reciting a litany of God-knows-what.

In any case, in 1972 former CIA officer Patrick McGarvey recalled that he was first welcomed to the CIA by being strapped to a lie detector machine and asked, "Do you still masturbate?" Stunned by the question, he was taken even further aback by his examiner's hot-tempered insistence that he answer. The questioner then proceeded with predictable follow-ups. For example, "Ever had a blow job?"

Prurient hazing aside, the CIA shares another trait with those secret societies with which it is so thoroughly enmeshed: money. Most secret societies are much more than social organizations. They are repositories of wealth as well as power.

The CIA maintains an impressive financial portfolio, which seems to serve a dual purpose. It bankrolls the CIA's many adventures and, through a network of "proprietary" companies, provides cover for clandestine activities.

Among the revelations in the Iran-Contra scandal was the fact that a CIA-run shrimp fishery, Ocean Hunter, was used as a drug-smuggling operation with proceeds going to the CIA-financed contras. The CIA also infiltrated Wall Street in the 1960s and 1970s through a thirty million dollar company called "Southern Capital." It has owned and operated airlines. Through a technology company called "Zenith Technical" in Miami, the CIA ran numerous operations against Cuba in the 1960s. The agency doesn't stop with its own companies either.

The CIA owned stock in ITT in 1970, at the same time it was staging the coup that led to the overthrow and assassination of Salvador Allende in Chile—an action that handed the South American country to ITT. Major oil companies are often inseparable from the CIA. In Venezuela, for example, according to investigative reporter Jim Hougan, "Exxon *is* the CIA." Smaller oil companies are, too. Zapata Oil, founded by George Bush, is believed by some to have been CIA connected.

Some executives look at fronting for the CIA as good business. Howard Hughes figured that if his company took CIA contracts, the CIA would be there to bail him out when he needed them. They may not have been there for Hughes (that's another story!), but they seem to be there for a more contemporary group of big-bucks brigands: savings and loan executives.

The CIA's most recent venture into the universe of high finance may be its most costly ever, in terms of raw dollars. The collapse of the savings and loan industry appears to have been caused at least in part by CIA hijinks, and it may yet cost the United States taxpayers one trillion dollars to reimburse the lost, federally insured money. What's more, some corrupt S&L executives are said to have "get out of jail free" cards supplied by the CIA.

None other than the director of the FBI, William Sessions, testified to Congress that "looting" had more to do with the S&L failures than the abstruse economic factors that fascinate official analysts. Sessions didn't say who pulled off this massive looting operation, but a lone investigative reporter from Texas, where S&Ls were rolling into oblivion like so many tumbleweeds, followed the money for five years. Along the way, he bumped into an array of CIA operatives and their mobster pals.

Pete Brewton of the *Houston Post* listed twenty-two savings and loan institutions where evidence pointed to plunder by the organized crime–CIA nexus. The CIA immediately denied the *Houston Post* stories, saying "that would be a violation of U.S. laws, and we do not violate U.S. laws."

The CIA maintains deniability on many of its more outlandish escapades by using contract agents rather than its own full-time personnel. That was how, in its old rough-and-ready days, the agency used the private detective firm headed by superspook Robert Maheu, who was also Howard Hughes' alter ego. Maheu's firm took on assignments the CIA deemed too sensitive to handle. It was the inspiration for the television series "Mission: Impossible."

If the CIA was involved in looting the S&Ls, it used its contract agents to do the work. One of the contractors, Brewton reported, was Farhad Azima, a pro-Shah Iranian who headed one of the largest charter airlines in America, Global International Airways. The airline borrowed money from an S&L in which Azima was a major investor, then declared bankruptcy. Global was either a CIA proprietary, or a heavy contract client of the CIA. Some of Global's pilots also flew for the defunct Air America, known to be a CIA company. One of Global's creditors was Southern Air Transport, a Miami company once owned by the CIA (the agency sold it to an ex-CIA lawyer), which supplied planes for shipping arms to Iran, and to the contras.

Global Airlines' biggest client was a company called "Egyptian American Transport and Services Company." (EATSCO), run by some of the same CIA men named by Daniel Sheehan as defendants in the "Secret Team" lawsuit—men who have been behind the darkest of the CIA's dark doings for thirty years: Ted Shackley, Edwin Wilson, Thomas Clines. According to Gene Wheaton, a private eye who once worked as an investigator at the Pentagon, EATSCO actually owned Fazima's Global Airlines.

Azima milked a Kansas City S&L called Indian Springs State Bank, according to Brewton's stories. Vision Banc Savings in Kingsville, Texas, was another CIA target, according to the Brewton series. It loaned millions for a failed Florida land deal to convicted money launderer Lawrence Freeman, a friend of Paul Helliwell—a CIA man from the agency's early days and an associate of William Casey. Brewton cites sources who told him that some of the money siphoned off by Freeman may have gone to covert operations.

Vision Banc Savings was owned by an alleged money launderer and occasional CIA contact named Richard Corson, Brewton's stories say. Brewton also reports that Freeman may have been a front man for Mike Adkison, who borrowed a total of one hundred million dollars

from Corson's bank and five other Texas thrifts. Ad
kison, according to Brewton's reports, is reputed to be a
international arms merchant who has sold arms to Iraq

A Florida-based newsletter called *Money Launderin*
Alert said in April 1990 that "a significant amount c
money obtained through fraudulent means from a num
ber of the nation's failed S&Ls were laundered throug
the accounts of CIA front companies . . . to fund co
vert operations."

Former CIA contract agent Richard Brenneke, th
same man who testified that he had flown George Bus
to a Paris meeting in 1980 to strike a preelection arms
for-hostages deal with Iran, told Brewton that mone
from S&L raids was being spirited to the contras. Re
porter Stephen Pizzo said that in researching his boo
about the S&L plunder, *Inside Job*, he and his collabora
tors came across the CIA "about a half a dozen times,"
but decided "that's not what we're writing about righ
now." They resolved to follow only the trails of mobster
(trails lengthy enough to consume any investigator'
time).

"Who knows how many those [the CIA connections
would have linked to," Pizzo said. "We just don'
know." Eventually, they wrote an article summing up
their CIA-S&L findings for *Penthouse* magazine.

The savings and loan fiasco, if it unfolds the way
Brewton's reports indicate, would not be the first time
the CIA has exploited the banking industry. Christic In
stitute counsel Dan Sheehan says that Bank of America
which came close to collapsing in the 1980s, suddenly
reversed its losses when the Iran-Contra scandal became
public. The suggestion is that B of A was being looted for
a contra war. Much better documented, however, is the
saga of Australia's Nugan Hand bank, a CIA operation in
every respect but its name. Under the agency's sage guid
ance, the Nugan Hand bank was a front for drug run
ning, a laundry machine for money coming from the

Shah of Iran and Ferdinand Marcos, and a channel for the CIA's covert funding of its preferred political parties throughout the world.

Nugan Hand met with a fate not unlike that of so many American S&Ls. More than fifty million dollars in debt, it folded. The fate of its titular owners was far worse than anything yet meted out to an S&L exec, however. Frank Nugan was shot to death, and Michael Hand disappeared.

Like all good secret societies, the CIA knows the ancient art of invisibility. The full story of the CIA-S&L affair may never come out. A former Justice Department prosecutor, quoted by Brewton, summed up the frustration of trying to apprehend the elusive CIA. "It's like trying to grab smoke."

Allegations against the CIA get wispier and wispier when puzzling over how the CIA performs the one duty dear to all conspiratorial societies, fomenting revolution. On the one hand, there's no question the CIA has been behind more toppled and subverted governments than could be catalogued here. Guatemala in 1954. Chile in 1970. Grenada in 1984. Iran. Greece. The Dominican Republic. Cambodia. Nicaragua. And of course, Vietnam. Those countries make up a pitifully incomplete inventory of nations whose governments have been installed, overthrown, or undermined by the CIA.

The subject becomes more ambiguous when we explore the CIA's support for terrorism. Terrorists (as modern revolutionaries are called) have become the arch villains of American folklore. In popular parlance as prescribed by government and the media, a "terrorist" is by definition a hater of America, so it seems beyond belief that an agency as fanatical as the CIA is about protecting American interests and enforcing the American will would have anything to do with terrorism.

Part of that problem of perception has to do with the American definition of "terrorism." Somehow, terrorism has come to be firmly linked to left-wing insurgency, as if right-wing terrorism did not exist. Though the idea of terrorism as a leftist phenomena is certainly perpetuated by official sources, to say simply that the media or government propaganda invented this definition and made it stick would be too facile.

The meaning of terrorism comes down to the meaning of "us" and "them." "They" are the poor, blacks, foreigners, and so on. "We" are American mainstream, white folks with a little money in our pockets. The reason the "we" seem so eager to accept that terrorism is a threat only from the extreme left is that the extreme left threatens "us." Since communism was concocted, Americans have been indoctrinated with the notion that the Left wants to take away all the things *we* treasure so deeply. The right wing, conversely and more comfortingly, is primarily concerned with *them*—minorities, the poor, foreigners—and directs its violence away from us. Right-wing terrorism isn't very terrifying because it doesn't terrorize *us*.

At least, that's how we've been instructed to think.

Despite the American delusion of terrorism as a left-wing phenomena carried out by radical Marxists lauding the people's struggle as they bomb department stores and gun down tourists, the right-wing "Black International" is actually far more entrenched. The movement was founded by Skorzeny and other Nazis, including "Butcher of Lyons" Klaus Barbie, and, perhaps most important, the enigmatic old guard Nazi financier François Genoud.

That conspiracy could not have formed, it's fair to say, without sustenance from the CIA. The CIA helped Nazis, Barbie among them, escape prosecution for war crimes. It used them as intelligence "assets," set them up with new lives and some of them with new identities. The right-wing terror network is still in evidence today.

Palestinian terrorist organizations are part of it. Their spark was lit by Skorzeny and his SS compadres backed by the CIA. Agency connections reveal themselves right up to the present. The CIA schmoozed with Ali Hassan Salameh, leader of Black September, mastermind of the 1972 Munich massacre at the Olympics. The agency was so keen to make Salameh an "asset" that it gave him an all-expense paid vacation in sunny Honolulu. Salameh's day at the beach came to an end when the long arm of Israeli vengeance got to him in 1979. But the Israelis waited to hit Salameh until they'd received clearance from the CIA.

Still more recently, as commandos backed by Iran and Libya were holding American hostages and staging suicide attacks against U.S. servicemen, a network of arms dealers based in the White House was arming Iran at the behest of CIA chief (and longtime intelligence agent) William Casey. That operation was the heart of the Iran-Contra scandal.

On December 21, 1988, just four days before Christmas, thirty-one thousand feet in the air over the countryside village of Lockerbie, Scotland, a Pan Am 747, whose nickname "Maid of the Seas" was painted across its cockpit, exploded. The passengers and crew, mostly Americans bound home for the holidays, were thrown into the air to their deaths, some of them still safety buckled into their seats. Several more people, residents of Lockerbie, died when the wreckage of the plane smashed in a blaze to the ground.

The bombing of Pan Am Flight 103 from London, originating in Frankfurt, was immediately pinned on Palestinian terrorists with links to the Iranian government. Not surprisingly to those initiated into the mysteries of terrorist conspiracies, the CIA showed up on the scene as well. The CIA connection to the horrific mass murder received far less publicity than did the equally shadowy Arab-Iranian involvement. From reading most news accounts, even to this day, one could miss mention of the CIA completely.

The stories, cover stories, and theories about the bombing of 103 have become numerous. Undisputed, though not often discussed, is the fact that CIA agents were passengers on the plane. There were at least four, possibly five. Some accounts say eight. But they were there. What were they doing on board a civilian airliner, these obvious targets for assassination? That they would be targets is made more likely by the nature of their mission. They were returning from Lebanon, where, it is suspected by most who bother to check, they were working on some sort of deal regarding the American hostages held by pro-Iranian kidnappers.

They could have been part of an effort to buy the hostages' release. Bundled, large-denomination traveler's checks worth more than half a million dollars were found by two farm boys at the crash site. Or they could have been planning a rescue operation. Searchers found a diagram of what appeared to be a building in Beirut, with exact locations of two hostages marked.

The conspiratorial story is much more complex. It came out in a report prepared by a former Israeli intelligence agent working as an international private investigator for a firm called Interfor. Pan Am hired him to do the investigation, and, based on what he found, the airline subpoenaed from the U.S. government a whole set of material. Most intriguing, Pan Am alleged that the CIA possessed a videotape of the bomb actually being placed on board the plane. The Interfor report calls that tape "the gem" of the investigation.

The Interfor report was reported on the front page of the *Toronto Star* and several London newspapers, some f which led their own journalistic investigations of the ombing. In America, it made the rounds of the alterna- ve press, written up in the *San Francisco Bay Guardian* nd San Pedro, California's *Random Lengths.* My paper, he San Jose *Metro,* also made some mention of it. But in he daily press and on television, nothing.

The unfortunate CIA squad on board Pan Am 103 are ctually the heroes of the Interfor report. That team, led y an Army major named Charles McKee—on loan to he CIA from the Defense Department—had in fact been 1 Lebanon on a top secret, hostage-related mission, the eport says. In their investigations, they zeroed in on a yrian drug smuggler named Monzar Al-Kassar, who had onnections high in the Syrian government. In fact, he vas married to Syrian President Hafez Assad's niece.

Al-Kassar also had connections in other governments. Like many international drug traders, he also dealt arms nd, as such, he was useful to the American Iran-Contra Enterprise." Richard Secord and Albert Hakim paid Al- Kassar $1.5 million to ship small arms to the contras. nterfor said he was earlier the go-between between the rench government and terrorists when a few French ostages were set free. According to the Interfor report, a nysterious "off the shelf" team of CIA agents lurking in West Germany, with their "control" at an unknown loca- ion not at Langley but in Washington, tried to use Al- Kassar for the same thing.

The McKee team found out about this other CIA op- ration. And they discovered that the other agents, in xchange for Al-Kassar's help, were protecting his drug- unning routes. Incensed, the McKee team boarded Pan Am 103, for home.

Unknown to them, presumably, they picked the flight sed by Al-Kassar for his drug smuggling. And on that light, Al-Kassar's terrorist friends decided to use the CIA cover of his drug route to plant the bomb. West German police, with the help of Israeli intelligence, found

out about it. They actually videotaped the bomb going
onto the plane. When the CIA agents covering for Al
Kassar phoned back to their "control" to ask what to do
they were told, "Don't worry about it. Don't stop it. Let
it go."

They did. 259 people died on the plane, eleven more
on the ground.

Late in 1990, allegations surfaced in the Italian press that
none other than the P2 Lodge was the real mastermind of
the Pan Am 103 bombing, to cover up its own role in
arms deals with Iran. I haven't seen that claim supported
or corroborated anywhere, but it wouldn't be out of
character for the P2. And it suggests a dizzying conspiracy theory: with P2 allegedly funded through an Italian
corporation whose parent company was in Panama (recall
Brenneke's allegations earlier this chapter), CIA man
George Bush somehow connected to the P2, and that
Panamanian parent company (according again to Brenneke) in existence right up through the end of General
Manuel Noriega's reign. Suddenly, from the depths of
international intrigue, the possible true motive for Bush's
1989 invasion of Panama creeps into light: to destroy
records that could link the CIA, and even himself, however indirectly, to the mass murder aboard Pan Am 103.
Of course, there's no evidence for any of that—just another demon raised from conspiratoriological hell.

Sometime after the crash, George Bush phoned Marga-
ret Thatcher. According to Jack Anderson, the two leaders agreed that the investigation into the bombing would
be "limited" in order to protect British and American
intelligence interests.

Another stray fact worth noting about Pan Am 103: In
addition to the CIA's McKee team, the plane was also
carrying Bernt Carlsson, the U.N. negotiator with South
Africa, who had just carved out a deal on Namibian inde-

endence. He was on his way back to New York to ink he pact. Needless to say, he never got to sign his name.

The Interfor report, when it's mentioned at all in the najor media, is usually dismissed. The lone exception as of this writing is a December 1990 feature piece in *Barron's*, a Dow Jones–owned financial weekly. The *Barron's* article was quite thorough, with one glaring exception. It never mentioned the McKee team. The title of the piece, "Unwitting Accomplices?," is also an odd one, given that the story *did* mention CIA headquarters' alleged instructions to "let it go," when warned of the bomb—hardly "unwitting." Leaving out the McKee team story obscures one possible motive in letting the bomb go: to eliminate agents who had learned too much about the drugs-hostages-arms connection.

Other than *Barron's*, no news organization that I know has even bothered to check out the Interfor report's allegations, save consulting their intelligence sources, who, as expected, deride it as a "spitball," meaning a hodgepodge of fact and fiction with no value as intelligence. I doubt that much of what the Interfor report says will ever be seriously examined. It tells a tale that, even for a conspiracy theory, is one of the darkest ever spun about the CIA. And its implications are even more daunting. If the report proved true, it would connect the bombing of Pan Am 103 to the Iran-Contra scandal; the bombing would become part of the Iran-Contra cover-up.

Iran-Contra, the real story, was costly enough without 270 lives added to the price tag. It's been alleged by the Christic Institute and others that Iran-Contra operators Richard Secord and Albert Hakim were hooked up with renegade CIA operatives Edwin Wilson and Frank Terpil. Wilson, Terpil, and Secord shared a mutual boss, "Blond Ghost" spookmaster Ted Shackley. But Secord has always angrily denied having anything to do with Wilson. Wilson and Terpil sold arms and explosives to Libya's

Colonel Qaddafi. They were indicted, convicted, and im
prisoned for it. Secord and Hakim were not. Nor was Ted
Shackley, an almost godlike figure in spook circles.
Shackley was Wilson's CIA supervisor. He had distinguished himself in Vietnam as a prime mover behind the
near-genocidal Phoenix program, in which the CIA killed
tens of thousands of Vietnamese civilians.

Shackley is author of a book, *The Third Option*, that
advocates in no uncertain terms U.S. covert operations to
control the politics of foreign countries. He is also widely
believed to have been a leader of the CIA's Golden Triangle opium smuggling activities, which he angrily denies.

When Wilson and Terpil were caught arming terrorists, Shackley was allowed to quietly resign his CIA
post. The CIA's deputy director at that time, who supported Shackley, was Frank Carlucci. After National Security Adviser John Poindexter was forced to resign
when accused of masterminding the Iran-Contra cover-
up, Carlucci got his job.

Iran-Contra and the Wilson affair got a lot of press,
although their significance was never fully explained in
the mass media. Less publicized are the CIA's strange
encounters with characters like Licio Gelli and its darker
weavings with the fascist terrorist cabal. Gelli is said to
have conspired with "Black" terrorist Stefano Delle
Chiaie to plan the Bologna train station bombing. The
European Black International in which Delle Chiaie was
a preeminent figure consisted of old and "neo" Nazis,
including SS officers, and other elements of European fascism and anti-Semitism. Among its list of accomplish-
ments, this same network was responsible for bombing a
Paris synagogue just weeks after the train station bomb
went off.

Delle Chiaie, as well as Gelli, had his own CIA
friends. Both are linked to the Mafia. No surprises there.
But both are also tied in with the "Red International,"
that is, with international left-wing terrorism. In recent

years, the two terrorist factions have become so close that the distinction is not much more than semantic.

In late 1990, around the time I was finishing this book, a story broke in Europe that put the CIA's connection to right-wing terrorism into focus. The story became a huge scandal in Italy, threatening to topple the Italian government. In America, it received limited play. The *Washington Post* ran an article headed "CIA Organized Secret Army in Western Europe." The *New York Times* offered its own summary of the affair, but did not mention the CIA.

The "secret army," European press revealed, was part of the CIA's "Operation Gladio," its Cold War project to organize the extreme right in Europe into an anti-Communist resistance. The German arm of the Gladio army was made up of former SS men. The Italian branch contained such sterling characters as Delle Chiaie and his P2 cohorts. The London *Independent* newspaper wrote that the killing of Italian prime minister Aldo Moro may have been carried out with the cooperation of these CIA-backed elements—namely, P2 members in the Italian government. Moro's kidnapping and execution were pulled off by the supposedly left-wing Red Brigade.

As early as 1969, the Black International held a summit conference in Barcelona, Spain, with good wishes from the country's fascist dictator, Francisco Franco. The summit was called to plan strategy for Yasser Arafat and his burgeoning cabal of Palestinian terrorists. Left wing? Or right wing?

The fact of the matter is, while it's easier to link the CIA to right-wing terrorism than to left-wing terrorism, the line between right and left is blurred beyond recognition. The alliance goes beyond their shared tactics of extreme violence aimed at oblivious civilians. Their new unity is known as the "Third Position," and its adherents rally around the slogan "Hitler and Mao united in struggle."

"Third Position" interlocks explain some apparent anomalies. Klaus Barbie, CIA-backed Nazi war criminal, was represented at his 1985 Paris trial by left-wing lawyer Jacques Verges. Verges became famous for using the courtroom as his platform for lashing out at Western imperialism. He married one of his most famous clients, Algerian bomber Djamila Bouhired, converted to Islam, and became a doctrinaire Maoist after traveling to China and meeting Chairman Mao himself. He is named in connection with many of the best-known "Red" terrorists. Yet he represented the most infamous Nazi war criminal since Eichmann, and has known François Genoud for four decades.

Left-right intercourse also explains why the hijackers of the *Achille Lauro* cruise ship demanded the release of Odifried Hepp, a prolific neo-Nazi terrorist then incarcerated in West Germany. In the early 1980s, Hepp planned and carried out attacks on several American army installations, NATO bases, and night spots where U.S. soldiers liked to hang out. Some of the attacks were attributed in the press to leftists. Sometimes, left-wing groups went out of their way to claim credit for the attacks.

Right and left lose their meaning in the swirling eddy of global insurrection. The connections are dazzling. They set the legend of the CIA in the same light as legends of secret societies from the Illuminati to the Hashishim to the Freemasons. They are committed not to national aims, nor to explicitly ideological ones. They are devoted only to their own subversive, secret agenda.

14

SHOTS FROM THE
BUSHY KNOLL

*Friendly fascism in the United States
would not need a charismatic, apparently all-powerful leader such as Mussolini or Hitler. . . . The chief executive, rather, becomes the nominal head
of a network that not only serves to
hold the Establishment together but
also provides it with a sanctimonious
aura of legitimacy. . . .*

BERTRAM GROSS, *Friendly
Fascism*

Not since Adam Weishaupt founded the Bavarian Illuminati on May 1, 1776, has one man been at the pinnacle
of such a massive pyramid of conspiracy theories as our
forty-first president, George Herbert Walker Bush. No
doubt about it; he has earned his way there.

If conspiracy theories came into some sort of vogue in
the mid-1970s, with the Watergate mystery unresolved,
the House Select Committee on Assassinations casting
shadows on the Warren Report, Senator Frank Church
displaying secret CIA death weapons on national TV, and
Trilateral Commissioner Jimmy Carter in the White
House, they seem even more apropos in the 1990s, with

haphazardly gesticulating, sentence-fragmenting, broc-coli-bashing, yet somehow sinister, Bush as chief executive. All the elements that incited dark innuendo in the cynical 1970s have come to life in one man. Called everything from a "veteran of the Kennedy assassination," to a Rockefeller stooge, to head honcho of Dope Inc., Bush's case history is a conspiracy researcher's textbook.

Bush serves as a concentric point for the two circles that are the focus of most American conspiracy theory. He is a product of the Eastern Establishment who also functions smoothly in the Southwestern cowboy clan of oil and adventurism. It's sometimes said that Ronald Reagan's presidency marked a shift in power away from the Eastern Wall Streeters to the space-laser cowboys of Texas, Arizona, and Southern California. Away from nuclear deterrence and into Star Wars. Away from effete Trilateralism into Red Menace machismo.

The two wings of the ruling oligarchy have been struggling for predominance for a long time—at least since Barry Goldwater slugged it out with Nelson Rockefeller in 1964. Reagan, rather than marking a final transfer of power, may have been a transitional president in the process of melding the two sects into one unified body of overlords. Getting Bush into office seals the marriage with a salty kiss.

Bush was chief of the CIA under Gerald Ford. Before entering government, he was a Texas oil boss. His name came up in the aftermath of the J.F.K. killing. He belonged to the Council on Foreign Relations and the Trilateral Commission and is an initiate into an exclusive secret society with occult, if campy, rituals.

The Christic Institute posits Bush as a key coordinator of the Iran-Contra "enterprise." There is ample documentation that Bush lied about his involvement in the scandal. He was never "out of the loop" as he claimed. How deeply is Bush involved in drug trafficking? His perduring relationship, gone sour, with Panama's former dictator Manuel Noriega suggests he knows something about the narco trade that he could hardly be expected to tell.

As CIA boss, he covered up the assassination of a Chilean diplomat in Washington, D.C., and the terrorist bombing of an airliner that killed seventy-three people. As Nixon-picked chairman of the Republican National Committee, he stonewalled for his patron president up until the day before Nixon resigned. "I owed Richard Nixon a lot, and as a matter of fact I still do," he shamelessly declared, in his 1987 autobiography.

A former CIA operative testified under oath that he piloted Bush to Paris in October 1980, where the then vice presidential candidate helped negotiate a deal with Iranian hostage holders—to keep holding hostages until Reagan was in office. As if hobnobbing with terrorists wasn't distasteful enough, fascists turned up in the infrastructure of Bush's 1988 presidential campaign—real live fascists of the same ilk imported by the CIA after World War II. They were part of the Republican "Ethnic Outreach" effort.

Right-wingers always wondered why Reagan picked Bush for vice president in 1980. The sunbelt-conservative cowboy and tweedy, bespectacled Brahmin made an asymmetrical pair. "The same people who gave you Jimmy Carter now want to give you George Bush," the hard liners warned when Bush was leading Reagan in the Republican primaries that year. In response to the pressure, Bush resigned from the Council on Foreign Relations, damning it as "too liberal," out of step with his newfound affinity for the radical right. He stayed on for a while on the Trilateral Commission, though.

Was Bush, like Carter before him, being groomed for the top job by invisible power brokers from the start? Though he would later derive unlimited mileage by invoking the malaise-laden spirit of Jimmy Carter to ward off Democratic opponents in the 1988 presidential campaign, the *L.A. Times* reported that in the 1970s Bush was bucking for a job in the Carter administration. Carter's national security adviser, Trilateral Commission founder Zbigniew Brzezinski, took a high profile role in Bush's 1988 campaign, advising on foreign policy. In 1980, his campaign was aided in no small measure by a group of disgruntled intelligence operatives known loosely as "Agents for Bush."

Once in vice presidential office, Bush flirted with a fast promotion. Curiously, Bush's son Neil had a dinner date with an old family friend the night that John Hinckley, with a .22 caliber bullet, almost facilitated George Bush's ascendancy to the White House. The old family friend was John Hinckley's brother, Scott.

Hinckley, as I mentioned in Chapter 10, was under the influence of mind-altering psychiatric drugs, and dabbled with neo-Nazi cultism. We looked at the theory that he was a mind-controlled assassin. But what about the theory that he was a mind-controlled patsy, not unlike—the speculation goes—Sirhan Sirhan? In the NBC news special reports immediately following the attempt on Reagan's life, correspondent Judy Woodruff said on the air, with considerable certainty, that at least one shot came from an overhang above Reagan's limousine. Later she said that the shot came from *a Secret Service agent* stationed on the overhang.

A shot from that angle would explain how a bullet got into the president's chest, when Hinckley would have had to fire straight through a car door to hit him at that angle. Later, the shot in the chest was explained as a ricochet. John Judge, seizing on Woodruff's on-the-scene report, calls it "the shot from the Bushy Knoll."

Neil Bush, almost a decade later, leapt to national infamy in the savings and loan scandal. Allegedly, while a director of Silverado Savings and Loan in Colorado, he voted to approve loans for one of his business partners. Another received a loan from Silverado that was never repaid, contributing to the thrift's demise. Neil was also involved with a Colorado company called Sun-Flo International, a dehydrated foods maker that functioned as a money-laundering machine for known drug dealers. The company's founder, a convicted drug trafficker, is quoted saying, "Bush's kid is in my hip pocket."

George Bush was also entwined with Sun-Flo, hosting one of its consultants on a 1982 African tour. Thus, the vice president, in the words of the alternative newsweekly that reported the story (most dailies missed it), "unwittingly helped promote a firm run by a convicted drug dealer."

Bush's help may have been unwitting, but maybe not out of character. In the public eye, he's an amiable, if slightly twerpy, family man. In the underground information exchange, he's a cunning, ruthless spook with a secret agenda. The real George Bush, say the suspicious, lurks in the shadow cast by his thousand points of light. Not "kinder, gentler," but "a dangerous threat to world peace." One person, one president, but viewed through two different lenses.

In his own mind, who knows when George Bush first decided that his mission was to become president of the United States? In reality, his fate was fixed when William Casey convinced Ronald Reagan to select Bush as his 1980 running mate. Bush and Reagan had some contentious encounters on the primary circuit, but Casey, Reagan's campaign manager, was an old buddy of Bush. Four years earlier, Bush and Casey worked together to produce a special intelligence document whose purpose was to exaggerate the alleged Soviet "threat." The Reagan administration used the document as a basis for its rabidly anti-Soviet foreign policy, and increases in military spending at home.

William Casey was an intelligence agent from OSS

days, a member of the Council on Foreign Relations, and a financial adventurer who rode the stock market like a bucking bronco. Legality and ethics not always his top priority, Casey was, by some accounts, apt to attempt a remodeling of public policy to suit his own prospectus. When Casey became director of the CIA, an inside joke developed that "CIA" stood for "Casey Investing Again."

With George's father, Prescott Bush (a World War I Army Intelligence agent) Casey cofounded a think tank in 1962 called the National Strategy Information Center, which got into trouble for financing publications issued by a CIA front company engaged in disinformation campaigns. Fourteen years later, Casey, dissatisfied with the CIA's modest estimates of Soviet military prowess (he was then on the president's Foreign Intelligence Advisory Board), got together with George Bush, then director of the CIA, to form a study group that would counter the conventional CIA wisdom.

The Bush/Casey group amassed evidence to support its predrawn conclusion that the Soviets were winning the arms race, and that the U.S. was malnourished by comparison. One of the study group's leaders was General Danny Graham, who went on to found High Frontier, the organization that effectively shaped Reagan's "Star Wars" policy.

The report cooked up by Bush and Casey's team served as a major rationale for the Reagan defense buildup. Who benefited from the defense buildup? Defense contractors and the companies they do business with—many of the country's largest corporations. Who sits at the top of those companies? Some of America's richest people, whom I'll be introducing in the next chapter. They're sometimes called "the Establishment." The Bush-Casey report was a gift to America's most wealthy and powerful. At the expense of everybody else.

That Bush would be a loyal member and servant of the

American ruling class is more than a matter of tradition, friendships, or family pride. Like so many of the elite and influential, Bush roots his power in private organizations that do business in dim corners, where the cleansing broom of public opinion cannot reach. Insulated from outside forces, the values and viewpoints formed in the cool remove of a secret society emerge fully formed into the light of politics. The public does not—and as far as the society's members are concerned, should not—understand where they came from, or their real motivations.

This is not to say that all members of a secret society conform to dogma. There is much dissent within societies, and sometimes war between societies. What their members share is a framework of belief, an image of themselves as an elect, a chosen people. To get into a secret society, they have been, quite literally, chosen. That framework guides the "brothers" to perpetuate their elite breed by any means available, and those means are plenary.

Bush belongs to Skull and Bones, a group "tapped" every year from Yale University's junior class. There are seven "Senior Societies" at Yale with long traditions of cornball cloak and dagger, college style, but Skull and Bones is the elite of the elite. Bush was a 1947 inductee. The society is more than just a glorified frat. It has a fat financial portfolio and a summer retreat on Deer Island available to Bonesmen for life. Most important, though, it provides a network of support and cooperation for some of the most powerful people in the U.S.

Bush is the second Bones president. William Howard Taft was the first. Other heavy-hitting Bonesmen include William F. Buckley; alleged leftist William Sloane Coffin; multinational business demigod Averill P. Harriman; Rhode Island senator John Chafee; one-time Nazi-sympathizer Henry P. Luce, who founded *Time* magazine; and numerous top-of-the-heap corporate and legal figures. Massachusetts Senator John Kerry, who has been

Bush's most dogged congressional pursuer on the Iran-Contra drug-smuggling trail, is also a Bonesman, oddly enough. McGeorge Bundy, an architect of the Vietnam War, is Skull and Bones too, as is Robert Gow, president of Zapata Oil, which was Bush's company in the 1960s.

It should hardly be a revelation that the roster of the CIA is speckled with Bonesmen. Besides Bush, a partial list would have to mention William Bundy, another Vietnam booster and vet of both the CIA and OSS. An enthusiastic proponent of "counterinsurgency" Bundy advocated preserving "liberal values" through "the use of the full range of U.S. power, including if necessary its more shady applications." Other Skull and Bones former intelligence agents include the aforementioned William F. Buckley, whose brother James is also a Bonesman and backer of CIA covert activity in Chile (though not CIA himself), and William Sloane Coffin.

The wife of a Bonesman once expressed her distaste for the society's clandestine fixation by calling it "a sinister unhealthy offshoot of the gentleman's code . . . a weird, CIA-like thing."

With headquarters in an iron-gated sanctuary, said to be adorned with skeletal remains of historical celebrities, the group's skull and crossbones insignia is explicitly Masonic, although I've never found a study linking Skull and Bones to the Masons. Its initiation rituals serve the purpose of all occult initiation rites: to break down the individual and build him up again as a member of the order.

Picture if you will George Bush lying naked in a coffin reciting his entire sexual history. The ritual, called "Connubial Bliss" (the naked-in-a-coffin part has never been confirmed), forces initiates to surrender their intimate secrets to the society, while at the same time encouraging that unbreakable male bonding of which sexual bull is so much a part.

The bond lasts forever. In 1985, when Bush was despondent about his political future, still languishing in

Reagan's long shadow, a cadre of Bonesmen showed up at his residence and took him into a private room for a similar confessional. After reportedly baring his insecurities, and receiving the unsparing critique of his comrades, Bush emerged rejuvenated. The future president, reconstructed in the Skull and Bones mold.

In the summer of 1988, well after George Bush had sealed the Republican nomination for president of the United States, the *New York Times* reported that a twenty-five-year-old memo had surfaced naming a "Mr. George Bush" as an agent of the CIA. This Mr. Bush, according to the memo, was passing information to the FBI about the Kennedy assassination.

Ten days later the *Times* reported that it was all a case of mistaken identity. The "George Bush of the CIA," circa 1963, was not the same George Bush running for president in 1988. The *Times* closed the case.

In November 1975, President Gerald Ford offered George Bush—the same George Bush who would later run for president, no doubt about it this time—the job of director of Central Intelligence. Bush, who'd been eyeing Ford's vice presidential nod for the 1976 election, suddenly scotched those ambitions and took the CIA job, to the bewilderment of some of his old friends. One Skull and Bones compatriot from Bush's class of 1947 asked him bluntly, "What the fuck do you know about intelligence?"

He knew enough to know his role: not so much the CIA's director, but its chief executive in charge of coverups. He took over the CIA in the midst of its most severe political crisis. Under attack from congressional committees, with former director Richard "The Man Who Kept the Secrets" Helms about to be investigated for perjury by the Justice Department, the CIA was in danger of finally facing its secret, saucy past in public.

Before Bush took office, he and outgoing director William Colby launched into a good-cop/bad-cop routine that ultimately bamboozled congressional probers. Using the conveniently timed assassination of CIA Athens station chief Richard Welch as a springboard, Colby dove into an all-out attack, charging critics of the CIA with wantonly risking the lives of hardworking, all-American agents. Meanwhile, Bush began a project of backslapping and hand clasping that ingratiated him with the CIA's adversaries on the Hill.

After a few months, the public mood had flipped from outrage at the CIA's dirty, sometimes deadly, tricks, to a groundswell of rally-round-the-boys, which cast Congress and the press as collaborators in league with terrorist assassins gunning for our men in the field. Or something like that. In any case, the propaganda gambit paid off. In early 1976, the Senate Intelligence Committee struck a hush-hush deal with Bush, agreeing to back off if Bush would only be so kind as to inform the senators, discreetly of course, of what the CIA was doing.

Bush put on a good show of holding up his end of the backroom bargain. He appeared before Congress almost once a week, on average, during his term as CIA director. But there was plenty he did not reveal. He stonewalled on the CIA's role in the Washington car-bomb slaying of a Chilean diplomat and in the aerial bombing of a Cubana Airlines jet that killed seventy-three people. Two anti-Castro Cubans were arrested for the airline bombing. One, Orlando Bosch, had been arrested just a few months earlier in connection with a plot to kill Henry Kissinger. The other, Luis Posada Carriles, turned up in 1985 working for the CIA in El Salvador. His immediate superior was Felix Rodriguez, George Bush's friend, the man who boasts of personally killing Che Guevara, then looting the corpse, and who is alleged in Senate testimony to have passed ten million dollars to the Nicaraguan contras from the Colombian Medellín cocaine cartel.

Bush also violated a direct order from President Ford to turn over documents that would have shed light on the CIA's use of the Drug Enforcement Agency as a cover for domestic activities, including MKULTRA, the mind-control operation. The CIA is barred by law from any clandestine or surveillance activities on American soil.

Bush's real job as CIA chief was to allow the agency to get back to the business of cloak and dagger without pesky congressmen getting in the way with all their whining and moaning about laws and ethics. To that end, he appointed some of the hardest of hardcore, old-guard covert operators to administer the CIA's "operations" division. Among them was Ted Shackley, long rumored to have been key in setting up the Asian Golden Triangle opium-smuggling outfit. Shackley's name became much more familiar a decade later. The Christic Institute, in its massive Contragate lawsuit, named him as a defendant, and alleged that he was the brains behind "The Enterprise," sometimes called "The Secret Team," an ongoing unofficial network of intelligence operatives deep into drugs and guns, assassination, and freelance counterinsurgency.

Shackley's associate Edwin Wilson was caught arming and training Libyan terrorists in September 1976. Wilson's "off-the-books" operation involved on-duty CIA agents, even though Wilson is now labeled a "renegade" CIA agent.

Bush's most famous acquaintance in the intelligence world would turn out to be Manuel Noriega, the Panamanian military man and $200,000 per annum CIA operative. Noriega would rise to the dictatorship of his country, develop a bad case of hubris, and turn his patrons against him. On December 20, 1989, President Bush ordered an invasion of Panama to get rid of Noriega and to "restore democracy."

During the 1988 presidential campaign, Bush's opponent Michael Dukakis ineptly attempted to make Bush's buddying up to the acne-scarred strongman a campaign issue. It probably should have been one. The U.S. government knew about Noriega's involvement with drug smugglers since the Nixon years, and Bush was claiming he had heard nothing about it until a federal grand jury indicted Noriega in early 1988.

According to a State Department official, the CIA had "hard intelligence" about Noriega's dope business by 1984. It's hard to believe that Bush, with his galaxy of CIA buddies and colleagues, was never told. Donald Gregg, Bush's friend since 1976, might have at least dropped a hint. A CIA man since graduating from Williams College, Gregg met Bush when they both worked at CIA headquarters.

Assigned to the vice president's staff in 1982, Gregg is alleged to have helped persuade Bush to use his office as a cover for a contra resupply program that involved switching planeloads of arms going out for planeloads of cocaine coming in to the United States. In his autobiography, Felix Rodriguez—named as a coordinator of the operation—denies that it ever existed.

These and many other murky circumstances led Noriega to boast that he "had Bush by the balls." Shrewd as the dictator was, Bush turned out to be shrewder. The pretext for the 1989 Panama invasion was supposed to be Noriega's "declaration of war" against the United States (he never made such a declaration) and attacks against U.S. soldiers by the Panamanian Defense Force (which was trained by the CIA). The attacks appeared part of an American provocation program. Just weeks before the invasion, Bush authorized three million dollars for a CIA operation against Noriega. A candid U.S. military officer in Panama admitted that U.S. troops goaded PDF troops into attacking Americans. "It was an attempt to tick them off, so they'd do something," the officer said, of American soldiers' repeated forays into off-limits Panamanian turf.

The final twist of irony, if it can be called that, to Bush's Panamanian adventure is that the "democratic" government installed by the U.S. was corrupt from the get-go. The new head of the army was another CIA functionary, according to reports, and the new administration does nothing to rout police involved in all kinds of underhanded schemes. In fact, one prosecutor was suspended after fingering a police chief in a kidnapping plot. Bushian "democracy" marches on.

The Panamanian combat was the first time the current incarnation of the U.S. military engaged in all-out urban warfare. The soldiers didn't fare too well, despite the clandestine presence of the Stealth bomber. Unfortunately, they expended much energy and ammo shooting at each other.

In the Reagan administration and his own, Bush was involved with federal planning for martial law and round-ups of terrorists and political dissidents, in league with Louis Guiffrida of the Federal Emergency Management Agency. Meld that fact with the Defense Department's surging enthusiasm for taking part in the ceaseless drug war—which appears more about rolling back individual liberties than curtailing drug use—and the scapegoating of inner city blacks for the nation's drug problem, and the Panama invasion looks unnervingly like a dry run for the domestic crackdown.

Just a thought.

CIA alliances and dalliances with dictators are just part of the complex constellation of contacts that codify into the George Bush cabal. It's hard to pick the most appalling of these people, but seven good candidates arose from the Republican "Heritage Groups Council," which has worked for years in the Republican party and aided

Bush's presidential campaign among ethnic groups. Among these unsavory characters: Laszlo Pasztor, a Hungarian Nazi collaborator who came out of the Arrow Cross party—one of many political organizations set up by the SS in Eastern Europe; Florian Galdau, member of the Romanian Iron Guard, another arm of the SS; Philip Guarino, an honorary American member of Italy's fascist-terrorist Masonic P2 Lodge; and Nicolas Nazarenko, who served in the German SS Cossack Division and who identifies Jews as his "ideological enemy."

Bush announced that criticism of these honorable men was nothing more than a political smear tactic, and he took no action against them. The Heritage Council was not a minor part of the Republican power base. According to one former chairman, it recruited eighty-six thousand volunteers to work for Reagan and Bush.

That group is my selection as Bush's worst association. Those of a more Birchian bent might select his Kissinger compadres, most notably Brent Scowcroft, his national security adviser, and Lawrence Eagleburger, deputy secretary of state. Both Scowcroft and Eagleburger refused at their confirmation hearings to make public the list of clients they had served while working for Dr. K's private "consulting" firm, Kissinger Associates. Potential conflicts of interest were abundant. Congress went ahead and confirmed the two anyway.

Scowcroft later surfaced in Peking, sent by Bush, toasting the Chinese leaders who had pulled off the Tiananmen Square massacre just weeks earlier. Bush's refusal to come down on China the way he did on, say, Panama, can be seen as a continuation of Henry Kissinger's China initiatives of the early 1970s. Bush was U.S. envoy to China back then, and people close to him say that, in that job and as ambassador to the United Nations, Bush simply took orders from Kissinger.

Maybe Bush's attitude toward China has at least a little to do with his brother Prescott, who works for a consulting firm involved in big business deals with the Chinese government. Said one U.S. diplomat of Prescott Bush's relationship with the Chinese, "He was smart enough not to mention his brother's name, and the Chinese were smart enough to make the connection."

As I was wrapping up the first edition of this book, Iraq invaded Kuwait and George Bush readied for combat once again. He spewed a slew of tenuous rationales for the massive U.S. buildup, but as can be expected when George Bush is involved, there was more to the story than presented for public consumption. The earliest clue appeared on October 21, 1990, two and a half months into the "Gulf crisis," when the London *Observer* featured a special investigative report suggesting that Bush encouraged Iraqi dictator Saddam Hussein to attack Kuwait.

Earlier in the year, according to the *Observer*, Bush sent a secret envoy to meet with one of Saddam's top officials. The envoy told the dictator's confidant "that Iraq should engineer higher oil prices to get it out of its dire economic fix," wrote the English paper. The story appeared nowhere that I ever saw in the American media.

Saddam took the envoy's advice, moving his troops to the border of Kuwait. U.S. Ambassador to Baghdad April Glaspie told Saddam, "We don't have an opinion on inter-Arab border disputes such as your border dispute with Kuwait."

"The evidence suggests that U.S. complicity with Saddam went far beyond miscalculation of the Iraqi leader's intentions," wrote *Observer* reporter Helga Graham. The leaked documents on which she based her piece "have built up a picture of active support for the U.S. president."

The story was quite a scoop for Graham. A year and a half later reporter Murray Waas, who'd been on the story for months in alternative media outlets like *The Village Voice,* finally penetrated the big-time dailies with a *Los Angeles Times* report on the Bush/Saddam lovefest.

"In the fall of 1989, at a time when Iraq's invasion of Kuwait was only nine minths away and Saddam Hussein was desperate for money to buy arms," Waas and collaborator Douglas Frantz wrote, "President Bush signed a top-secret National Security Decision directive ordering closer ties with Baghdad and opening the way for $1 billion in new aid."

The Waas-Frantz exclusive revealed a pattern of Bush's support for Saddam dating back to Bush's vice-presidential days and running practically until the moment of Iraq's invasion. "As late as July 1990, one month before Iraqi troops stormed into Kuwait City, officials at the National Security Council and the State Department were pushing to deliver the second installment of the $1 billion in loan guarantees," the article said.

Two years before the invasion, at a time when (according to Waas's reporting) Bush would have been meeting with Iraqi officials and pressuring American banks to fork over money for Saddam, Peter Dale Scott wrote an article for Pacific News Service detailing Bush's role in an international oil-price rigging scheme. The story was named one of the year's ten best "censored" stories by "Project Censored," an annual competition to recognize important stories that the big media skip, spike, or suppress. On the sands of Saudi Arabia, the petroleum president was at work once more.

After the conflict began in earnest in January 1991— more a one-sided assault than a "war," really—more information started to seep out. The silence of the American media with regard to anything but "sorties" and "smart bombs" was stupefying. But had they paid attention they could have picked up on the type of information contained in *Secret Dossier,* a book by highly respected foreign correspondent Pierre Salinger and French journalist Eric Laurent.

Salinger and Laurent took a matter-of-fact tone and were clearly reliant on Jordan's King Hussein as a source (the often startling allegations in the book also beg the question of why Salinger, one of ABC's top overseas reporters, didnt' report the stuff on his network). Nonetheless, a little reading between the lines illuminated "The Hidden Agenda Behind the Gulf War" (the book's subtitle). Salinger and Laurent's information, though it hardly proves that the Kuwaitis prodded Iraq into attacking at the behest of their American protectors, does seem to support that hypothesis.

The invasion of Kuwait could have been averted at a peace conference in late July 1990, *Secret Dossier* reports. Iraq would have been mollified if Kuwait met its request for a $10 billion loan to cover expenses in the Iran-Iraq war. Saddam felt he was owed something for staving off the spread of Iranian-style Islamic fundamentalism.

Kuwait's answer was more like a taunt than a refusal. "After much discussion the [Kuwaiti] Crown Prince agreed, in principle, to a loan of $9 billion," Salinger and Laurent report. "His refusal to grant the extra $1 billion struck the Iraqis as a deliberate attempt to humiliate them."

No problem, said the oil-bloated Saudis, who were more than mildly interested in assuaging the livid Saddam and preventing an invasion. We'll kick in the extra billion. But just when the difficulty appeared resolved, the Kuwaitis pulled another fast one.

"We must decide on the exact demarcation of our borders," the Crown Prince told the Iraqis. Without warning, he'd raised the sorest issue between the two nations.

What was going on? A piece of paper dated November 22, 1989, seized from the Kuwaiti Foreign Ministry by pillaging Iraqis, seemed to indicate a complicated situation. The internal Kuwaiti memo reported a meeting between a high Kuwaiti official and the CIA—which was confirmed by the CIA though it scoffed at the document as a phony. At that meeting, the memo said, the CIA urged Kuwait to "pressure" Iraq into settling the border dispute.

Shortly after the invasion, in another set of negotiations, Iraqi Foreign Minister Tariq Aziz accused Kuwaiti Sheikh Sabah Al Ahmad of being "an American mercenary who's been working for the CIA for years," to which the Sheikh responded by fainting—two times.

George Bush's administration and military were ready for action when Iraq rolled into Kuwait. Too ready, perhaps? Just a week before the invasion the army ran through a simulated Middle East operation called "War Flag '90." In the war game, despite that real war seemed imminent in that region, Joint Chiefs Chairman Colin Powell omitted names of the various Gulf states from the game map and redrew borders to disguise the nations involved. "Exceptional tact," declares Salinger, with a possible touch of sarcasm.

Bush was his manipulative self in the early days of the crisis, playing Arab nations against each other. He told Jordan that the United States would do nothing for forty-eight hours, then turned around and, through the State Department, sent a threatening message to Egypt. Take a "firm stand" against the invasion or Egypt will "no longer be able to count on America."

At the United Nations, Bush threw money at some countries and bullied others to build his "coalition," legitimizing what might otherwise appear to be another episode of American swashbuckling. "Yemen's ambassador was informed that his would be "the most expensive no vote you ever cast," if that country balked at the U.S.-backed "use of force" resolution, reports a radio journalist who covered the proceedings.

Why would Bush play such a costly and conspiratorial game? The obvious reason is the political boon he bestowed upon himself with "victory in the Gulf." Another possibility was revealed by former Watergate investigator Scott Armstrong. There is a $200 billion secret agreement between the U.S. and Saudi Arabia, Armstrong documented, assuring a permanent U.S. military presence in the Middle East through a staggering program of covert base-building. The deal, says Armstrong, creates a "premixed, dehydrated war machine: Just add American troops and (fresh) water." However, it also ties the U.S. military to the Saudi monarchy because if the royal family loses power the big bucks deal is blown.

"Earlier versions of these agreements had set the stage for U.S. intervention in the Persian Gulf war, probably making it inevitable," wrote Armstrong. And more ominous: "These secret agreements . . . make U.S. involvement in future Middle East conflicts unavoidable."

On January 16, 1991, Bush ordered a massive bombing attack against Iraq. In the ensuing saturation media coverage of the war, mentions of the Glaspie green-light to Saddam Hussein cropped up in passing but by and large there was little discussion of U.S. policy toward Iraq prior to the conflict.

My paper, *Metro,* was an exception. We ran a piece by *Village Voice* reporter Murray Waas detailing how Glaspie's attitude toward Iraq's "border dispute" with Kuwait was hardly an anomaly. In the months leading up to the invasion, administration officials repeatedly swore off use of force against Iraq. Secretary of State James Baker even went so far as to offer what sounded like a rationalization for Iraqi use of chemical weapons. He reported to a Senate committee Saddam Hussein's explanation that chemical weapons were his only deterrent against nuclear attack.

"I am not taking sides," said Baker—an astonishing statement in light of events that followed. "I am just stating that."

Metro also ran my little story about how Silicon Valley's original high-tech company, Hewlett-Packard, sold computers to Iraq knowing that they would be used in ballistic missile development. Numerous U.S. companies, I reported, sold military technology to Iraq right up until the international embargo came down after the invasion of Kuwait. German corporations were far worse offenders. Those companies under the jurisdiction of America's close ally were directly responsible for Iraq's chemical weapon-making ability.

Was Bush deliberately trying to get the U.S. into a war, to satisfy yet another cryptic agenda? Waas wrote off the Bushian pro-Iraq stance as a diplomatic blunder, albeit one of history's worst. Perhaps so. The Vietnam war was half-a-decade old when the Pentagon Papers leaked out to confirm what a sizable segment of the country suspected: the administration's public reasons for throwing the country into that war were simply sham.

Perhaps someday a "Pentagon Papers II" will appear, exposing how the country was fooled into the Persian Gulf war. I rather doubt it, however. Whatever his reasons for risking thousands of American lives (and taking thousands of Iraqi lives, including innumerable civilians) he is managing the war-propaganda well. The press is tightly controlled and seems to accept its bitter medicine with disturbing calm. Even enthusiasm. Meanwhile, Bush beats away on his theme of us against *him*, Saddam Hussein. It's the U.S. against a lone nut. How strangely fitting.

I'm sorry to admit that I've only skimmed the surface of the Bush file in this chapter. When I scanned a data base of newspaper articles from the years 1987 through mid-1990, the single largest subheading in Bush's entry was "investigations." In time, his life and career will be the subject of hundreds of books. As a Kissinger protégé, Nixon stooge, oil baron, CIA agent, Reaganite, Trilateralist, invader of foreign countries, coddler of fascists, family friend of a brainwashed assassin, president of the United States, and member of a secret society, there is no realm of conspiracy theory that cannot find a comfortable spot for George Bush. He is an *embodiment* of conspiracy. Maybe some of those future books will show that those eccentric, incredible theories were tinged with the flavor of truth, and the part he played in reshaping America will be illuminated a little bit brighter.

15

JUST A GROUP OF CONCERNED CITIZENS

In a subtle and civilized way they create an environment in which ideas are absorbed almost by osmosis and in which one draws the strength which comes from being with a group of individuals who form a community in this best sense.

HENRY KISSINGER, singing the praises of his colleagues on the Council on Foreign Relations

The November 13, 1989, issue of *U.S. News and World Report* magazine contained an announcement that slipped quietly by amidst news of the fall of the Berlin Wall and the lifting of the Iron Curtain. Innocuously stated, it heralded an equally startling revolution. "After nearly a century," the magazine proclaimed, "the Rockefeller 'thirst for dominion' may be quenched."

The announcement was prompted by the sale of Rockefeller Center—legendary real-estate development in the center of Manhattan—to Mitsubishi, a Japanese corporation. Also sold was fifty-one percent of the Rockefeller Group, the company that coordinates the Rockefeller family's dazzlingly diverse holdings. The press recorded the transaction as evidence of Japanese encroachment into American affairs. Little mention was made of the long alliance between the Rockefellers, American industrial rulers, and Mitsubishi, which plays a similar role in the Japanese corporate state. The press also failed to scrutinize the assumption that the Rockefeller organization is actually "American." In fact, it is global, and the guiding philosophy of the family in its business dealing is not nationalistic, but "one world."

Nor was it widely noted that while direct influence of Rockefeller family members over the day-to-day operations of the "domain" may have diminished with the sale, the organism fertilized and nurtured by the Rockefellers lives and grows. This being, with a mind of its own by now, is sort of a supersociety, on top of the society in which the average American lives. It goes by many names, most of them chosen by people not part of it: the American aristocracy, the faceless oligarchy, the power elite, the ruling class. The Establishment.

How powerful is this high society? What kind of influence does it have over our daily affairs?

Many of these people hold the highest positions in government and in big business. They sit on the boards of banks and control the money circulating around the world. They decide what gets manufactured, and how much. Educational institutions and mass media outlets are under their control, which means the information we receive—the very stuff of our thoughts—is also shaped by this elite, this "Establishment." This conspiracy.

America is arranged as a republican democracy in which elected representatives of the people make enlightened decisions through a consensus process. Because the American system is supposed to allow an equal voice for all, wealthy society is dismissed by many otherwise serious thinkers as having no undue influence over the governance of society at large.

For conspiracy theorists, there is no question that the ruling elite rules. American government as we know it is but a servant, indentured to this ruling system of which the Rockefeller clan is a central component.

The class is not just people; it is institutions: social clubs, prep schools, universities, "think tanks," councils, and committees; multinational corporations; Harvard and Yale; Exxon and Mobil; the RAND Corporation; the Council on Foreign Relations (CFR); the CIA—all temples of the ruling elite. The John Birchers aren't the only ones who see these organizations as secretive conclaves of the world's most powerful people. David Rockefeller pleads innocence, calling the conspiracy theories "foolish attacks on false issues."

Defending one such organization, the Trilateral Commission, which he founded, Rockefeller said, "[F]ar from being a coterie of international conspirators with designs on covertly ruling the world, the Trilateral Commission is, in reality, a group of concerned citizens interested in fostering greater understanding and cooperation among international allies . . . in such an uncertain and turbulent world climate . . . we must—all of us—work together to help frame a foreign policy that best reflects the courage and commitment that are the cornerstones of this great nation."

Rockefeller's "We Are the World" rhetoric appears more than a little disingenuous with a perusal of the Trilateral Commission's membership list—which included, when Rockefeller made that speech, the president of Mitsubishi. "All of us," in Rockefeller-speak, means leaders of established corporate giants, along with academics willing to do the grunt work of preparing reports and papers to give the corporations a scholarly justification for existence.

The stock comeback to the conspiracy theory is to point out that, in reality, members of the alleged ruling class have a hard time agreeing on lunch, much less on strategy for global conquest.

One of the elite's superstars, Henry Kissinger, feuded

with his colleagues on the CFR, particularly McGeorge Bundy, whom Kissinger regarded as something of an intellectual lightweight and closet anti-Semite. For that matter, George Bush, who reached the zenith of elite aspirations, resigned in protest from the CFR calling it "too liberal." Bush also turned in his Trilateral Commission credentials, feeling that association with the Rockefellers was becoming a political liability as he sought the presidency in 1980.

David Rockefeller has said he finds the charge that Trilateralists are of one mind "totally absurd." He has said that there is no such thing as a "Trilateral position" on issues. There is no "Trilateral conspiracy." The commission is merely a forum for discussion and has no power anyway.

"If 'conspiracy' means that these men are aware of their interests, know each other personally, meet together privately and off-the-record, and try to hammer out a consensus on how to anticipate and react to events and issues," writes sociologist G. William Domhoff, "then there is some conspiring that goes on in CFR, not to mention the Committee for Economic Development, the Business Council, the National Security Council and the Central Intelligence Agency."

There is no necessary contradiction between the fact of diverse opinion within the elite, and a conspiracy among the elite. The institutions of the elite "conspiracy" act like a blender, taking the jumble of opinions, personalities, and interests and stirring them into a smooth consensus. Forming a consensus from competing interests is the *purpose* of the Trilateral Commission, the CFR, and like bodies.

Furthermore, seemingly contradictory points of view within the Establishment are not as different as they might seem. On an obvious level, the membership of groups like the Trilateral Commission and the CFR is largely composed of businessmen. Funding comes from big business, businesspeople, and business foundations. It is therefore reasonable to conclude that, in general, these groups are not inclined to take up viewpoints which could be characterized as "antibusiness." The debate centers mainly around which policies are best for big business, not whether policies favoring big business are best.

The Rockefellerian apologia, that the goal of his commission is to promote a foreign policy "concerned with the most basic needs of the nation as well as its enduring aspirations," may well be sincere. But in Rockefeller's rarefied world, there can be little difference between the national interest and the objectives of international finance and trade. As Bill Moyers said, after shadowing Rockefeller for a week, "In the world of David Rockefeller it's hard to tell where business ends and politics begins."

Beyond the relatively simple requirements of self-interest, there is something else about the elitist worldview that bonds the Establishment together—the guiding philosophy of "management." "The peace and prosperity of the Trilateral world is not threatened by aggressors, spendthrifts, socialists, or other human types—only by problems," explained one of the rare mainstream journalists to write about the Trilateral Commission at any length.

To the Trilateralists (and I'm using that term more or less interchangeably with "elitists," etc.), the world is a perpetually pumping machine in need of constant adjustment. Their purpose is to make these adjustments. They don't view themselves as "a coterie of international conspirators" because the way their world works "makes conspiracy redundant" (to quote Moyers again), with power wielded through handshakes and luncheons.

Since the system is set up for the good of all, the managers are not rulers, but servants. Servants have no power. There is no such thing as power; there is only the system and its managers. When Rockefeller waves off talk that he and his Trilateral pals are running a global conspiracy with himself as "cabalist in chief," he is sincere. At the same time that he was flying all over the world—never worrying about customs, passports, or the other formalities of international travel—greeting Communist premiers, lunching with despots, striking deals with oil sheiks, Rockefeller probably saw himself as nothing more than a "concerned citizen" trying to do his best for the system—a system with an elite group of managers at the controls.

The elite's conspiracy of shared belief leads to a conspiracy of action. The Trilateralist conspiracy theory got its most public airing during the administration of President Jimmy Carter. Carter portrayed himself as a political outsider, not a false picture as far as Washington was concerned, but he was a member of the Trilateral Commission and it was at the Rockefellers' knee that the Georgia peanut farmer learned his foreign affairs.

During the 1976 presidential campaign, Hamilton Jordan, Carter's top adviser, was heard to promise, "If, after the inauguration, you find Cy Vance as Secretary of State and Zbigniew Brzezinski as head of national security, then I would say that we failed. And I'd quit."

Brzezinski was David Rockefeller's operative who did the scut work to organize the Trilateral Commission in 1972. Cyrus Vance was one of the most respected "commissioners," a Wall Street lawyer, Johnson administration official, and director of IBM, Pan Am, and the New York Times Company. After the inauguration, Hamilton Jordan was appointed Carter's chief of staff. Vance was named secretary of state, and Brzezinski became national security adviser. Jordan did not quit.

Twelve years later, when George Bush, another former commissioner, was scoring heavily in his presidential campaign by comparing his opponent Michael Dukakis to Jimmy Carter, Brzezinski popped up again—in Bush's camp. He endorsed Bush and advised him during the campaign on foreign policy matters. The press and public made little note of this irony, and never scrutinized the Trilateral connection behind it.

In its own literature, the Trilateral Commission lists "collective management" of global "interdependence" as its objective. Although Rockefeller may insist that he wields no real "power," and here in the United States his name rarely appears in the news, citizens of other nations have some difficulty with his demure attitude toward his own world position. In some countries, particularly in Latin America, where loans from Rockefeller's Chase Manhattan Bank propped up tyrannical regimes, his mere presence causes riots. Rockefeller's 1986 visit to Argentina set off the worst domestic uprising that country had seen in years.

Lobbying by David Rockefeller and Henry Kissinger influenced Jimmy Carter to allow the deposed shah of Iran into the U.S. for medical treatment. Carter's decision touched off the seizing of the American embassy in Tehran. The subsequent 444-day hostage crisis mutated American politics, allowing Reagan and establishmentarian George Bush to assume the country's top two elected posts.

It is one of the many paradoxes of American conspiracy theories that Rockefeller forces would put Carter in office, then help to depose him four years later. Perhaps David Rockefeller is right; the alleged conspiracy doesn't work as smoothly as imagined by those who launch "foolish attacks" on Trilateral integrity. Or perhaps the Trilateralists simply saw a better opportunity with Ronald Reagan as figurehead and Establishmentarian George Bush as deceptively obsequious second banana. The Reagan administration turned out to be as thoroughly shot through with Trilateralism as Carter's. But that is a matter for later in the chapter.

The Trilateral Commission was founded in 1972. David Rockefeller raised the idea for the new roundtable group at a meeting of an older one, the Bilderbergers.

Named for the Bilderberg Hotel in Holland where the group held its first get-together in 1954, the Bilderberg Group is a traveling convention of the world's richest people who gather to talk about how to get richer. The Bilderbergers are more secretive than the Trilateral Commission, perhaps with good reason. Their president until the mid-1970s was Prince Bernhard of the Netherlands. The Bilderbergers thought it best that he resign when his name surfaced in the Lockheed bribery scandal.

Apparently, Lockheed, one of globe's biggest multinational military contractors, paid the prince millions to convince the Dutch government to buy its planes. The Lockheed affair, which involved several multinationals in a web of bribery, spying, and other sordid affairs, shed at least a little light on the dirty dealings of big business. "Respectable" corporate executives stood exposed as no better than mobsters—worse, because they committed crimes on a worldwide scale. Those activities may well be the sorts of things hashed over in the cozy confines of the Bilderberg.

All the Bilderbergers are American and European. Letting in Japanese elites is a Trilateralist innovation. While it was hatched at a Bilderberg meeting, the Trilateral Commission owes an equal debt to its more direct predecessor, the Council on Foreign Relations (CFR), perhaps the most elite of elitist think tanks.

The CFR sits in a building called the Harold Pratt House at 68th Street and Park Avenue in Manhattan. Initiates of elite society wander in and out: presidents, chiefs of staff, secretaries of state, directors of Central Intelligence, industrialists, financiers, media moguls, academic authorities. Solar plexus of the conspiracy, the CFR was incorporated on July 29, 1921, after two years of planning by some of America's most influential people. At least, they thought they were influential until they went to the Paris Peace Conference of 1919.

Edward M. House, President Woodrow Wilson's close adviser and power behind the throne, organized one hundred of the crustiest members of the upper crust into a group called "the Inquiry," which met secretly in New York, putting together Wilson's strategy for the peace conference. To their horror, Wilson snubbed their carefully composed counsel. They watched in blushing disgruntlement while European leaders had their way with the American president at the negotiating table.

Thomas W. Lamont, an official of the Morgan Bank and the U.S. Treasury, was particularly perturbed. He took his concerns to his aristocratic British counterparts and the idea that later became the CFR began to coalesce. Morganites already had an elite foreign policy group of their own, the Round Table.

CFR members pepper U.S. government employment rolls. When CFR mainstay John J. McCloy (sometimes called the "chairman of the Establishment") was personnel chief for the secretary of war, he admitted he did most of his recruiting off the CFR roster.

The CFR's membership swelled to more than two thousand by the 1980s, but it still admits just five percent of applicants and recruits many members out of the government. Late CIA director William Casey was rejected on his first try, even though he was a well-heeled Wall Street speculator. But in 1973, when he became an undersecretary of state, the CFR sent Casey an invitation and he joined.

Casey's background in the intelligence community probably didn't hurt him in the CFR's eyes. CIA directors John McCone, Richard Helms, William Colby, and

George Bush were all CFR members. Traditionally, the CIA has drawn its top agents from the same social circles where the CFR finds its members. Pipe-puffing Allen Dulles, the CIA's most storied director and a Warren Commission member, dates back to Edward M. House's "Inquiry" group. The CIA counts on CFR members to front for its cover organizations, and CIA officials feel comfortable revealing the touchiest information at CFR meetings.

It was within the catacombs of Harold Pratt House that American policy makers were first introduced to the idea that nuclear war could be "winnable," so uninhibited is the Establishment in its search for new and more efficient world management techniques. The CFR has its own publishing house and, in 1957, it hit the best-seller list, not that it needed the money. The best-seller was *Nuclear Weapons and Foreign Policy* by Henry Kissinger. "Limited nuclear war is in fact a strategy which will utilize our special skills to best advantage," wrote the young German scholar. "Our superior industrial potential, the broader range of our technology and the adaptability of our social institutions should give us an advantage." Dr. Strangelove on the CFR.

Kissinger's scary opinions are made more so by his origins. Long before he became Richard Nixon's national security adviser, Gerald Ford's secretary of state, or Lyndon LaRouche's personal Lex Luthor, Kissinger was a protégé of Nelson Rockefeller, who mentored the young professor and supported him financially. In the Nixon administration, when Kissinger was making a public show of disassociating himself from Rockefeller—Nixon's personal enemy—he was sneaking documents out of the White House to Rockefeller's estate.

Nixon and Rockefeller were arch rivals. Tricky Dick hated the "Eastern Establishment," which he thought looked down its elevated nose at him. So how and why did he get Henry Kissinger on his side? Or was the Big K a Rockefeller mole all along, guiding Nixon's foreign policy in the CFR-Trilateral "One World" direction it eventually took?

Just as the Establishment is at the center of conspiracy theories, the Rockefeller family is at the center of the Establishment.

"The Rockefeller family is the most powerful family in the United States," writes sociologist Holly Sklar, an authority on Trilateralism. "Rockefeller power lies in the many interlocking corporations, financial institutions, foundations and leading individuals they control."

The Rockefeller strategy of owning a piece of everything is typical. Interlocking corporate directorates are rampant among the Establishment, giving further appearance of a conspiracy.

Sklar wrote a decade before the Rockefellers unloaded Rockefeller Center, Radio City Music Hall, and fifty-one percent of the Rockefeller Group on Mitsubishi. Nonetheless, the list of Rockefeller investments was and still is impressive. In the 1970s, when Nelson Rockefeller became vice president, the family portfolio included Exxon, Mobil, Standard Oil of California, Standard Oil of Indiana, Eastern Airlines, the Chase Manhattan Bank, Metropolitan Life Insurance, and several of the nation's largest philanthropic foundations. Nelson Rockefeller tried to soothe conspiracy panic when he was appointed vice president. "We have investments, but not control," Rocky told the Senate committee confirming him. "I hope that the myth or misconception about the extent of the family's control over the economy of this country will be brought out and exposed and dissipated."

Rocky had run for president twice already, in 1964 and 1968. His lust for the high office was no secret. So in 1974, when, in the aftermath of Watergate, Nelson Rockefeller became an appointed vice president to an appointed president—the famed "heartbeat away"—even the sober minded could be forgiven for wondering if maybe there was something to those Rockefeller conspiracy theories after all. When two separate assassins came a bullet away from putting Rocky in the Oval Office, they could be forgiven once again. If not for a couple of jammed pistols, Nelson Rockefeller would have fulfilled his dream of becoming president—without winning a single vote.

The Rockefellerian elite is generally referred to as the "Eastern Establishment." It is centered on Wall Street and nurtured in New England prep schools and Anglophilic Ivy League universities. As we saw earlier, the Eastern Establishment is the bane of anti-Communists, who see the Rockefellers aiding and abetting, in fact, masterminding, the international Communist conspiracy. Under President Reagan, the Council on Foreign Relations, the Trilateral Commission, and the rest of the Eastern Establishment was usurped by a more hard-right, uncompromising, intellectual and financial elite based in the South and West. The Trilateralists, who always advocated absorbing the Soviet bloc into the capitalist New World Order (it was the Third World that was never invited in), slipped into the shadow of Stanford University's Hoover Institute, the intellectual hub of anticommunism and right-wing theorizing.

As it happened, the Rockefeller crew had the last laugh. With George Bush as president, the Communist countries have been subsumed into the "free" world and talk of a "New World Order" is uninhibited.

Much of the financial backing for the Southwestern Establishment—sometimes called the "Cowboys," as opposed to the Eastern "Yankees"—came from Texas oil barons. This was the same Southwestern Establishment involved, as we saw a few chapters back, in a scenario allegedly behind the assassination of President Kennedy. But the cowboy/Yankee division is not that simple.

The overlaps and interlocks between the two factions stretch across the oil business into the CIA, which draws its upper echelon agents from the CFR, yet spent decades enforcing the raunchy anticommunism of the Southwesterners. The blend became smoothest in the Reagan years, when William Casey ran the CIA. He slithered in and out of the two spheres—detesting the "Eastern Establishment" while making a fortune on Wall Street, the Establishment's breast, and sitting on the CFR. The "Reagan Doctrine" of interventionist foreign policy, of which Casey was operational manager, was debated within the administration between Secretary of State George Schultz, former president of the multinational construction company, Bechtel Corporation, and Trilateral Commissioner Casper Weinberger, Reagan's defense secretary.

If we need further proof that George Bush is the ultimate conspiracy president, note his easy transition between the cowboy and Yankee cliques. He literally claims two homes, one in crusty New England, another in tobacco-stained Texas. He comes from an aristocratic Connecticut family and, with his father's financial backing, made his first name for himself in the oil-sodden circles of Houston wealth. In the CIA, he was equally at ease with rootin'-tootin' Bay of Pigs–hardened Cubans like Felix Rodriguez, and their Williams College–educated tutors like Richard Helms and Donald Gregg. Disunity between the Northeastern and Southwestern elites may have once been a mitigating factor against total takeover by elites of the political system. But Bush brings the two camps into one tent.

The confluence of interests between the "Yankees" and the "cowboys" comes down to one thing: power. Which is more or less synonymous with money, because money is the most important tool with which humans control other humans. The "Establishment" conspiracy theory sees the raw pursuit of power by the wealthy as the only real motive for the conspiracy. Just as one Kennedy assassination theory points to the Southwestern Establishment, another pins the crime on the Rockefeller set.

The difference becomes almost semantic as the conspiracy theory becomes increasingly all consuming. The idea of powerful elites who conspire to control the masses is what Neil Wilgus calls the "Illuminoid" theory, the theory that sees secret societies behind all the major events of political history.

"If the Illuminati begat the Round Tablers who begat the CFR who begat the Bilderbergers who begat the Trilateral Commission, then perhaps," writes Wilgus, "this is the ultimate answer to the Kennedy and other assassinations."

Could it be that David Rockefeller's "group of concerned citizens" can trace its heritage back hundreds, maybe thousands, of years? We've already seen how the CIA functions as a secret society, how the CFR feeds the CIA, how the universe of elite elements can coalesce in one limited conspiracy—the J.F.K. assassination—with incalculable sociopolitical, economic, and even psychological effects. Is there any noumena behind these phenomena, or are they simply phantoms? Do the shadows of history play tricks on the eye?

Peter McAlpine's witty little volume *The Occult Technology of Power,* purporting like a modern version of *The Prince* to be a how-to handbook for the power elite, draws the same connection as did Wilgus's work.

"Perhaps the most accurate overview of our intelligence community can be achieved by visualizing it as a 'nationalized secret society,' " says the book, written in the first person as if by a master conspirator to his son, about to inherit the covertly controlled empire. "Our predecessors, in their struggle against the old order of kings and princes, had to finance secret societies such as the Illuminati, Masons, German Union, etc. out of their own pockets. . . . How much easier it is for us, inheri-

tors of a fully developed state-capitalist system! By ap
pealing to 'national security' we are able to finance a
erect secret societies of a colossal scope."

Contemporary American conspiracy theories tend
downplay the secret society angle. European conspira
theories pay secret societies much more attention. But t
archetype is there. The CIA and the Trilateralists both
the model. There have been secret societies forever,
seems, and they still exist today. Maybe they are nothin
but coincidentally similar groups that sprout from tin
to time in response to the pressures of each particul
historical time and place. Or perhaps the "technology
power" has been "occult" since early civilization, whe
humans first began to control nature and those most in
portant creatures of nature—other humans.

16

FROM MYSTERIES
TO MASONRY

*The true student does not speak of the
work he is engaged in nor of his experiences, or the degree of his development
other than to his master.*

Rosicrucian secrecy oath

The meaning of "secret society" has become somewhat
foggy over the centuries. Ancient secret societies were
politically and religiously subversive. If their existence
was uncovered, they would be wiped out.

More modern secret societies often don't bother to
keep their membership rolls secret. Freemasonry, for example. Few Masons are shy about revealing their alle-
giance. They wear their Masonic pins and rings proudly.
Anyone who wants to spend the time at a good library
can find voluminous Masonic books spelling out rituals
and Masonic etiquette in detail. The same is true for the
Rosicrucians, the "Order of the Rosy Cross," who claim
an Egyptian heritage. One latter-day Rosicrucian order
offers its secrets by mail order in magazine classified ads.

So what's the big secret? In the summer of 1988, the
Masonic Grand Lodge of New York took out an advertisement in the *New York Times* asking just that question:
"Why do some people still think Masonry is a secret society?" This was followed by text explaining the pure-

hearted purposes of the Masonic order, "the oldest a[
largest fraternity in the world." The appearance of t[
advertisement cum apologia was something of a curiosi[
in itself.

The exact origins of Freemasonry aren't one hundr[
percent clear. The standard account is that the socie[
metamorphosed out of medieval labor guilds. How
union of bricklayers could become haven to freethinki[
professors and philosophers is still mysterious. Freem
sonry on the continent was very much a spiritual e[
deavor. Not exactly atheistic, it was not explicitly Chri[
tian either. Lodge activity included speeches and resear[
into the nature of man as a moral being, and the furthe[
ance of human fellowship. The motto of the French rev[
lutionaries—"Liberty, Equality, Fraternity"—was t[
Masonic motto.

At the same time that lodges were pondering ho[
mankind might be made free and equal, they were al[
elitist. In England, Masonry took a different directio[
from its continental counterpart. The royal family a[
the aristocracy was largely Masonic.

In America, Masonic lodges don't have the aristocrat[
airs their European counterparts retain. Typically Amer[
can, they're largely places to strike up business contac[
rather than ruminate on the perfectibility of human na[
ture. Nonetheless, how many Americans know that si[
teen American presidents were Masons? Couldn't it b[
possible that the social contacts they made in their lodge[
and the beliefs passed on through Masonic rituals, ha[
some influence over their presidential decision makin[
For George Washington, and the other Masonic foundin[
fathers, they did. They went so far as to base the urba[
design of Washington, D.C., on Masonic mystical princ[
ples.

The average person isn't aware of those principle[
Nor do many understand them. Even reading about M[
sonry in books is not equivalent to the experience of be[

ing initiated. All secret societies have some kind of ritual that must be experienced to be understood. Membership may be public knowledge, beliefs may be recorded in books, activities may on occasion be advertised, but the secret of a secret society is the shared experience of the members.

These days, secret societies have as much in common with social clubs as with the cults and mystical orders that are their ancestors. The classically fashioned secret society is an association of true believers. Usually, a "grand master" rules the society with absolute authority. The society itself is as repressive as the social order it opposes. Some societies have taken their fanaticism to extremes. The Russian Skoptski, or Castrators, are the best example of devotion to the esoteric cause. The members castrated themselves in order to more readily attain enlightenment.

Few secret societies get that carried away. But, throughout history, clandestine groups, hidden cabals, and secret societies have been accused of manipulating events and shaping the social order. The Bavarian Illuminati were thought to have fomented the French Revolution. The Knights Templar, precursors of Freemasonry, became Europe's controlling bankers and landlords in the Middle Ages, until they were accused of practicing the black mass and worshipping a disembodied head known as "Baphomet." The authorities exterminated them.

"The world is governed," said Queen Victoria's prime minister Benjamin Disraeli, "by very different personages from what is imagined by those who are not behind the scenes." Disraeli, no paranoid, was nonetheless a firm believer in the power of secret societies over political events and the course of history. Adolf Hitler held a similar belief. He may well have been the tool of such societies himself. The Nazi party and the SS, in particular, were patterned after secret societies. The occult motivations of the Nazis is a touchy topic, not widely discussed among academic historians—which means, of course, that this book will cover it extensively in the next chapter.

Secret societies have indeed had an unseen hand in shaping the world, probably since the beginning of recorded history and definitely since the dawn of the modern era. Has the truth been hidden for thousands of years? Have the few who comprehend this secret knowledge been using it to control the world? Or have the initiates been the oppressed ones, guarding the truth from the power mongers who are threatened by its existence? Either way, truth is concealed. Ordinary people meander through life with delusions, and no understanding of the human predicament.

The history of conspiracy theories, then, is the history of secret societies. The history of secret societies is the history of conspiracies. And that is the history of civilization itself.

What follows does not claim to be a comprehensive history of secret societies. By the very nature of secret societies, that history can never be written. If it were, what might it reveal? The fanaticism and paranoia basic to human nature, or the greatest conspiracy, the *only* conspiracy in the history of the world: the conspiracy against truth.

"Illuminati" has become like a secret society brand name. When a Bavarian professor named Adam Weishaupt founded a meta-Masonic order by that name on May 1, 1776, he had every intention of changing the world. His legacy instead has been a voluminous library of literature not by him but about him, from anti-Semitic tracts naming Weishaupt as the pawn of a centuries-old Jewish plot, to acid-tripping novels with the Illuminati as metaphysical secret agents, sort of a gnostic SMERSH.

According to assorted scribes, the Illuminati are behind the French Revolution, the Bolshevik Revolution, the American Revolution, the pope, the Kennedy assassination, Charles Manson, the Rockefeller dynasty, the New Age movement, UFO visitations, and the Universal Price Code. The odd inscription "57 Varieties" on Heinz Ketchup has been called an Illuminati code phrase. And if you ever see the word "fnord" in the *New York Times*, watch out. You'll know the Illuminati are on the scene.

The Illuminati saga has understandably become a favorite of freaks—hate groups on one extreme, dorm-room Dungeons and Dragons devotees on the other. For John Birchers, the Illuminati are "the conspiracy above communism," an enemy to be suppressed. For the pop philosophers, "Illuminati" is a game, a puzzle whose pleasure is in the solving, not in the solution.

In actual fact, the existence of the Bavarian Illuminati was a minor scandal of the late eighteenth century. The group plotted ambitious political stratagems. As far as the general public knew, its influence was stifled in 1790 when the Bavarian government outlawed the group and seized its records. That fourteen-year time span gave the Illuminati opportunity to infiltrate governments and in some way tie itself to the French Revolution. If that were the society's only achievement, the Bavarian Illuminati would be a force for social transformation. Whether the Illuminati's influence extended further, possibly into perpetuity, has been the subject of much debate, speculation, and fantasy.

Weishaupt, founder of the Illuminati, was a law professor at the University of Ingoldstat in Bavaria and was accepted into Freemasonry in 1774. Weishaupt had been taught by Jesuits, had some Jewish background, and supported the Protestant cause for a while, but finally got fed up with all religion. He'd studied paganism while a student and drew up a plan for a secret society modeled on pre-Christian mystery cults.

Weishaupt's godfather was librarian at the University of Ingoldstat. He stocked books of a freethinking bent condemned by Jesuits, who had held a tight rein until then on the parameters of intellectual debate in Bavaria. Weishaupt was just twenty-six when he was appointed to his professorship, a chair that had been held for ninety years by Jesuits.

In the same year, 1775, Weishaupt joined the "Lodge Theodore of Good Counsel," a somewhat radical Masonic organization in Bavaria. Like most continental Masonic lodges of the day, the Lodge Theodore devoted its proceedings to dissertations on the attainment of human happiness and perfect morality. During the Enlightenment, we often forget, rational thought and mystical practices were not yet divorced. Science, philosophy, and mysticism were all one discipline. Masonic lodges were the laboratory.

Weishaupt was one of the Lodge Theodore's most rambunctious members. He rejected established authorities and believed man should live in an enlightened state of nature, free from restrictions imposed by European society. His political program was to alter civilization to make his utopia possible. He founded the Illuminati, alternately known as the "Order of Perfectibilists," out of his annoyance with the limitations of Masonry. But he knew he needed Masonry, and he believed in it. The Illuminati was not a breakaway from the Freemasons, but a secret order above the Masons. Masonic lodges were Weishaupt's recruiting grounds. Once an initiate had mastered the tenets of Freemasonry, through its ritual "steps," he was (unknown to himself) a candidate for induction into the Illuminati.

Weishaupt was inspired by the Jesuits, the Catholic order whose teachings he rebelled against but whose structure he admired. The same intellectual discipline demanded by Jesuits was requisite for all Illuminati. Only when each new member was thoroughly versed in the principles of each stage of "illumination" would he be ready for initiation into the higher mysteries. Some never were. Only when members climbed to the top of the staircase of degrees were they told the true purpose of the Illuminati: world revolution.

The Illuminati began with five members. Within eight years, the order had franchises throughout Europe and, by some estimates, four thousand members. The society had agents inside parliaments and aristocracies and had infiltrated Masonic lodges all over Europe—and at the same time was itself infiltrated by police. When informers exposed an Illuminati scheme to overthrow the Hapsburg dynasty in 1784, the government began its first crackdown on secret societies.

Some writers maintain that Weishaupt was a nonviolent revolutionary. This seems doubtful now—or, if he was, his followers were not. The Comte de Mirabeau, an instigator of the French Revolution, is reported to have been an Illuminist. Illuminati pamphlets, rife with esoteric symbolism, were strewn through the streets of revolutionary France.

"Illumination" is the objective of most secret societies. Mysticism is the belief in and practice of transforming one's consciousness through meditation, yoga, intensive study, drugs, sex, sacrifice—any form of ritual whose purpose is to produce a direct experience with the sacred. The "sacred" is just another way of saying "reality" or "the truth." Secret societies are not religions per se, but they all hold some concept of a higher truth.

Weishaupt's Illuminati aimed to induce not merely the personal transformation of its initiates, but the transformation of the whole human society. A quintessential conspiracy—a quintessential conspiracy theory.

Weishaupt based his Illuminati on ancient mysteries, goddess-worshipping cults that flourished in Greece and Rome. The mysteries of antiquity were not as rabble-rousing as Weishaupt's brainchild. For adherents, they were refuge from corrupt society, offering freedom in their festivals and belonging in their rituals. And, most of all, transcendence of the one dire inevitability that faces all of us: death.

The sacred secrets of the mysteries were the secrets of life and death. In the view of religious scholar Hyam Maccoby, human sacrifice was a commonly practiced sacred ritual among early Jews and Christians. The sacrificial priest was a "sacred executioner," who brought death to one victim for the greater good, or rebirth, of the tribe.

The Old Testament, says Maccoby, carefully covers up the history of human sacrifice among the Hebrew tribes. The New Testament, in a rather startling reversal, rejoices in sacrifice.

Interviewed by Patrick Tierney in his book *The Highest Altar,* Maccoby explains how he broke a "biblical code," revealing the numerous murder stories in the Old Testament as ritual sacrifices. The most obvious example is Abraham's sacrifice of Isaac, his son, at the command of the god Yahweh. The biblical story contains a deus ex machina allowing Abraham to spare the boy. Other versions of the story, from Jewish oral tradition, have a bloodier end. Furthermore, he says, the biblical story contains no criticism of a child sacrifice. Abraham was unnervingly placid about Yahweh's rather extreme request, as if children were sacrificed all the time.

For the sacrifice, Abraham was blessed by Yahweh, becoming the father of an entire people. Through death, a rebirth. In some versions of the story, Isaac himself is resurrected. Tierney notices "how similar [the Abraham myth] is to the many child sacrifices at the origins of other religions." He lists Greek, Mayan, and Dogon tales in which killing and rebirth of children are acts of primal creation.

The killing of Abel by Cain is usually taught as the "first murder." Cain had been offering vegetable sacrifices to God, while Abel's animal sacrifices netted much greater results. So, according to Maccoby, Cain turned around and sacrificed his own brother. As a reward for this supreme offering, Cain is given his own city, which he dubs "Enoch" after his son. Cain's descendants become musicians, artisans, and livestock breeders, "inventions typically ascribed to godlike culture heroes in every primitive society," writes Tierney. By his sacrifice, Cain was rewarded; humanity was rewarded by the civilization he founded. Death, and rebirth.

The mystery schools were filled with sacrificial rites, real and symbolic. Cultic rites often entailed eating the body of a sacrifice, or consuming a communal meal with food substituting for a god's body. Sound familiar? The Last Supper fits the pattern.

For the ancient mystery cults, death and rebirth were "the basic idea of an initiation ritual." Mystery cults were the earliest secret societies. Not really religions, the way religions are defined today, they were ritualized groups devoted mostly to the worship of the Great Goddess and the Fertility God in all their permutations. The names of gods changed from culture to culture, but ancient religion was richly cross-pollinated. Mythical personalities were nearly indistinguishable. Sacrifice was an important part of the mystery rituals. There are conspicuous similarities between modern secret societies and their ancient forebears.

This is not to say that secret societies are bastions of "that old-time religion," human sacrifice. Rituals of *symbolic* death and rebirth are common. Masonry's most important myth is one of human sacrifice: the murder of Hiram Abiff, godlike architect who built the Temple of Solomon. To be admitted to the Masonic "third degree," a member acts the part of Hiram in a playlet of this ritual killing, after which the initiate is reborn as a "Master Mason." Under one interpretation of Masonic mythology, Hiram is an incarnation of Osiris, the Egyptian god of resurrection. In one rite of Masonic initiation, the novice lies down in a casket. In Egyptian mythology, Osiris was murdered by being shut in a casket.

It is worth noting that the Temple of Solomon—the most sacred of Masonic symbols—appears not to have been a monument to Yahweh, the Hebrew god, but to the heaven goddess Astarte, of whom Solomon is identified as "a follower." The goddess figure was also known as Isis, Ishtar, Demeter, or Ashtaroth, all of whom had mystery cults devoted to their worship (under Christianity, Ashtaroth became a demon, and male). To the Greeks, Osiris was Dionysius, god of renewal—and of wine—who had a cult of his own. Either the original Masons deliberately concocted myths modeled on these ancient archetypes, or the Freemasons are the latest stage of secret society evolution beginning in the earliest civilizations.

One theory suggests that raising Lazarus "from the dead," one of Jesus's many "miracles," was actually a death-rebirth initiation rite. The entombment of Lazarus was his rite of passage, and his resurrection by Jesus was the final stage of his initiation. Taken literally or not (and not all early Christians did), the tale of Jesus's own crucifixion describes a death-rebirth ritual.

Jesus is the most important historical figure of the past two thousand years. He is the most enigmatic figure as well. There is no small question as to whether such a person actually lived, and, if so, what kind of person he was. Although his era was tense and active, politically and intellectually, no contemporary historian mentions him except for a writer named Josephus—but most scholars believe that the mentions of Jesus in Josephus's work are forged interpolations.

There are two possible explanations for the absence of a Holy Paper Trail. First, Jesus never existed—he is a purely fictional character. Second, and more likely in my view, is that historical writings about Jesus have been censored to insure that no extant information could contradict the "official" biography of Jesus that gave the Church a rationale for power. Under either scenario, the story of Jesus holds many dangerous secrets.

As sage a source as Saint Augustine acknowledged that the "true religion" existed long before Jesus appeared, "from the very beginning of the human race," in fact. Christianity, he said, was a continuation of this primeval tradition. If Jesus was real, he was an adherent of the "true religion." If he was made up, then his story would likely be another in a long line of allegorical stories meant to convey the principles of this religion of creation, of life and death.

The story of Jesus, in its broad outlines, matches many myths that came before. Lloyd Graham, in his bluntly titled book *Deceptions and Myths of the Bible*, points out that what he calls "the pagan and mythic nature of the Christ story" repeats the Greek myth of Hercules. Both were born of virgins, sons of gods, called "savior," and died martyr's deaths. Graham also sees similarities between Jesus and Bacchus, who incidentally was the god figure to a breed of mystery cults. The specific historical source for the Jesus myth, says Graham (who contends that Jesus is a fictional character), was the Indian legend of Krishna. Graham maintains that there are no less than sixteen "Christs" who predate Jesus, whose stories could have been rewritten as the New Testament Gospels.

Among these resurrected gods was Attis, whose cult was one of the most well attended of the Greek mysteries. Patrick Tierney notes that the Attis cult had a stronghold in the town of Tarsus. That town of Tarsus was home to Saint Paul, the ideological founder of Christianity. The death and resurrection of Attis also reverberates with Christlike connotations. Attis was supposed to have died and been resurrected around the time of the spring equinox, for example, just like Jesus. The time between death and rebirth was three days, just like Jesus. The festival of Attis includes a "communion meal."

According to Tierney, the Jesus story is out of sorts with Judaism of that era, which was repulsed by human sacrifice. But "it fits perfectly with the cult of Attis."

Another mystery idol, the bull god Mithras, shared something with Jesus: a birthday. Both were born on the winter solstice. The cult of Mithras was popular among Roman soldiers.

Just because his story fits a pattern of age-old mythology doesn't mean that Jesus was not a real person. In 1966, *The Passover Plot* became a best-seller with its case that the real Jesus was a political revolutionary who orchestrated the last few weeks of his life, including his own crucifixion, to fulfill Old Testament prophecies.

In 1983, another book, *Holy Blood, Holy Grail,* took that argument much further. The authors of that book, Michael Baigent, Richard Leigh, and Henry Lincoln, make a case that Jesus did, indeed, plan the whole thing. Traditional lore has it that a few of Jesus's key disciples made their way to France following the crucifixion. Among them were the mysterious Joseph of Arimathea— a wealthy landowner said in the Bible to be a "secret disciple"—and Mary Magdalene. Evidence supports the view, the book contends, that Magdalene was a mystery cultist, or former cultist, who became Jesus's wife. They base this opinion on passages from the scripture itself, including Mary Magdalene's display of spousal obedience at the resurrection of Lazarus, her brother. That would make him Jesus's brother-in-law.

The crucifixion itself, the *Holy Blood, Holy Grail* authors argue, was staged. Jesus may have survived it. His surprisingly quick death and removal from the cross (under Roman custom, crucifixion victims were denied burial, left to rot on the cross) indicate that the crucifixion of Jesus was not routine. More unorthodox, the Roman governor, Pontius Pilate, discharged the body to the care of Joseph of Arimathea, the "secret disciple." The crucifixion itself, reading between the biblical lines, took place in a private garden far from public view. Could Pilate, a corrupt thug, have been bribed to participate in this contrivance?

Legend also has it that when Joseph and Mary escaped to France, they brought with them "the Holy Grail," whatever that may be. Baigent, Lincoln, and Leigh theorize that "Holy Grail" is actually a mistranslation of a word that means more precisely, "royal blood." In other words, the Holy Grail is the bloodline of Jesus—the heirs to the throne of Israel. Jesus had a rightful claim to that throne. In the Gospel according to Matthew, he is described as a descendant of King David and King Solomon.

The Holy Grail in popular lore is usually described as the cup from which Jesus drank at the Last Supper, but there's no more evidence for that claim than for any other. Historical genealogist Noel Currer-Briggs identified the Grail with the Shroud of Turin (a strange sheet imprinted with a quasi-photographic likeness of a crucified man, the shroud has until recently been passed off as the burial cloth of Jesus).

In the early Grail Romances, which were widely condemned by church authorities, who spotted the pagan heresy immediately, the Grail is a cup of plenty. Food, drink, and eternal life are the rewards to anyone who can grasp its meaning. The Grail is a fertility symbol, a life giver. Death and rebirth.

Whatever the Grail is, it is a secret. Given the symbolism-drenched, allegory-thick description of the Grail in epic poems from the Middle Ages, the Grail is as much an experience as a physical object. The Grail Romances describe it as a cup or a stone, but also as a series of visions and a riddle—"Whom does the Grail serve?" Evidently, the Grail represents some sort of secret knowledge that must be experienced to be comprehended.

The Holy Grail is forever associated not only with
Jesus, but with King Arthur—yet another mythical icon
who fits the bill as a "Christ." The earliest Grail Romances were Arthurian tales spun by Chretien de Troyes
in the twelfth century. In these poems, the Grail has no
Christian connotations. That came later. Those who
dwell on such arcania tend to agree that the Grail myth is
pagan, not Christian, and has ancient origins.

In Chretien's poems, the Grail is guarded by a group
of knights called Templars. It seems likely that these were
the same Knights Templar who appeared out of nowhere
in the Holy Land sometime early in the twelfth century,
claiming to be a tiny band of "poor knights" numbering
just nine. Over the following two centuries, these "poor
knights" encompassed Europe with their banking/real-
estate empire, backed by their own military might.

The Templars were founded in the city of Troyes,
Chretien's hometown and home to the count of Cham-
pagne. Esoterica and mysticism flourished in the count's
court.

King Phillippe of France, on Friday, October 13, 1307,
ordered the destruction of the Templars. The knights
were arrested, tortured, and burned at the stake. The entire operation took seven years. It concluded with the
Templar grand master, Jacques DeMolay, roasted alive on
a spit. Phillippe's motive was probably money, but there
was more to it. The Vatican sanctioned the operation even
though the Templars were knights of the Church.

Among the charges of heresy brought against the Templars was their worship of a severed head. The Grail
myth, according to Arthurian historians, evolved from
pagan Celtic head-hunting cults that worshipped severed
heads. To the Celtic tribes, chopped-off heads brought
fertility and protection from enemies. From the death of
the choppee came life.

The Grail myth, in which the Grail is an experience of
truth, is also decidedly gnostic. Gnostic gospels tell of

Jesus faking his own crucifixion. He laughs as some anonymous poor sap is nailed up in his place. The Islamic holy book, the Koran, also contains this ghoulish "substitution" scenario. On the docket of indictments against the Templars was the allegation that they shunned Christianity in favor of infidel Muslim beliefs.

Despite the barbecuing of their grand master, it is highly likely that the Templars were not totally eliminated. Survivors went underground, coming under the protection of Scotland's bad-boy king Robert Bruce. From there, the Templars preserved their heritage by forming a secret society. At the time, it was secret in every sense of the word. The metamorphosis of the Templars is much debated, but with each new study seems more and more plausible. There are too many similarities between the Templars and the society that eventually took the name "Free and Accepted Masons." Freemasons.

Freemasonry in American history is not hard to spot. George Washington was an avid Mason. His funeral in 1799 was a major public event, and featured full Masonic honors. As president, Washington had been sworn in by a Masonic grand master. When the cornerstone of the Capitol building was laid in 1793, the ceremony was unabashedly Masonic. When the Marquis de Lafayette, a Mason, made his historic visit to the young United States in 1825, he was welcomed by lodges from city to city. Masonic banquets in his honor were widely covered by the press.

The great seal of the United States is gorged with Masonic symbolism, from the "eye in the pyramid" to the "Novus Ordo Seclorum" banner announcing the dawn of a New Age. Benjamin Franklin was inducted into Freemasonry in 1731. He belonged to the first official American Masonic lodge. Franklin's travels brought him

into contact with other secret societies. On trips to En
gland, he'd often drop in on the Friars of St. Francis o
Wycombe, otherwise known as the "Hell Fire Club."
The "club" was the creation of Sir Francis Dashwood,
notably decadent aristocrat and occultist who was
member of the British parliament. Dashwood also be
longed to a Druidic cult (though he would be expelled)

As a visitor to the Hell Fire Club, Franklin likely too
part in the strange goings-on there. Dashwood was some
thing of a porn buff. His secret society was a cover fo
sex orgies and, according to some accounts, Satan-wor
shipping Black Masses with a naked woman serving a
the blasphemous altar. In the years leading up to th
American Revolution, Franklin and Dashwood worked
together to come up with a nonviolent way to smooth
over differences between the colonies and Dashwood'
friend, King George III.

Their efforts came to nothing, of course, but the par
ticipation of Masons in the war for American indepen
dence didn't stop. Almost every one of the signers of the
Declaration of Independence was a Mason. The U.S.
Constitution was also framed to fit Masonic precepts o:
liberty, equality, and fraternity.

Masons fought on both sides in the revolutionary war
which helps explain why the British lost. Surely the
mighty British Empire could have suppressed a poorly
armed colonial rebellion if it had so chosen. On the bat
tlefield, and in the generals' quarters, the unwillingness of
British Masons to slaughter their colonial brethren, with
whom they were sworn in fraternity, weakened British
resolve. Masons who took other Masons prisoner would
not hold them long. In that sense, the American Revolution was not merely a rebellion of disgruntled taxpayers
against their colonial lords, but a rebellion of Masons
against the established social order. The "Novus Ordo
Seclorum" that would be the American republic was the
result.

After the revolution, as the republic developed, Masonry enjoyed an era of what historian Ronald Formisano called "an uneasy legitimacy, even as it attained an unparalleled prominence and acceptance."

The explosion came in the 1820s, when Masonic membership grew well into the thousands, with hundreds of lodges cropping up throughout the colonies. Formisano, while doubting that Masonry was a "political conspiracy," acknowledges that Masons "did occupy many more positions of leadership in government and in publishing relative to their numbers than did the rest of the population. . . . Masonic activity, like church activity, was a way of aiding a political career."

As the Masons accrued political power, their arrogance swelled. They flaunted their power, taunted critics, and flouted the law. In the fall of 1826, Masons in upstate New York caught wind of a local newspaper publisher's idea for a book "exposing" Masonry. They embarked on a program of intimidation to stop the book. Finally, they kidnapped and probably murdered one of the aspiring authors, William Morgan, who disappeared (no body was found). There was a long string of trials, but a tight cover-up prevented any Masons from receiving more than light penalties.

The Morgan affair was one, albeit the most egregious, of many incidents in which Masons displayed contempt for laws and norms governing noninitiates. Anti-Masonic backlash left Masons chastened. Within a decade, the lodges had either curtailed their political agitating or had taken it underground.

Roughly 160 years later, on February 11, 1988, Masons were in the White House again. High officials of the Washington, D.C., grand lodge were in the Oval Office to honor Ronald Reagan, who, like presidents Ford, Truman, Franklin Roosevelt, Harding, Taft, Teddy Roosevelt, Garfield, Andrew Johnson, Buchanan, Polk, Andrew Jackson, Monroe, and, of course, Washington, was Mason.

With all this Masonic activity in disturbingly hig places from the very dawn of our beloved nation, it' only natural to think that at least some of what went o in the secret chambers of the Masonic temple had an in fluence over what happened in government. If the fram ers of the Constitution applied their Masonic educatio to affairs of state, why wouldn't their successors do th same? Right-wing conspiracy theorists have no doubt c it. F.D.R. in particular is singled out as an Illuminatus— more than a mere Mason. F.D.R., according to som sources, belonged to another secret society known as th Ancient Arabic Order of Nobles and Mystics, in whicl he supposedly held the title "Knight of Pythias." Th Comte de Mirabeau—Illuminati and force behind th French Revolution—had also been an adept of the "An cient Arabic Order," as had Francis Bacon, who founde his own school of philosophical Masonry. It was F.D.R who ordered the pyramid and eye insignia onto the dolla bill. More importantly, it was F.D.R., with his New Dea who first introduced socialism into the American econ omy.

Socialism, as we saw in our chapters on the Bircher and conservatives, is looked upon as the first step towar one world government. The ultrarightists, many funda mentalist Christians, and some even further right see so cialism as nothing short of a conspiracy guided by th ultimate "Illuminatus," the Angel of Light, Lucifer him self. The "one world government" would be a worl united under the rule of the Devil.

Some of these theories, as usual, get lost in the strato sphere. I blame that more on the effects of secrecy tha on the fanaticism of the conspiracy theorists. When gov ernment is zippered shut with secrecy to begin with, an an unusual number of powerful people in the governmen belong to a secret society, speculation becomes difficul to keep in check. Indeed, it should not be kept in check. Freewheeling, independent thought is the only real antidote to secrecy's chief weapon, propaganda.

In any case, while secrecy in itself is destructive, its aims don't have to be. The ideals of liberty, equality, and brotherly love are laudable enough. There are worse beliefs on which to base your country. On the other hand, if the secret societies' goals are so benign, why all the cloak and dagger? Because the goals are not always benign.

Soon after the Civil War—a war in which brother fought brother, real brothers and Masonic brothers—a group of southern Freemasons and like-minded non-Masons got together to form a new secret society. The purpose of the society was to preserve the Southern way of life shattered by the confederacy's defeat. The new society was not officially Masonic, but it incorporated Masonic-style initiation rites, symbols and argot words. These founders were not a bunch of stereotyped Southern yokels. They were sophisticated and educated. For the name of their society, they went to classical Greek and took the name *kuklos,* which meant "circle."

The name was soon Americanized, taking the pronunciation "Ku Klux." Then they mixed in some Templarism, fancying themselves a chivalric order, defending the old white South. They called themselves Knights of the Ku Klux Klan.

Not even Freemasons themselves know much about the beginnings of their fraternity. The most common explanation is that the society grew from stonemason guilds of the Middle Ages. Researcher John J. Robinson rebuts that claim. The labor guilds were meticulously Christian, he writes. The Freemasons were heterodox from the start, requiring only a belief in a nonsectarian Supreme Being.

The temple from which the Knights Templar get their

name is the Temple of Solomon, Freemasonry's most important symbol. In their mythology, they claim a direct descent from its architect. The temple itself sat on Mount Moriah, a low hill in Jerusalem, where, according to tradition, Abraham sacrificed (or almost sacrificed) his son. The very "rock of ages" where the human sacrifice took place was housed in the temple. Remember that the temple itself was probably a tribute to the goddess Astarte, to whom Solomon's erotic "song" is a paean.

According to Robinson, the new secret society created by the Templars set to work immediately. In 1385, there was a nationwide peasants' uprising in England. Appearing spontaneous, the revolt was too widespread and too well coordinated to have been anything but a planned conspiracy. Rumors floated through the country of a "great society" organizing the rebels. The society's existence was confirmed, but its connection to the revolt was unclear; as unclear as the connection between the Bavarian Illuminati and the French Revolution four hundred years later.

In *Holy Blood, Holy Grail,* Baigent, Leigh, and Lincoln find a great society that they posit as the guiding hand behind both the Templars and the Masons. This group called itself the Priory of Zion *(Priuere de Sion)*. It is a real society, and it had something to do with the French Resistance in World War II. The three authors trace its existence back to 1099, and its original headquarters to an abbey on Mount Zion, right outside Jerusalem. They were set upon their quest when investigating the mystery of Rennes-Le-Chateau. In 1885, a country bumpkin priest named Sauniere took over an abbey in a small town in the south of France, Rennes-Le-Chateau. Quite by accident, he discovered in the church a secret "treasure." The "treasure," whatever it was, made him rich, but the treasure was not money.

Sauniere also found encrypted documents, which, when deciphered, stated that the treasure belonged to

Dagobert II, a seventh-century French king of the Merovingian dynasty who was assassinated by agents of the pope.

Without recounting the entire book-length argument of *Holy Blood, Holy Grail,* here are its conclusions: The Merovingian dynasty was the kingdom created by the heirs of Jesus upon their arrival in south France—the Merovingian kings were direct descendants of King Solomon, and of Jesus; the Priory of Zion was created to preserve the Merovingian bloodline—the Holy Blood which is also the Holy Grail; the Templars were agents of the Priory of Zion—guardians of the Holy Grail, a secret truth tracing back to the Temple of Solomon and before, to the earliest days of humanity on earth.

If the Freemasons are descended from the Templars, and the Illuminati from the Freemasons, then the conspiracy theorists are not far wrong with their ravings about a transmillennial line of Illumined ones leading back to the Garden of Eden.

Of course, there can be no single, unimpeded conspiracy over thousands of years. But there have been secret societies for that long, and many of them claim a heritage going back that far. There's a feeling, in secrecy, of being different, of being in possession of something sacred no one else has. There is a feeling of power. That is why secret societies, though ostensibly religious, mystical, or simply social, are by their nature political.

"When linked, secrecy and political power are dangerous in the extreme," notes ethicist Sissela Bok. But has there ever been power without secrecy? Until we find a regime that holds power while allowing full and free publicity, then power itself is "dangerous in the extreme."

17

CONSPIRACY NATION

*Every thing secret degenerates . . .
nothing is safe that does not show how
it can bear discussion and publicity.*

LORD ACTON

Anyone who has seen *Raiders of the Lost Ark* has a notion of the ties between Nazis and the occult. That flick and its second sequel, *Indiana Jones and the Last Crusade*, in which Nazis scour Europe in search of the Holy Grail, have some relation to reality. The Nazis did perform strange excavations in France looking for mystical relics—presumably the Grail, or maybe Templar treasure. Even people who don't like cartoony adventure movies may be vaguely aware that the swastika was an ancient magic symbol signifying light, which the Nazis reversed to symbolize darkness.

Nazi preoccupation with mythology is good Saturday matinee fare, but the origins of nazism in Germany's occult underworld are not usually looked upon as a legitimate topic for study by historians of the Second World War. On the one hand, we have the sweeping but wholly conventional poli-sci analysis à la William L. Shirer's *Rise and Fall of the Third Reich*. On the other, there's the psychohistorical outlook typified by *The Psychopathic God* by Robert G. L. Waite, which attempted to explicate nazism with reference to Hitler's fifty percent deficit in the testicle department—a new twist on the lone nut theory.

Academic minds tend to force the most irrational phenomena into the frame of reference found in a college bookstore: politics, economics, sociology, and, of course, abnormal psychology. All such approaches seem almost designed to isolate Nazi Germany from the continuum of history and confirm that it can't happen here. This is a comforting notion, conducive to detached, scholarly analysis of the role of secret societies peopled by true believers, whose motives were not only irrational but antirational, which falls outside the spectrum of temperate discourse on modern history's darkest period.

I'm not arguing that Germany's rotting economy, its stratified class structure, the impotence of its Weimar government, or even the mental and genital abnormalities of the Nazi führer have no place in understanding the Nazis. They have a big place. But without the highly organized, perversely passionate, subterranean occult movement that gestated in Germany around the turn of the century, all of those elements could not have congealed into nazism.

More than a political party, the Nazi party was very much a cult. Like most demagogic religious sects, its rank and file was spellbound with the courage of demented convictions, and its leadership was financed and supported by powerful people whose main interest was accumulating more power. The finely tuned machine of brainwashing, fanaticism, and secrecy is perfect for that purpose.

Germanic occultists, like the Ku Klux Klan, were in love with religious warriors, holy knights. They were disgusted with even-keel, post-enlightenment rationalism, which cut man off from his spiritual nature and turned him into a timid species of accountants and clerks. The Middle-Ages were their romantic ideal. Squalor, plague, ignorance, and malnutrition—endemic to the Middle

Ages—meant nothing to these incipient Nazis. All they cared was that spirituality in those days was transcendent. Templars and Teutonic Knights were their heroes. In this German version of medieval mythos, the Grail was the pure blood of prehistoric gods, and it was carried by only one race, the Aryan. Everyone else was subhuman, Jews and nonwhites especially. The holy knights, according to this lore, were guardians of the Aryan bloodline. Aryans, the occultists believed, were descended from a race of giants who ruled earth long before recorded time. The supercivilization had a Great Fall. Only Aryans perpetuate the holy heredity.

Jorg Lanz von Liebenfels and Guido von List, two Austrian mystics, were the ideological grandfathers of nazism. Lanz formed, in 1900, a society called the Order of New Templars (ONT). The ONT, and the societies that evolved from it, ultimately the Nazi party, was a core for industrialists, lawyers, publishers, and other powerful individuals who needed a means to consolidate control of German society. Their security at the top of Germany's power structure was threatened by insurgent communists.

The ONT published *Ostara,* a magazine chronicling the eternal war between godlike Aryans and the bestial subhumans. Comic book paintings of luscious blonde bombshells in the clutches of furry ape men adorned its pages. The psychosexual subtext of these quaint racial theories was difficult to miss. Among the readers of *Ostara* was a young Austrian painter and fan of the occult, Adolf Hitler.

Eight years after Lanz founded his New Templars, List started a group he called *Armanen.* He took the swastika as the *Armanen* emblem. In 1912, the two societies merged to form the *Germanen Orden,* direct forerunner to the Nazi party. While Hitler was still watercoloring postcards in Vienna, this coven of wealthy occultists was incubating the racial, nationalist, quasi-pagan theory that would become law in the Third Reich.

In 1918, members of the *Orden* started a new secret society, called *Thulegesellschaft,* the Thule Society. The legend of "Thule" was a variation on the Atlantis myth. Thule was supposed to be a nation of superbeings with a utopian civilization. It flourished until 850,000 years ago, when it was wiped away by a cataclysmic flood. The flood itself was symbolic of the "Fall," but the Thulians —or Atlantians—had brought it upon themselves by mating with creatures of a lower race.

The Thulists appropriated this tale from the writings of Madame Blavatsky, "theosophist" housewife-turned-guru who created a cult in nineteenth-century New York City. Blavatsky's writings are gospel to more recent "New Age" groups. The Thule Society adapted Blavatsky to their own prejudices. The supermen, they believed, were forerunners of the Aryan race. The subhuman creatures became Jews. To overcome their own debased nature and become supermen once more, the Aryans must overcome the Jews.

Like apocalyptic movements for millennia before them, the Thulists were fervently messianic. Unlike many of their precursors, they weren't happy waiting for the messiah to appear. They went out and found him.

In 1913, Hitler moved out of Austria, settling in Munich for what he said in *Mein Kampf* were "political reasons." Actually, he was avoiding conscription—a draft dodger. Nonetheless, he ended up enlisting with enthusiasm in the German military. Though a commoner and a private, Hitler received preferential treatment at every stage of his military service. Perhaps he was an intelligence officer. He may already have been an agent of the Thule Society. After a prolific stint as an anticommunist informer, in which he sent scores of his army pals to their executions, he was sent to university anticommunism seminars paid for by the Thulists. He joined and eventually took over the German Workers Party, which was founded, funded, and controlled by the Thule Society.

In 1919, Hitler met Dietrich Eckart, a drunkard, drug addict, small-time playwright, and socialite. Despite his character flaws, Eckart had a powerful mind and a powerful personality to go along with lots of money. He published an anti-Semitic magazine and belonged to the Thule Society's "inner circle," the members most involved in the Thule's political program.

"Their meeting was probably more decisive than any other in Hitler's life," writes Wulf Schwarzwaller in his biography, *The Unknown Hitler*. "Eckart molded Hitler, completely changing his public persona." Under the occultist's tutelage, Hitler transformed from a temperamental painter, who spent more time pigging out on coffeehouse cake than at his easel, to a shrewd, forceful orator —a dangerously persuasive propagandist.

From his deathbed in December, 1928, Dietrich Eckart issued a command to his fellow adepts of the Thule Society: "Follow Hitler!" he implored. "He will dance but it is I who have called the tune. Do not mourn for me. I shall have influenced history more than any other German."

Hitler's 1941 pogrom against occult groups is often mistakenly taken as evidence that the occult was at best an incidental influence on nazism. The crackdown, in all likelihood, was damage control following the famous flight of Rudolph Hess, one of Hitler's closest confidants. Hess, for reasons still not entirely clear, stole a plane and made a solo flight without Hitler's knowledge to Britain, where he was captured. One story has Hess lured there by British intelligence in a plot masterminded by Ian Fleming, the spy who later turned writer and created James Bond.

Hess belonged to the Thule Society. Reportedly, the

British intelligence service was interested in what he knew about the occult's hold on Hitler and the Nazis. Fleming allegedly wanted Aleister Crowley to act as the interrogator. Crowley is undoubtedly the most notorious occultist of the twentieth century. His secret society, the *Ordo Temple Orientis,* attracted, as so many of these groups do, people from the top of society in any country where it set up shop. Crowley himself was terribly decadent. A happily heroin-addicted, bisexual Satan worshipper, he asked people to call him "The Beast 666." Crowley believed that he was literally the antimessiah of the apocalypse. Or at least he wanted people to believe that he believed he was.

Crowley was also an intelligence agent. He claimed to have worked for the British Secret Service in the First World War. He may have been working for Germany as well. He renounced his British citizenship and took openly pro-German positions, even writing pro-German propaganda. Though British intelligence officials denounced him, he was not prosecuted and developed (or continued) a relationship with the British government between wars, feeding information to MI6 (one British spy outfit) about German occult activities.

The Nazi government may have been based on occult principles, but it was not the only government with an interest in every secret thing.

"We find it difficult to admit that Nazi Germany embodied the concepts of a civilization bearing no relationship at all to our own," note Louis Pauwels and Jacques Bergier. "And yet it was just that, and nothing else, that justified this war."

Pauwels and Bergier wrote *Morning of the Magicians,* a book that aroused a fracas in the early 1960s by finding occultism seething beneath every layer of modern life, particularly in the Nazi era. While I'm not sure I endorse their view that "nothing else justified this war," their point is well taken: The war against the Nazis was not only a war for territory, money, or even power. It was a war to decide whether a "humanist" or a "magical" view of the universe would dominate planet earth. "This truth was hidden from us by German technology, German science and German organization, comparable if not superior to our own," says *Morning of the Magicians*. "The great innovation of Nazi Germany was to mix magic with science and technology."

Both the American and Soviet governments wanted a taste of that toothsome mix. Once Hitler was safely beaten, they competed fiercely for the services of Nazi scientists. The U.S. seems to have been more successful winning commitments from Nazis like Wehrner Von Braun, rocket scientist and SS major once described by Allied intelligence as a "potential security threat." The government cleansed Von Braun's wartime record, brought him into America, and put him to work on projects that culminated in the Saturn V rocket—the booster that lifted Neil Armstrong and the Apollo 11 crew to the moon.

Von Braun was the most famous of the Nazi scientists imported after the war. Most were described by the government as "ardent Nazis," but those pejoratives were scratched from their files. Operation Paperclip (so named because secret files on the scientists were denoted by a simple, everyday paperclip) employed seemingly supernatural German expertise to construct the American war machine. The Paperclip Boys were the plasma of the military-industrial complex.

Meanwhile, the newly formed CIA was busy recruiting SS spy-master Reinhard Gehlen and "Hitler's favorite commando" Otto "Scarface" Skorzeny. Under cover of U.S. intelligence, these two and their minions did more than anyone to keep the ideals of the Third Reich alive and pave the way for a Fourth Reich. Gehlen manipulated intelligence information to portray the Soviets in the worst possible light. With his CIA collaborators, he started the Cold War and kept it going.

While Gehlen played the U.S. government—and American public opinion—like a flute, Skorzeny globe-trotted. He established Nazi power bases in South America that nurtured the continent's many dictatorships.

Skorzeny did a similar favor for the Middle East. Gamel Abdel Nasser came to power in Egypt with help from Skorzeny and an elite corps of former SS storm troopers. Always the good Nazi, Skorzeny never gave up on the twisted dream of wiping out Jews. He set up the earliest Palestinian terrorist groups, trained them, and sent them on commando raids into Israel. Without the American-backed entrepreneurship of this disfigured Nazi, the Middle East would probably be a much more stable place than it has been for the past four decades.

From the Order of the New Templars to the Thule Society to the SS, the CIA, and the PLO, the intersection between government and secret societies continues to make our world an uncertain, terrifying place. The Nazi conspiracy rolls on.

Nazi Germany, impregnated with occultism, was a state founded in conspiracy, by conspiracy, for conspiracy. A relatively small group of people with hidden motives, using propaganda, mind control, and terror, carried out a plan to take over a country and the world. The German secret societies succeeded in conjuring up a massive social transformation, at a staggering cost in human lives. The ever-present, grim irony of secret society revolutions, nowhere more evident than with the Nazis, is that the great transformation, while it may overturn governments, makes conditions secure for the hidden powerful. Secret society revolutions happen when the secret oligarchy feels threatened.

The Thule Society was a magnet for rich businessmen

and aristocrats, who provided it with considerable finan
cial wherewithal to carry out its ambitious conspiratoria
schemes. Without funding from big business, Germa
and international, the Nazis never could have sprung
from the Thulists' loins. "It is even partly true that Hitle
was able to sell an evil idea like anti-Semitism simply
because he had the support of wealthy contributors," say
the authors of *Who Financed Hitler*. Nazism was occult
ism, but it was also fascism; it carried out Mussolini'
dictum "Fascism is corporatism."

Craven Jew-hater Henry Ford, inventor of the auto
mobile company if not the automobile, was such a doting
patron of Hitler's that the führer once offered to impor
some shock troops to the U.S. to help "Heinrich" run fo
president. Alfred Rosenberg, the Nazi party's siniste
mystic laureate (his extreme racial theorizing was found
by the Nuremburg tribunal to be so instrumental in na
zism that he was hanged), was friends with petroleum
magnate Henri Deterding—managing director of Roya
Dutch Shell and one of the world's richest men. Almos
every major industrial concern in Germany, oil compa
nies, agricultural firms, banks, and shipping companies
made sizable donations to Heinrich Himmler's *Schutz
staffel*, the SS, the Nazis' elite corps, which itself wa
fashioned as a secret society.

I. G. Farben, the gargantuan chemical cartel, was on
of the new Reich's stolid financial supporters. There wa
plenary profit in nazism for Farben, and all of Hitler'
corporate investors. The cartel's contributions were espe
cially egregious. It manufactured Zyklon-B, a poison gas
for use in the gas chambers. Auschwitz was a slave-labo
camp for an on-site Farben factory. I. G. Farben and it
associated companies were among the passel of Nazi cor
porations that did business with the most powerful Wal
Street law firm of the 1930s and 1940s, Sullivan and
Cromwell. Their chief contact at the firm was an attorney

named John Foster Dulles, who became secretary of state in the Eisenhower administration.

"Sullivan and Cromwell thrived on its cartels and collusion with the new Nazi regime," say the firm's chroniclers. In 1933 and 1934, when the Nazis' brutal course was obvious, Dulles led off cables to his German clients with the salutation "Heil Hitler." In 1935, he scribbled a screed for *Atlantic Monthly* dismissing Nazi state terrorism as "changes which we recognize to be inevitable." Dulles's brother, Allen Dulles, was also a partner in Sullivan and Cromwell. He later founded the CIA and recruited thousands of Nazi SS men into the new "department of conspiracy." Much to Foster's consternation, he never met Hitler, while little brother Allen was granted that thrill.

Sosthenes Behn met Hitler, too. Behn was the founder of International Telephone and Telegraph (ITT) and virtual inventor of the multinational corporation. He met Hitler in 1933, the first American businessman to receive an audience with *der Führer,* while striking up deals with German companies. At the same time, he filed classified reports on their activities to the U.S. government. American spy or not, Behn allowed his company to cover for Nazi spies in South America, and one of ITT's subsidiaries bought a hefty swath of stock in the airplane company that built Nazi bombers.

Behn recruited Nazis onto ITT's board. His closest Nazi friend, Gerhard Westrick, visited New York at Behn's expense in 1940—when the Nazis were conquering Europe without much resistance. The agenda of Westrick's visit: to talk American corporate leaders into forging a German-American business alliance. These sorts of activities could easily be dubbed treason on Behn's part, but by 1944 and the Allied liberation of France, he was celebrated as an American hero. Allen Dulles—who supplemented his legal income as a U.S. intelligence agent— appears to have been the magician behind this miracle rehab, helping Behn set up his relationship with the U.S. military. Later, Dulles was an originator of the idea that multinational corporations are instruments of U.S. foreign policy and therefore exempt from domestic laws—a theory that has been a secret government policy since the mid-1950s. Behn also gave money to Himmler's SS.

The Nazis were able to weld corporatism to occultism seamlessly, which may say something about the similarity between the two. "The oligarchs of agricultural kingdoms wrapped themselves in witchcraft. . . . As industrial capitalism accumulated power and wealth the old mysteries were replaced and dwarfed by the new mysteries of high finance, market manipulations, convoluted and lucrative legalisms, pressure-group politics, and a labyrinth of new bureaucracies," writes Bertram Gross.

But it also says that for the Nazis, the occult served both idealistic and pragmatic purposes. Himmler was immersed in occultism, but though he believed the stuff, he also used it as a method of mind control. When he began the corps, he needed a large membership to consolidate power. He recruited about sixty thousand. Membership was literally for sale to the wealthy, and "honorary" membership was available for as little as a mark per year. There was no way to unify such an unwieldy legion, so once the SS had established itself as the most powerful faction of the Nazi state, Himmler purged his rolls of anyone ideologically impure, or racially suspect (members had to draw up a family tree going back more than a century to prove their pure Aryan, non-Jewish, lineage). He also banished or killed all the SS homosexuals he could spot, and there were quite a few.

The SS was still absent a coherent ideology to bind its remaining members in strict obedience. Himmler found one in his own neopagan beliefs. He renovated Wewelsburg Castle, a Westphalian fortress, and made it his own Camelot. He installed an oaken round table where the twelve "knights" of his inner circle would gather for initiations and rites. Like all cult leaders, Himmler was skilled in using ritual and esoterica to strip away the individuality of his followers. Whatever humanity the SS soldiers possessed was subsumed by their mission to exterminate "lower races" and stand guard over the Reich. The storm troopers became robots programmed to kill.

Himmlerian mind control didn't die when Himmler bit his cyanide capsule. While real live Nazis like Skorzeny and Gehlen frolicked about the world causing merry mischief, their younger admirers kept the occult spirit of nazism alive in right-wing hate groups and Satanic cults.

The popular image of right-wing "neo-Nazi" groups as Neanderthal thugs is somewhat misleading. The rank-and-file skinheads may be a little on the slow side, but the movement's leaders tend to be voracious readers, researchers, and theorists, after a fashion. Just as they are, perhaps correctly, the subject of conspiracy theories, they've developed anti-Jewish, anti-Masonic, Illuminati-style theories of their own that display an unsettling level of detail—all in the tradition of Thulian master-race paganism.

White Aryan Resistance chieftan Tom Metzger—a regular on "Geraldo"-style daytime talk shows—is anti-Christian as well as predictably anti-Jewish. He and his skinhead disciples call themselves pagans, and adhere to the ancient Germanic religion. They find affinity in the "Christian Identity" religion, which began in England in the nineteenth century and now flourishes in cornfield churches of the Midwest. The Identity churches are only "Christian" in the sense that they count Jesus as an Aryan. White Europeans, they say, are therefore the true biblical "Jews," and the "race" that calls itself Jewish is really a conspiracy of subhuman imposters.

Unlike the conspiracy theorists profiled in the first part of this book (with the possible exception of Lyndon

LaRouche), Nazi and neo-Nazi groups use their conspi
acy theories, like Himmler, as a technique of control, t
mobilize a group to a common goal, to move people t
actions they might not otherwise carry out. More br;
zenly occult variations on the same theory turn up i
Satanic cults.

The Manson family was portrayed in the mass med
as a group of crazed hippies, of flower children gor
mad. In the mass mind, Charles Manson is associate
with the political left—ironic for a Hitler-worshippin
racist. Like Hitler, who learned his oratorical skills at th
knee of Dietrich Eckart, Manson picked up his powers c
persuasion in the occult underground of San Francisc
circa 1967. His "I am Christ, I am the devil, Christ is th
devil" rants could have been lifted from sermons by Rol
ert DeGrimston, British émigré and leader of the Proces
Church of the Final Judgement.

The Process, which may have had Manson as membe
was a Satanic cult that sprung up in the 1960s and spu
tered out by the early 1970s. But does it still exist? Maur
Terry's book *The Ultimate Evil* makes a case that th
Process didn't die. Instead it faded away in a Satanic dia
pora, forming offshoot cults that link into a loose natio
wide conglomerate of dope dealing, S&M porn, and ritu;
murder. The Son of Sam killing spree that terroriz\
New York in the late 1970s was Terry's focus. He allege
that the murders were carried out by a conspiracy of cul
ists based on Long Island with connections across th
country. One of the Sam murders, Terry contends, w;
committed by a character called "Manson II," famou
among Satanists as the occult underworld's top hit man,
friend of Charles Manson himself.

The Tate-LaBianca murders, crimes that won the orig
inal Manson his infamy, may not have been randor
"Helter Skelter" slayings, according to Terry and ▪
Manson biographer Ed Sanders. They appear to hav
been murder for hire. But who would hire Manson an

why? Could it have been the same people who hired Manson disciple Lynette "Squeaky" Fromme to shoot President Ford? Namely, someone in the U.S. government, according to Michael Milan, who says he was once a hit man for J. Edgar Hoover.

Here we get into the grayest of conspiratorial speculations, foggy even by the standards of conspiracy theory. Contentions that the intelligence community is somehow aligned with Satanism, using cults as indoctrination for mind-controlled robot assassins, are backed up by only gossamer strips of information. Milan's claim that the Manson family "took the contract" on Ford; Maury Terry's implication that New York police may have been in on the Son of Sam murders (taken together with known facts about the CIA's infiltration of big-city police departments); and the name of the drug dealer who led the Matamoros death cult, the nasty devil worshippers who murdered a med-school student in a Mexican shack a few years ago, allegedly turning up in the address book of downed contra pilot, Eugene Hasenfus, a CIA contractor.

The most curious case, to my mind, is that of Michael Aquino, another frequent talk-show guest who bears an uncanny resemblance to Mark Lenard, Mr. Spock's father on "Star Trek." Aquino founded and leads the Temple of Set, an offshoot of Anton LaVey's Church of Satan, which was the first Satanic church ever to receive tax exemption. The Temple of Set takes a dour turn on LaVey's dime-store pseudopagan buffoonery. Unlike LaVey, Aquino never sought publicity. He got it anyway, when he was accused of molesting children at a military day care center on San Francisco's Presidio base.

Aquino was never tried on any charge, and he vehemently denies any crimes. He sued the city of San Francisco for defamation of character after an investigation failed to turn up any evidence that he or his "Temple" was involved in child molestation. Aquino is nonetheless an odd bird with thought-provoking connections.

Aquino is always careful to distance himself publicly from nazism, but he is so fascinated by Hitler and Himmler that he once made a pilgrimage to Wewelsburg Castle, the site Himmler planned as home to his mystical order. He carried out some form of black magic ceremony there, amidst the SS relics. When the Presidio scandal became news and Aquino's name surfaced, the Pentagon denied that he was in the Army. This was in 1981, at the same time that the Army was granting Aquino his Top Secret security clearance. In reality, Aquino is an Army specialist in psychological warfare. He wrote an article on "MindWar" and PSYOPS (psychological operations) and their use in controlling mass populations. America's failure in Vietnam, he believes, was a failure to apply the effects of "MindWar."

In the conspiracy theory, the epidemic of Satanism across America stems from the U.S. government deploying MindWar against its own people.

"Some things are secret because they are hard to know, and some because they are not fit to utter. We see all governments as obscure and invisible." So declared Francis Bacon, founder of his own school of Masonry, and of the inductive "scientific method." Bacon didn't issue that utterance with any intention of condemning government secrecy. The governance of men, he believed, was necessarily a secret affair. People are incapable of understanding what government does. And some things that government does, it is best that the governed never know.

When governments are involved in terror and murder, it is not hard to understand why they keep secrets from their people. Nor is it surprising that Francis Bacon, given his immersion in secret societies, would feel the way he did. If Bacon's reasoning holds true, it might be better to have no government at all.

A government that is obscure and invisible will inevitably, like the Nazis, be a government based on conspiracy. The very act of keeping government secrets is a conspiracy.

Secret government—and by Bacon's cold logic, all governments are secret—divorces everyone in society except the secret keepers from any genuine understanding of the circumstances that govern their own lives. Conspiracy theory is an attempt by a few minds to reclaim some understanding.

In this part of the book, I've tried to piece together as many slabs and slices of information that I could find to support the kinds of conspiracy theories that got me interested in the subject. These are American conspiracy theories, many with long historical roots, but, nonetheless, distinctively contemporary conspiracy theories. These are theories born in a country too big and diverse to govern, but permeated totally by government. A country whose basic ideal is individual freedom, where daily life is dominated by authority. From the runaway power of the presidency to the tyranny of workplace management, liberty is strangely difficult to come by. We've substituted the multicolored spectacle of consumerism for control over our own lives, and we're supposed to think that because we have so much stuff available for purchase we have the freedom to choose. But you can't fool everyone. Conspiracy theorists may not always be right, but they are not fooled.

The information in this section is not supposed to be an argument for any particular conspiracy theory, although there seem to be plenty in here. I've been trying to present a *way of thinking* about a society where information is controlled, ergo, understanding is impossible. Conspiracy theories are a guide to life in a strange and threatening America: a conspiracy nation.

Conclusion

THE THRESHOLD OF BELIEF?

*Every government is run by liars and
nothing they say should be believed.*

I. F. STONE

*We go around in circles in the night and
are consumed by fire.*

GUY DEBORD,
Title of his last film

The Firesign Theatre, a surreal comedy ensemble popular on college radio stations a long time ago, once made an album called "Everything You Know Is Wrong." The Firesign Theatre may have been right.

All the anomalies, all the horrors, all the conspiracies that we've just journeyed through—can they be true? Is the nation really that malevolent? That insane?

I hope not. But the point is, we just don't know. We all have our belief systems about the world. Whatever doesn't fit into our systems, we ignore. I look at the foregoing trip through the conspiracy nation in the spirit of Charles Fort. Fort believed that there are phenomena that conventional science is not able to explain; I look on conspiracy theories as the stuff that conventional political science refuses to deal with.

The science and philosophy of Charles Fort is ethereal

stuff. Conspiracy theories are about politics—the reality of day-to-day life. Surely the truth of who, or what, governs America should be accessible. People created this nation. People run it. Someone, somewhere must know what's going on. Why can't everybody? Conspiracy theories begin with that very question. The truth is being kept from us.

In *Friendly Fascism*, a book describing what can only be called a conspiracy between big business and big government to rule America, Bertram Gross makes it a point to declare, "[T]here is no single, central conspiracy." Perhaps not. There is no council of twelve running the world, no Illuminati board of directors that plans every war, every election, every fluctuation in the economy, every piece of legislation.

There are, however, many councils, many boards of directors. In most contemporary American conspiracy theories, there is no "single central conspiracy." Instead, there is power and powerful people who will do anything to keep their power. Power is a fact of life in America, but most Americans are far removed from it. Secrecy is power's chief tool. Government seems distant, yet somehow domineering. We are increasingly isolated from one another—stuck in front of computer and television screens, prisoners behind windshields. There is a frustrating feeling of disconnection to modern American life. Are our lives really absurd? Or are we just being deceived? Conspiracy theories try to put the pieces back together.

What if AIDS was deliberately created? Biological warfare by the American government against its own people. Such experimentation would hardly be unprecedented. From the LSD MKULTRA experiments (see Chapter 11) to the 1950 spraying of infectious bacteria onto San Francisco from Navy ships, various government agencies have exhibited no reservation about trying out new chemicals and toxins on U.S. citizens. Some of these literally sickening experiments were instigated by ex-Nazi doctors. The government brought over biologists as well as rocket scientists from the Third Reich. Former government lawyer John Loftus, in his book about imported SS war criminals, *The Belarus Secret,* speculates that Lyme disease may be the result of one ex-Nazi–inspired biowarfare test.

Why not AIDS, then? Or does it cross the threshold of belief to suppose that our government, even one isolated element of it, could commit such an atrocity?

The conspiracy theory of AIDS sees the disease as a vast eugenics exercise, not that it would take Nazis to dream up a eugenics program. Back in 1904, the philanthropic Carnegie Foundation, founded by founders of the American industrial system, bankrolled eugenics experiments at a bioresearch lab in Cold Spring Harbor, New York. The American preoccupation with weeding out "inferior" humans continues to this day, in softer forms. The IQ test was first administered by scientists (and I use the term loosely) whose initial interest was identifying "the feebleminded."

AIDS's proclivity for hitting the underprivileged and marginal members of society is hauntingly reminiscent of the "great pellagra cover-up" in the early twentieth century. No one I've heard of suggests that pellagra—a fatal disease rampant until the 1930s—was deliberately created. It almost might as well have been. The real cause of the disease, malnutrition, was discovered in 1914, but ignored. In 1917, a national commission announced that the disease was hereditary, attributable to the same bad genetics that, in the minds of government eugenicists, caused the poverty of most of the disease's victims. Not until the Depression hit, and the previously well-off found themselves in dire financial straits and therefore susceptible to malnutrition, was the disease finally brought under control.

What, then, is the truth about AIDS? Much government-sponsored research is secret. The rest is esoteric, understandable only by other scientists. Public comprehension of science is scant, depending entirely on third-party interpreters and "experts," who have agendas of their own. Not only is general scientific knowledge therefore minimal, more importantly, few people understand how science works. We think we're getting objective truth, when what we're really seeing is a political, acerbically personal process involving billions of dollars, reputations and egos, and belief systems that censor large slices of fact and theory. Is AIDS the result of a demonic scientific experiment? Who knows? I tend to doubt it myself. But could it be? Of course it could, because if it were, no one in a position to do anything about it would believe it.

The process of everyday politics also looks strangely like a conspiracy. Despite the presence of cable television cameras in the Senate and House of Representatives, few meaningful decisions are made in public. Legislative votes are public, of course, so there is a degree of accountability, but coalitions are made in private, and deals are cut in closed meetings. Presidential decision making is absolutely unencumbered by public scrutiny.

In 1989, just a month or so after the Tiananmen Square massacre of prodemocracy demonstrators in China, President Bush sent two envoys secretly to meet with the Chinese government, to reaffirm American-Chinese ties.

The envoys, probably not coincidentally, were two former employees of Henry Kissinger, National Security Adviser Brent Scowcroft and his deputy, Lawrence Eagleburger. Kissinger's "consulting" firm has extensive business ties to China. When Bush was ambassador to China, it was said that he did almost nothing, leaving the driving to Henry, as it were. Bush's own brother has a "consulting" business link to the Chinese government.

When reporters, in an uncharacteristic display of indignation (perhaps more at being left out of the story than at the predictable breach of trust) challenged Bush, he uncorked an impassioned defense of his right to do business in secret, a theme he has hit upon repeatedly during his presidency.

Bush is hardly unusual among presidents in that regard. But when business like Bush's China mission takes place in secrecy, can so-called conspiracy theorists really be blamed for surmising that the whole thing was a Kissinger scam? Kissinger's clients include the world's largest corporations. What does that say about the apparent conspiracy? The Bush cronies' covert China junket appears as one more installment of the ongoing conspiracy of the wealthy, powerful, and very, very private against the average person.

The number of people who can find out firsthand what goes on inside the presidential administration, in Congress, the halls of academe, research labs, and corporate boardrooms is tiny. The rest of us must rely on the communications media, news, and entertainment. News has *become* entertainment. Television is the main source of news, and the only real purpose of *any* commercial television program is to deliver an audience to advertisers.

The programs and the advertisements become indistinguishable, both serving the purpose of massaging the viewer into the mood to consume. If there were no such thing as official U.S. government propaganda, America would still be in the grip of the most powerful propaganda apparatus in human history: the advertising industry. Advertising is not usually thought of as propaganda, because it has no obvious political slant. All the better to brainwash you with. In fact, advertising sells a political ideology as fully developed and as potent as anything pushed by Joseph Goebbels. The ideology is consumerism.

There are two types of propaganda identified by Jacques Ellul, whose book *Propaganda* is a definitive work on the subject. There is propaganda of integration (sociological propaganda) and propaganda of agitation (political propaganda). Advertising is both. It presents a coherent set of values and standards, which serves the purpose of molding (integrating) disparate "propagandees" into a coherent group with shared ideals—in this case, the equation of happiness with consumer products. And it "agitates" its targets into performing specific acts for the benefit of the political system—namely, purchasing things, an act without which industrial capitalism, our political system, would perish.

Conflation of advertising and propaganda spawns USC professors Ian Mitroff's and Warren Bennis's book title, *The Unreality Industry*. The advertising and entertainment industries have teamed up to instill America with a culture based upon outright falsehoods and manipulations of fact. We worship celebrities whose public personas bear little relationship to their real identities, then we purchase products designed to make us identify with the artificial celebrities. The process perpetuates until we're living in a mirage. Or perhaps it's more like a hologram because the illusion is deliberately created.

What becomes of our own identities in this haze of consumption? We lose them, as we submerge ourselves into the mass culture. Striving to create ourselves in the images presented to us by advertising, we lose touch with reality.

Isn't there one branch of the media devoted expressly to the truth? Aren't newspapers and television news programs still devoted to letting us know what's really going on in our world?

Forget for a moment that all major news media are beholden to advertising for their existence. Forget that about twenty national and multinational companies own the bulk of America's newspapers and magazines. Reporters rely so heavily on "official sources" for their news, and are so slavishly credulous of the information those sources feed them, that otherwise "respectable" news media are easily infiltrated by the CIA. In one particularly infamous incident, *New York Times* correspondent C. L. Sulzberger, nephew of the paper's owner, reprinted a CIA press release, called a "briefing paper," verbatim under his own byline.

The CIA infiltrates and even operates newspapers in the capital cities of numerous foreign countries, and disinformation appearing in those papers often "blows back" into the American press. One CIA-planted story, linking Italy's Red Brigades to the Soviet KGB, was used by author Claire Sterling in her book *The Terror Network* to support her conspiracy theory that the Soviet Union was the hidden hand behind international terrorism. Her book and its KGB conspiracy theory was scooped up by Reagan's first secretary of state Al Haig (another Kissinger protégé), who used it to justify administration policy in Central America.

The Reagan administration also ran an "Office of Public Diplomacy," which, despite its soothing nomenclature, had as its true purpose a propaganda campaign to persuade and pressure major news organizations to provide favorable coverage of the Nicaraguan contras and defamatory coverage of the then-ruling Sandinistas. The propaganda campaign worked, and, lest anyone protest that "propaganda" is too strong a term for the Reagan administration's program, authors Martin Lee and Norman Solomon have uncovered internal White House memoranda using exactly that word.

If everything you know is wrong, how do you know what's right? There are no final answers—only questions. Conspiracy theorists ask those questions. They are intellectual outcasts, often social outcasts. But they are not aberrations. In a society woven together by propaganda and "unreality," whose own government and economic

establishment operates in secrecy, there will always be
conspiracy theorists. Eventually, we all may be.

The night that I sat down to write this concluding chapter, Meir Kahane was gunned down outside a Manhattan
hotel. I wasn't particularly saddened by his death. Rabbi
Kahane was the founder of the Jewish Defense League, an
anti-Arab racist who led a movement to drive all Palestinians out of Israel, a religious zealot and theocratic fascist.
Despite his repulsive qualities—or probably because of
them—he was one of the most visible, widely quoted,
frequently interviewed Jewish political leaders in the
world outside of the Israeli government (though for a
short time, Kahane was a member of the Knesset). His
murder was more than another in New York's homicide
wave of 1990. It was a political assassination.

There had not been, to my memory, an assassination
of a political leader on American turf since the killing of
John Lennon ten years earlier. Those loath to count the
ex-Beatle as a "political leader" would have to look even
further into the past. Even after writing this book, I still,
somewhat naively it turns out, expected extensive coverage of Kahane's assassination on the evening's newscasts.
I wanted to know who killed Kahane; whether the assassin belonged to any significant organizations; what significance there was to the timing of Kahane's murder, coming as it did with America and perhaps Israel preparing
for war against Iraq; what kind of trouble had Kahane
been stirring up recently; what happened to his security,
which I assumed must have been tight. And a long list of
other questions, none of which I saw so much as a comment upon the night of Kahane's killing. Why not?

Maybe the problem was me. Kahane was a hated man.
It's perfectly plausible, especially in crazy old New York,
that some angry Arab would pick up a gun and blow his
head off. Was I being paranoid in asking those questions?

Frustrated at the impoverished news coverage, had I become infected with the twisted anger of a conspiracy theorist?

If a conspiracy theorist is someone who sees the world dogmatically, a single conspiracy behind everything, then I've never been one and, after wallowing in conspiracy theories for more than two years, I'm still not. There are plenty of conspiracy theorists who fit that description, and the dogmatist is the popular stereotype of conspiracy theorists—the "large number of Americans who . . . have taken to an extreme the desire to find connections between events. . . . They don't react to new information and ideas by adapting. They try to squeeze the world into their systems." Paranoids. Simpletons.

I went into this project suspicious of all stereotypes. There had to be more to conspiracy theories than nuttiness. I've come away believing that there is. As I watched the thirty-second reports on the assassination of Kahane —the highlight of each being a gory shot of blood-smeared New York pavement—I wondered how the questions I wanted asked were any more simplistic than what I was seeing on television.

What I've come to believe is that the seeming "paranoia" of conspiracy theorists is not necessarily the result of some underlying mental dysfunction or of stupidity. The conspiracy theorists I interviewed for this book, with almost no exceptions, were nothing if not highly intelligent.

The dysfunction is with American society, maybe even civilization as a whole. The structure of civilization itself requires mass adherence to faith in the institutions that built civilization and make it run. The institutions are innumerable: science, politics, communications, education, arts, government, business—it all comes down to a faith in authority.

We have to believe the institutions are functioning in our best interests. We have to believe what the people

within those institutions assure us to be true. If not, we're
sentenced to a life on the edge, filled with frustration,
indignation, confusion, and perhaps what society calls in-
sanity.

The conspiracy theorists I encountered question our
authorities, and, because they do, they skirt the fringes of
society.

Anthropologist Jules Henry took it for granted that
"our civilization is a tissue of contradictions and lies."
He used the term "sham" for the everyday deceptions we
need to survive in this corrupted society. Henry argued
that mental illness, a concept of which he was highly
skeptical, is simply the refusal to accept that "sham is
reality." In the case of conspiracy theorists, that refusal
starts with questions, and often concludes in a highly developed worldview that is incompatible with the "sham."

Henry would have understood conspiracy theorists
well. "Sham gives rise to coalitions because usually sham
cannot be maintained without confederates." In other
words, to keep civilization afloat requires a conspiracy.
"In sham," Henry goes on, "the deceiver enters into an
inner conspiracy against himself."

Conspiracy theorists resist joining the "inner conspiracy." They can't lie to themselves, like Colin Wilson's
"outsider" who "cannot live in the comfortable insulated
world of the bourgeois, accepting what he sees and
touches as reality." The more they strip through the
sham, the madder they appear.

"I anticipate a geometric increase in madness," says
Jules Henry, "for sham is the basis of schizophrenia and
murder itself."

To understand conspiracy theorists, I now believe, is
to first understand that civilization is a conspiracy against
reality.

The Conspiracy Decade

Nineteen ninety-one was the most conspiracy-rich year in my memory, a good year for the first edition of this book to come out. Not since Watergate did conspiracy theories infiltrate the nightly news the way they did in 1991. The nineties promise to be the Conspiracy Decade.

On the short list: the ever-growing BCCI scandal; George Bush and the alleged "October Surprise" deal to hold fifty-two American hostages; CIA Director-to-be Robert Gates's links to Iran-Contra; America's arming of *Iraq* before the Gulf War; the State Department's "green light" to Saddam Hussein's invasion of Kuwait (was the whole thing a setup?); the strange death of lone-wolf journalist Danny Casolaro who was supposedly digging for links amongst the lot of them. Oliver Stone's *JFK* assassination conspiracy flick topped it off. As weirdly reticent as the media was about BCCI, a terrorist-funding, drug-money laundering, CIA covert-op financing international racket *cum* financial institution, the venom and volume of its vitriolic response to *JFK* was equally unsettling.

When I began this endeavor in 1988, I was pretty sure that a sympathetic book about American conspiracy theories would be timed well. With George Bush in the White House (by August '88 I was sure he would be), the "Reagan Revolution" starting to wear thin with the cave-in of its ersatz economic boom (and a nagging case of Iran-Contra), troubled times were beginning to boil and bubble. If as Tom Wolfe wrote, the "Me Decade" was the Third Great Awakening, I figured the Conspiracy Decade would be the fourth one. This time, rather than a narcissistic/solipsistic journey to the center of self, Americans

are pondering their place on the face of this globe, peer
ing outward. In a society where so little seems to make
sense, where so much is kept secret yet so many apparent
conspiracies persist in surfacing, any mass effort at "de
coding reality" (an early title for this book) is bound to
ignite a wildfire of conspiracy theories. And indeed it
happened. By the time the Paragon House hardcover of
Conspiracies, Cover-ups and Crimes hit bookstores in
early October 1991, I was already feeling a little bit left
behind.

In an attempt to catch up, I've added a few short inter
polations to the text, summing up some of the big-name
conspiracies that tripped off the *zeitgeist* tongue in the
past year. A comprehensive book about conspiracy theo
ries wouldn't be quite complete without *JFK* or the aftermath of the Gulf War. Yet even with the new material I
still see the book as something of a period piece. I always
intended it to be, even more than a book of conspiracy
theories, a book *about* conspiracy theories; a book about
an American way of looking at the world in the early
1990s, that peculiar, unhinged epoch—but not the American way transmitted by the "mainstream" media.

To document an undocumented trend, I felt I'd have
to go beyond my standard method of journalistic research. I would do the interviews and the somewhat formidable volume of reading, of course, but not "objec-
tively." I chose to alter my own point of view. To best
understand how my subjects were thinking, I chose to
think as they think; to interpret things in a, well, *paranoid*
way. The effect of this experiment on my own mental
state? A certain amount of paranoia, I confess. I've come
to believe paranoia in regulated doses is healthy in these
times.

Readers will find new material in sections about
George Bush and the Gulf War, and about President
Kennedy's Vietnam policy. As to the latter, I had origi-
nally cited no more than the staple of assassination con-

spiracy theorists—former Pentagon-CIA liaison officer Fletcher Prouty's reading of National Security Action Memoranda 263 and 273. Prouty argues that comparison of the two Kennedy Administration documents—one issued before the president's death, one right after—indicates a policy flip-flop just days after the assassination. Kennedy planned to end American involvement in the war. Johnson shifted into full gear. For some theorists no more proof is needed that Kennedy was killed by a military-industrial conspiracy.

In November 1991, when this book was new on the stands and Oliver Stone's *JFK* movie was still a couple of months away, an article by Robert Sam Anson adorned the cover of *Esquire,* and it took aim at Prouty. Anson linked Prouty to the far-right Liberty Lobby and stated unequivocally that Prouty's interpretation of NSAM 273 was wrong. The paper represented "no real change in Kennedy policy," Anson said.

To refute Prouty, Anson relied on John M. Newman, author of the then-forthcoming *JFK and Vietnam,* and a technical advisor to Stone. I have also relied on Newman's book for my new passage on J.F.K.'s Vietnam policy. Perhaps Anson had not read Newman's manuscript at the time, because he omits one of its most important facts.

Prouty, according to Anson, bases his theory on a November 21, 1963, draft of NSAM 273, that is, a draft penned while Kennedy was still president, just a day before his assassination. But the draft Lyndon Johnson actually signed on November 26, four days after Kennedy was killed, was not the same document. In fact, it had been "altered *significantly,*" Newman says, in his own italics.

Readers of Anson's account, probably far greater in number than readers of Newman's scholarly book, would never know that key fact. They would come away believing that Prouty was a fabricator (instead of merely an exaggerator) and that the main piece of circumstantial evidence suggesting a military motive for the assassination was naught but hot air. Newman tiptoes around the Dallas matter, but his book leaves no serious doubt that Kennedy was bent on getting the hell out of Vietnam and that Johnson trashed that plan while the slain president's body was still on ice.

Anson (who'd written about the assassination in a conspiratorial vein in the past) was somewhat sympathetic to Stone and Newman, and even he blew it on the Vietnam issue. Innocent oversight perhaps. Other media committed more egregious distortions.

Newsweek, in a cover spread that denounced Stone's movie as "propaganda," also sniped at Newman. The national mag told its readers that Newman's evidence consisted of no more than the memories of "two antiwar senators" who say that Kennedy confided his pullout plans to them. Thus, in one quick stroke, the magazine consigned Newman's meticulously sourced 500-page tome, based upon thousands of government documents including many unavailable to earlier scholars, to the dustbin of historical gossip.

Nicholas Lemann, an otherwise astute writer, summed up the center-establishment viewpoint in (of all places) *GQ,* when he wrote, "Not only is the Garrison-Stone case for the greater importance of the Kennedy assassination essentially a fantasy, it's strange they feel it has to be made at all. Even if Kennedy wasn't planning to end the Vietnam War, his death was still a great tragedy. Garrison and Stone are trying to make it into something more; the main turning point in American history—which it wasn't."

In my chapter "Coup D'État in the U.S.A." I discussed something I dubbed the "process" theory of history, the conviction that history proceeds through an impervious and orderly process. If I didn't make myself clear, take a look at Lemann's paragraph—and there it is!

Lemann, an eminently skilled scholar, fortifying conventional wisdom with superficial evidence, dismisses out of hand the Stone/Garrison/Newman hypothesis that the assassination *did* lead to escalation of the Vietnam war. Why? A lapse in scholarly standards, perhaps due to the less-than-rigorous forum offered by *Gentleman's Quarterly*? Maybe a little bit, but for the most part I think that Lemann (as well as Tom Wicker in *The New York Times* and a host of others) simply refuse to believe that American politics can be altered by something as alien to the sober-minded process as a presidential assassination. It doesn't compute.

Nor is this syndrome the exclusive purview of centrists. Gary Indiana, writing in the left-wing *Village Voice*, opined that "It's hard to conclude that Kennedy was philosophically much different from Nixon," and Alexander Cockburn in *The Nation* devoted copious verbiage to attacking Berkeley professor Peter Dale Scott's version of the Kennedy-Vietnam hypothesis. Apparently, leftist doctrine mandates that any American president is a priori an imperialist running dog, ergo the notion that Kennedy did not thirst for combat in Vietnam is intolerable.

"It fits the left-wing point of view that it doesn't make any difference who is the president because they're all capitalists," said Scott in an interview with my *Metro* colleague John Whalen. "Which, paradoxically, is very close to the mainstream establishment point of view, that they're all defending the American public interest and so on. So that for neither the center nor the left can the anomalous event of the assassination have any real impact on politics."

The reaction to Stone's movie and Newman's book was instructive and, I felt, served to confirm the underlying point of this book: that "perception is theory laden," as we used to say in philosophy class. Given any set of facts, the interpretations of those facts are as diverse as the folks doing the interpreting.

A bit more of a surprise, though it further supports the same thesis, was the babbling reaction the book elicited from one of its subjects. Of those I heard from, most were generally favorable. Except for David Emory, who was able to broadcast his reaction to my very neighborhood via his Sunday night "One Step Beyond" radio show on KFJC, the college station which has given him a forum for more than a decade.

For more info on Emory, check out Chapter 7. He felt that what you'll read there was a vicious attack (never mentioning that the bulk of my personal information about him came directly from interviewing him). He also harped on the absurd (and false) claim that I "ripped off" his research without proper footnoting. As far as I have ever been able to determine, his research consists primarily of reading books, newspapers, and magazines. Apparently he failed to understand that reading a book does not give one ownership rights to its contents.

In one instance he asserted that my section on Jonestown, in which I cited a speech made by Joseph Holsinger (an aide to assassinated congressman Leo Ryan), could only have been lifted from his program because, Emory cliamed, he is the only person in the world with a copy of that speech. The ironic note is that I actually didn't hear Emory so much as refer to the speech until long after I'd written that section, and my copy of it I *purchased* from none other than John Judge, another character in Chapter 7 and perhaps the only extant human who Emory seems to despise more than me.

Anyway, to make an extremely long and tiresome story short, Emory's obsession with the book, and with me personally it would seem, culminated (though not concluded) with two consecutive five-and-a-half-hour broadcasts—*eleven solid hours* of otherwise valuable airtime—devoted to lambasting me. Feigning the high road,

Emory pretended that my alleged "hit piece" didn't bug him. He did feel moved, however, to describe me as a "frontrunning yuppie pantywaist," whatever that means.

He was merely doing a public service, he demurred, by alerting his listeners to the fact that the hardback publisher of *CC&C*, the financially troubled but well-intentioned Paragon House, is owned by the Unification Church; the Moonies to you and me. Dreadfully sinister, indeed. He didn't mention that he began ranting against the book (calling me a "bastard" on the air, among other well-reasoned comments) the very first night he received it, October 6, 1991, at least a month before he knew anything about Paragon's insidious "connections." Nor did he ever bother to do any research into Paragon, beyond reading one sentence in one article in one issue of *Covert Action Information Bulletin*, which merely stated the fact of the publisher's ownership. Later, perhaps feeling a trifle odd over burning up such a sizable chunk of airtime on a personal vendetta for an imagined slight, Emory concocted a complex scenario melding Paragon, the Moonies, right-wing tax protesters, the anti-Semitic "Identity Christianity" movement, John Judge, and most amusingly, the alternative newsweekly where I work, *Metro* ("a masturbation vehicle for yuppies," he colorfully described it) into some kind of arcane yet malevolent plot directed at him personally. There was "as a result of this situation," Emory mused, "a possibility of physical violence and/or mind control" directed against "yours truly" (as he likes to refer to himself). "That's one of the reasons I felt this broadcast had to be done." After all, as he pointed out, "mind control isn't espresso."

For all his Firesign Theatrelike surreality Emory (whose program I stopped tuning in once his bilious diatribes against me became tedious) illustrates another of my pet themes: that conspiracy theory and its opposite are no more than competing paradigms dependent not so much on fact but on psychological, *irrational* adherence.

The purported rational basis for accepting one paradigm over another stems from the political power base of its believers. It's not difficult to notice Emory's irrationality, but compare his mental contortions to those of the anti-*JFK* press gang. You'll find they differ in tone far more than in content. Belief is by nature irrational, and what passes for rationality is a matter of style, a willingness to abide by unwritten standards of conventionality.

Callers to the numerous radio shows I've done since the book came out ask me one question with greater frequency than any other: If all of these conspiracies are real, what can we do about it? Do we take up arms and overthrow the powers-that-be? Or throw up our hands in impotent despair?

The answer lies not in accepting every conspiracy theory in this book as gospel truth (I don't think I can quite face the responsibility of writing a gospel just now) but in understanding the real point of studying conspiracy theories. Namely, to prove that no knowledge is certain. As Socrates said, the wisest man knows but one thing: that he knows nothing. My purpose in *Conspiracies, Coverups and Crimes* was to prove Socrates correct by collecting the craziest (by societal definition) group of thinkers I could find—conspiracy crackpots—then building a case that they might, just maybe, be on to something. If *they* could come close to the truth, close enough to make so-called responsible citizens darn uncomfortable, then the rest of us intellectually self-satisfied types can't be nearly as smart as we think.

Once we grasp that axiomatic yet oddly elusive fact of political epistemology we've opened ourselves up to a new way of seeing the world. I believe that change is taking place in the Conspiracy Decade. Dark and troubling as conspiracy theory can be—who knows?—maybe the Fourth Great Awakening will finally rouse this country from a lengthy slumber.

Notes

INTRODUCTION

Bertram Gross quote: *Friendly Fascism*, p. 5.
New York Times assassination editorial appeared 1/7/79.

CHAPTER 1

Thornley and Oswald's relationship in Marines and after: my
  interviews with Kerry Thornley; Thornley, *The Dreadlock
  Recollections.* Thornley testimony to the Warren Commission
  in *Hearings before the President's Commission on the Assassination of President Kennedy, Vol. 9.* Thornley *Affidavit*, 1/8/
  76. "Oswald, as Only a Marine Buddy Could Know Him"
  by Kerry Thornley; series in *Men's Digest*, 1965 (no months
  on my copy). Thornley, *Oswald;* "Outfit eightball" quote
  from *Oswald.*

Thornley's reaction to J.F.K. assassination: *Affidavit.*

"Breeding experiment" quotes: my interviews with Thornley.

Landlady snickering quote: letter from Thornley to me.

Bob Black on Thornley: *Rants*, p. 201.

Bowling alley birth of Discordian Religion: my interviews with
  Thornley.

Principia Discordia first published on Jim Garrison's Xerox machine: Wilson, *Cosmic Trigger*, p. 165.

"Poor man's *Ugly American*," quote: *Affidavit.*

Thornley in New Orleans, Bourbon House incident: *Affidavit.*
  Garrison's suspicions; "second Oswald": Garrison, *On the
  Trail of the Assassins*, pp. 74–78. Calls Thornley an Oswald
  "look-alike": ibid. p. 274.

Weisburg asks for touched-up photos: "Photo Touch-Up
  Charged" and "Weisburg Admits 'Touch-Up' Letter; Denies

Connection" by Tom Raum, *Tampa Times-Tribune*, 11/27–28/68.

"Was Thornley an agent . . .": Garrison, op. cit. p. 77.

Thornley denies he's a CIA agent: "Deputies Arrest Thornley on Fugitive Warrant," by Tom Raum, *Tampa Times-Tribune*, 2/22/68.

"As luck would have it . . .": Garrison press release, 2/21/68.

"very funny . . .": *Affidavit*.

Thornley travels to Mexico: Thornley's Warren Commission testimony.

Oswald in Mexico: Summers, *Conspiracy*, chapter 19; Groden and Livingstone, *High Treason*, photos.

Thornley's alleged New Orleans intelligence connections: Garrison, op. cit. pp. 72–73.

Bannister, Ferrie, and Oswald: Summers, *Conspiracy;* Groden and Livingstone, *High Treason.* Note: Material on the relationship among these three turns up in just about every book about the Kennedy assassination.

Thornley meets Bannister: *Affidavit.*

Thornley's relationship with Lifton: my interviews with both; *Affidavit*; Epstein, *Counterplot*.

Roselli says CIA "killed . . . president": *Affidavit.*

"Gary Kirstein" recollections: my interviews with Thornley, and his letters to me; *Affidavit*; Thornley, *The Dreadlock Recollections.*

"Did the Plumbers Plug J.F.K., Too?": Thornley refers to this article in his introduction to *The Dreadlock Recollections.* He says it was published in a newspaper called *The Great Speckled Bird,* but he gives no date of publication.

Attacked by men in ski masks: *Cosmic Trigger,* pp. 152–54.

Thornley quotes on mental programming, his mother, Vril Society, and Nazi breeding experiments are all from my interviews.

"Nazi Connections to the J.F.K. Assassination," by Mae Brussell. *The Rebel,* 11/22/83.

Discordian philosophy: Wilson, *Cosmic Trigger;* Hill and Thornley; *Principia Discordia.*

Concluding Thornley quotes: interview.

CHAPTER 2

Background material on News Election Service from research, including interviews, compiled by me and summarized in my article, "Compute D'Etat" in San Jose *Metro,* 9/28/89.

The Colliers' Votescam theory and peregrinations in pursuit of: Collier and Collier, *Votescam;* my interviews with Ken Collier.

"There isn't one single person in public office who earned their way there . . .": my interviews with Ken Collier.

Dade County election: *Miami Magazine,* July 1974, reproduced in *Votescam.*

Background on the Colliers: "The Great Vote Fraud Conspiracy" by Mike Clary, *Miami New Times,* 6/29/88.

The Colliers' *Spotlight* articles were reprinted in one special supplement, *The Stealing of America,* 8/84.

Home News articles are reproduced in *Votescam* and described in "The Great Vote Fraud Conspiracy."

The Colliers' book proposal: *Votescam.*

"It was a random thing . . .": KAZU-FM, Carmel, California, interview with Ken Collier, May 1988.

"What do they do?": ibid.

Staffing of NES: my interview with Paul Hain, former NES official.

The Colliers' suspicions about "master computer": my interviews with Ken Collier.

NES conceived: "Networks Plan Nov. 3 Vote Pool," *New York Times,* 6/8/64. "Many television executives . . .": ibid. "Master tally boards . . .": ibid.

NES performance: "News Media Pool to Speed Returns," *New York Times,* 11/1/64; "News Media Pool Sets Vote Marks," *New York Times,* 11/4/64.

Erroneous data in 1968 election: "Vote Computers That Failed are Under Analysis," *New York Times*, 11/7/68; "Nixon Popular Vote Lead Is Increased," *New York Times*, 11/8/68.

"Nixon has more power now . . .": my interview with Ken Collier.

Computers tabulate fifty-four percent: Hoffman, *Making Every Vote Count.*

"If you did it right, no one would ever know": "Electronic Elections Seen as an Invitation to Fraud," *Los Angeles Times*, 7/4/89.

Voter turnaround estimate belongs to the Colliers.

Bush wins New Hampshire despite bad polls: "New Hampshire Confounded Most Pollsters," *Washington Post*, 2/18/88.

The Colliers' Sununu theory: *Votescam.*

Shouptronic background: *An Election Administrator's Guide to Computerized Voting Systems, Vol. 2*, ECRI Report, 1988.

Naegle quote from my interview with him.

Shoup fined and sentenced: "Counting the Votes" by Ronnie Dugger, *New Yorker*, 11/7/88.

"We had to get Reagan elected . . .": ibid.

Forty percent figure from my interview with computerized voting entrepreneur Robert Varni.

"heap of spaghetti code . . ." and "shell game": "Machine Politics" by John W. Verity, *Datamation*, 11/1/86.

The Colliers' videotape alleged chad-related vote fraud, sue Republican National Committee: interviews with Ken Collier; "The Great Vote Fraud Conspiracy"; *Votescam.*

"He acted without jurisdiction . . .": testimony of Kennety F. Collier before U.S. Senate Judiciary Committee, 8/6/86.

The Colliers' allegations about Scalia and Nixon, and "He never invoked that as a reason for Watergate": interviews with Ken Collier.

NES as a CIA operation related to Kennedy assassination: my interviews with Ken Collier.

Jim Collier's stomach tumor: "The Great Vote Fraud Conspiracy."

"It's not even a quest . . ." and "Ultimately, it might come out . . .": my interviews with Ken Collier.

CHAPTER 3

LaRouche's formative years, Trotskyism, Operation Mop-Up: "Politics and Paranoia: The Strange Odyssey of Lyndon LaRouche" by Frank Deane and Randall Rothenberg, *The Nation*, 8/16/80; King, *Lyndon LaRouche and the New American Fascism*, chapters 1–5; my interviews with LaRouche.

"seating arrangements of the French National Assembly . . .": "Secret Agent Man" by James Ridgeway, *Village Voice*, 10/13/87.

"The problem with most conspiracy buffs . . .": my interview with LaRouche.

The clearest statement of the "moral imperative" appears in Kant's *Critique of Practical Reason*.

"promotion of scientific knowledge . . .": my interview with LaRouche.

"Wherever populations have become more rational . . .": LaRouche, *There Are No Limits to Growth*.

SDI as "my proposal": my interviews with LaRouche.

LaRouche's condemnation of the empiricists appears in almost every book or major article he has ever written.

"irrational hedonism": *There Are No Limits to Growth*.

"Henry's career . . . as a tool of Chatham House . . .": my interviews with LaRouche; LaRouche's British conspiracy theory is his central theme, stated most explicitly in *Dope, Inc.*, as well as in interviews and in almost everything he has ever written.

For a more complete history of the Templars, Masons, etc., see Chapter 16. "The leading controllers of the opium war . . .": *Dope, Inc.*, p. 61. See also chapter 9 of *Dope, Inc.*, in which LaRouche's "investigating team" explains how "the entire world drug traffic has been run by a single family since its inception" and how "the family religion" is the gnostic "Isis

Cult." See Chapter 16 of this book for a history of mystery cults and secret societies.

"Who's the conspiracy theorist . . . ?": my interview with Odin Anderson.

LaRouche's network of organizations and holdings: *The LaRouche Cult: Packaging Extremism,* an Anti-Defamation League Special Report, Spring 1986.

Executive Intelligence Review's scooping propensity is acknowledged even by Dennis King, LaRouche's fiercest journalistic adversary. See King, *Lyndon LaRouche and the New American Fascism,* p. 161, for King's account of how *EIR* got the scoop on the Iran-Contra affair.

". . . we are able to think better . . .": my interview with LaRouche.

The "Get LaRouche Task Force" hypothesis is stated most succinctly in the introduction to and Appendix A of *Railroad!* by LaRouche's rather misleadingly named "Commission to Investigate Human Rights Violations" (the "commission" is concerned exclusively with violations of Lyndon LaRouche's rights). The Boston trial received national press coverage. Copies of numerous newspaper accounts are in my possession, but for the curious reader's, and my own convenience, widely reported facts will be attributed to this LaRouche-produced book, a straightforward account of LaRouche's legal ordeals consisting mainly of reprinted court documents and FOIA releases (copies of many FOIA documents, including most of the important ones, are also in my files).

"The government got caught . . .": my interview with Anderson.

North-Secord memo: "North Memo Reveals Other Intrigues," *Philadelphia Inquirer,* 3/10/88.

Government informers as actual perpetrators of the crimes is LaRouche's central defense, which he was prohibited from using at his subsequent trial in Alexandria, Virginia, the trial at which LaRouche was convicted following the Boston mistrial. See *Railroad!* for a full account.

LaRouche and North competing for cash: "Search for Dollars Links LaRouche, North," *Lowell [MA] Sunday Sun,* 7/12/87.

LaRouche accuses Kissinger of organizing frame-up: my interviews with LaRouche.

Kissinger letters to Webster: *Railroad!*, pp. 546, 548.

"Politics of Faggotry" flyer: King, *Lyndon LaRouche and the New American Fascism*, p. 140.

Webster memo asking for investigation: *Railroad!*, p. 550.

"We opposed it because it stank . . .": my interviews with LaRouche. "You don't . . . start shooting up Jesuits": ibid.

Nancy Reagan as "an idiot," President Reagan as "pussy whipped": "Secret Agent Man."

Kissinger as LaRouche's adversary and LaRouche's allegation of Kissinger's "land scam operation": my interviews with LaRouche. Also from my interviews, Grateful Dead as a "British intelligence operation," and ultimate purpose of "this Satanism business."

Episcopal canon alleged by LaRouche to visit "Mineshaft" club: "The Indictment of LaRouche's Enemies," *New Federalist*, 2/17/89. *New Federalist* is LaRouche's successor paper to *New Solidarity*, which was closed by the government. LaRouche didn't write the cited article, but given the nature of the LaRouche organization it's quite certain that nothing he'd denounce makes it into his paper.

Confrontation with Nancy Kissinger recounted in Johnson, *Architects of Fear*, p. 191.

Masturbation prohibited: "Politics and Paranoia" by Deane and Rothenberg.

LaRouche's attitude toward sexuality is explicated in *Lyndon LaRouche and the New American Fascism*. LaRouche recognized that "personal life" and sexuality in particular were the greatest obstacle to total political commitment, according to his hostile biographer Dennis King. LaRouche sought, often using brutal techniques, to deprive his underlings of their sexual identities, or any sexual opportunities, promising to "take your bedrooms away from you," King, p. 25.

"Another word for it: New Age . . ." and LaRouche's comments on conspiracy: my interviews with LaRouche.

Judge's speculation that LaRouche is "put up by the Rockefellers": my interviews with Judge.

LaRouche's meetings with foreign leaders are recounted in *Lyndon LaRouche and the New American Fascism.*

For Carter's connection to the Trilateral Commission, se
Chapter 15.

LaRouche's CIA and administration contacts: "The LaRouch
Connection" by Dennis King and Ronald Radosh, *The Nev
Republic,* 2/6/84.

LaRouche's anti-Bush campaign: *Lyndon LaRouche and th
New American Fascism,* pp. 124–25.

"very much involved" with beam weapon: my interviews wit
LaRouche.

Dinner with NSC aide and use of Mitch WerBell: "Th
LaRouche Connection" by King and Radosh.

LaRouche's group was sued by *U.S. News and World Repor
for impersonating the magazine's reporters.

Souter, Rizzo relationships with LaRouche: "David Souter an
Lyndon LaRouche" by James Ledbetter and James Ridge
way, *Village Voice,* 9/18/90.

Boston jury agrees that government may have been involved i
fraud to discredit LaRouche, takes straw poll: "LaRouch
Jury Would Have Voted Not Guilty," *Boston Herald,* 5/5/88

CHAPTER 4

All of the material on William Bramley comes from my inter
views with him. Some quotes are taken from his book, *Th
Gods of Eden,* and are so noted in the text. See also my articl
"Alien Notion," from San Jose *Metro,* 6/21/90. Also, fo
more on secret societies, see Chapter 16 of this book.

All John Keel quotes are from *UFOs: Operation Trojan Horse
his definitive book. Charles Fort catalogued lights in the sk
in *The Book of the Damned.*

Roswell incident, absence from Project Blue Book: Randle, *Th
UFO Casebook,* pp. 5–11.

Robertson Panel: Good, *Above Top Secret,* pp. 335–39.

UFOs as psychotronic technology: Vallee, *Messengers of Decep
tion,* p. 21.

I AM" movement and fascism: ibid. pp. 192–93. William Dudley Pelley led the "Silver Shirts," and American fascist party before World War II. Pelley, who was interned by the government during the war, was also a mystic who helped two of his students, Guy and Edna Ballard, found I AM. After the war, Pelley started an occult group called Soulcraft, which also included George Hunt Williamson (aka Michel d'Obrenovic), a contactee. Pelley's own difficult-to-obtain writings are said to contain oblique references to UFOs. Pelley also associated with another contactee, George Adamski. The ideology of this cadre was standard "master race" stuff, with the twist that the "master race" are aliens who have left their descendents on earth. The "star children" turn up in the canons of various "New Age" groups and cults.

CHAPTER 5

"There's hope . . .": my interviews with John McManus.

Welch as dictator: In section eight of *The Blue Book of the John Birch Society*, Welch explains that the society is to be "monolithic" and under the "complete authoritative control" of one man, Robert Welch. By the way, Welch's family business survives as a leading grape juice bottler.

John Birch's bio: Vahan, *The Truth about the John Birch Society*, pp. 13–16.

Welch's education, business, fascination with Birch: "Salesman of the Right," *New York Times*, 4/1/61; Dudman, *Men of the Far Right*, p. 67; *The Truth about the John Birch Society*.

Birch's parents support JBS: "Birch Parents Support Society," *New York Times*, 4/2/61.

Origins of Birch Society: *The Truth about the John Birch Society*, chapter 2; *Men of the Far Right*, chapter 5.

The Politician likened to *Mein Kampf*: "The Americanists," *Time*, 3/10/61.

Welch's allegations about Eisenhower, others: quoted from *The Politician* in *Men of the Far Right*, and *The Truth about the John Birch Society*. Welch also called Eisenhower's brother,

Milton "a communist" and speculated that Milton may in fact have been Ike's "boss."

Goldwater's reaction to *The Politician: The Truth about the John Birch Society,* p. 85.

Characterization of Welch and descriptions of his monotonous, irascible speaking style rely on Schomp, *Birchism Was My Business.* Author was one of the Birch Society's few paid staffers. Also, "Coast Reaction Mixed on Welch," *New York Times,* 4/14/61.

"most heated public controversy . . . since McCarthy": *The Boston Traveler,* quoted in *The Truth about the John Birch Society,* p. 41.

Walker controversy: "Walker Resigns from the Army," *New York Times,* 11/3/61; "Birch Unit Ideas Put to U.S. Troops," *New York Times,* 4/14/61; *Men of the Far Right,* chapter 4. For Walker's role in Kennedy assassination scenario, see Chapter 10 of this book.

NAM censures Birch Society: "Birch Council Member Denies Censure Vote," *New York Times,* 4/14/61.

"We should use a rifle . . .": "Salesman of the Right," *New York Times.* "If you measured . . .": my interview with McManus.

Birch concentration in Idaho: "John Birch Society 'Wages War for Minds' in Idaho," *Idaho Statesman,* 3/24/85; in Oklahoma: "Still Keeping Watch," by Mike Easterling, *Oklahoma Gazette,* 4/26/89. Total Birch membership: "Area Man Leads Birch Society 'Youth Movement,' " *Norfolk Virginian-Pilot,* 2/2/85. Summer camps: "Swimming, Campfires and Anticommunism," by Ron Grossman, *San Jose Mercury-News,* 9/18/89.

"We've got truth on our side . . .": my interview with McManus.

"Early in our history . . .": Bunzel, *Anti-Politics in America,* p. 41.

Origins of the Know-Nothings: Bennet, *The Party of Fear,* pp. 105–16. Buntline as founder: Coates, *Armed and Dangerous,* p. 26.

"There is abundant proof that a foreign conspiracy . . ."

"Startling Facts for Native Americans Called Know-Nothings," pamphlet published in New York, 1855, p. 66.

Jack Chick comics are available through Amok Books; for background on Jack Chick, see Johnson, *Architects of Fear.*

Know-Nothings in elected office: *Armed and Dangerous*, p. 28.

"advocating the largest freedom . . .": "Address of the Executive Committee of the American Republicans of Boston to the People of Massachusetts," 1845, p. 11.

". . . a conspiracy above communism . . .": my interview with John McManus.

"why the Communists . . . celebrate May Day.": ibid.

Allen quote on Adam Weishaupt: *None Dare Call It Conspiracy*, p. 80; a brief history of the Illuminati is in Chapter 16 of this book.

Welch's ideas about Illuminati, and rejection of term "Supercom": "And Some Ober Dicta" by Robert Welch, 1976, pamphlet mailed in Birch Society copies of the book *Wall Street and the Rise of Hitler.*

"marketplace of ideas . . .": "A Member of the CFR Talks Back" by Zygmunt Nagorski, *National Review*, 12/9/77.

"The reality of socialism . . .": Allen, *Say No to the New World Order*, p. 21; How the *Insiders* built the Soviet Union is the theme that runs throughout *None Dare Call It Conspiracy* and most of Allen's writing.

McManus radio interview on KGO-San Francisco, 11/26/90.

Bertrand Russell called "British pro-Communist socialist," ADA called "Fabian Socialist": Smoot, *The Invisible Government*, p. 121.

"Our Jewish members were very upset . . .": my interview with McManus. List of anti-Semites in Birch Society from Anti-Defamation League of B'nai B'rith, *Extremism on the Right.* The former employee critical of Birchian anti-Semitism is Schomp, author of *Birchism Was my Business.*

"No one has anything to fear . . .": my interview with McManus.

CHAPTER 6

Pat Buchanan made his "anti-Christian" accusation on an episode of the Cable News Network program *Crossfire* in August, 1988.

"I'm not a conspiracy theorist . . .": my interview with Ted Temple.

"The growth of big government . . .": Sorman, *The Conservative Revolution in America,* p. 144.

Willard Givens is quoted in Stormer, *None Dare Call It Treason,* p. 123.

NEA as friendly to Soviet totalitarianism: Reed, *NEA: Propaganda Front for the Radical Left.*

"The real goal . . .": McManus, *The Insiders,* p. 18.

Jesse Helms's rant: *Congressional Record,* 12/15/87.

Reagan's early political career as GE spokesman is summarized in Wills, *Reagan's America,* and Dugger, *Reagan: The Man and His Presidency;* Reagan's key speeches are reprinted in *Reagan Speaks,* including the "evil empire" speech.

Bush as having "more input into policy" than Reagan, Schultz as "errand boy for the commercial establishment," and "follow the money": my interview with Howard Philips.

Irvine's connections to ACWF, WACL: Anderson and Anderson, *Inside the League,* pp. 86, 157; AIM's crusades are carried out in its twice-monthly newsletter "AIM Report," which often includes preprinted postcards addressed to corporate sponsors of programs AIM doesn't like, allowing AIM readers ease in participating in pressure campaigns; the anti-"Shootdown" effort started in "AIM Report" of January (Issue A), 1990. Irvine in that issue finds it very incriminating that the NBC censor to whom he complained about "Shootdown" "acknowledged that he read *The Nation.*" Irvine's comment about major TV networks "ill-equipped to screen out . . . propaganda inimical to our country's interests" is from the "AIM Report," January 1989, Issue B.

For other Irvine connections, see "Accuracy in Media" by

Louis Wolf, *Covert Action Information Bulletin* #32. Before Irvine, AIM was run by Abraham Kalish, a former employee of the U.S. Information Agency, the government's department of propaganda.

CHAPTER 7

Material on David Emory and Judge is based primarily on my interviews with them.

Mae Brussell's career, threats against her, her death: "All Things Conspired" by John Whalen, San Jose *Metro*, 11/17/88. "Conspiracy Theorist Mae Brussell Dies," by Ann W. O'Neill, *San Jose Mercury-News*, 10/5/88. "In Our Hearts" by John Judge, *World Watchers International*, Fall 1989.

Mae Brussell and *The Realist:* Brussell's second and third *Realist* articles were published in 1974. The second was titled "The Senate Committee is Part of the Cover-Up," and detailed alleged martial law plans cooked up by the Nixon administration and known to, but concealed by Senator Sam Ervin's Watergate investigating committee. (This allegation doesn't seem so outlandish in light of its echoes more than a decade later during the Iran-Contra hearings when Texas congressman Jack Brooks tried to ask about Oliver North's role in drawing up a plan to suspend the constitution. Brooks was silenced by committee chairman Sen. Daniel Inouye. For more on North's plan and other martial law scenarios see Chapter 11.) Brussell's third *Realist* piece was "Why Was Patricia Hearst Kidnapped?" Krassner's refusal to publish Brussell's footnotes to the "Patricia Hearst" article, and financial disputes, severed the relationship between Brussell and *The Realist*.

"I'm an existentialist," quote, "candidate is selected" quote from Mae Brussell radio interview, KPFK Los Angeles, 3/2/88. Nazis: "The Nazi Connection to the John F. Kennedy Assassination," by Mae Brussell, *The Rebel*, 11/22/83.

Emory on guns from "One Step Beyond" broadcast, KFJC, 10/22/89. Emory tape titles from *The Dave Emory Archive Cas-*

sette Catalog, Archives on Audio, P.O. Box 170023, San Francisco, CA 94117 (1990).

Tom Davis quotes: from my interview.

Quotes on Mae Brussell Research Center: "Conspiracy Theorists Ponder the Mae Brussell Question," by Greg Beebe, Santa Cruz *Sentinel,* 2/28/92.

Chapter 8

Because Garrison did not answer my written request for an interview, and on the phone his secretary told me he was "too busy" to talk to the press, I've reconstructed a narrative of Garrison's career and his case against Clay Shaw from the sources below; most contain overlapping information (although their points of view differ greatly), which is why in most cases I haven't listed individual citations.

Epstein, *Counterplot;* Flammonde, *The Kennedy Conspiracy;* Garrison, *On the Trail of the Assassins;* James and Wardlaw, *Plot or Politics?;* "The Case of Jim Garrison and Lee Harvey Oswald," by Gene Roberts, *New York Times Magazine,* 5/21/67; "The Garrison Commission on the Assassination of President Kennedy," by William W. Turner, *Ramparts,* 6/67; "Is Garrison Faking?," by Fred Powledge, *The New Republic,* 6/17/67.

Jack Martin described as "full of that well-known waste material . . .": James, *Plot or Politics,* p. 48.

Martin allegations about Ferrie, characterization of Ferrie as CIA contractor, eccentric: op. cit.; also Groden and Livingstone, *High Treason;* Summers, *Conspiracy.*

Ferrie as amateur cancer researcher: Flammonde, *The Kennedy Conspiracy,* p. 19.

Killing of Aladio del Valle: Groden, *High Treason,* p. 118.

"I continued to believe that Shaw had participated . . .": Garrison, *On the Trail of the Assassins,* p. 250.

Garrison sculpts Russo's testimony: Flammonde, *The Kennedy Conspiracy,* p. 302.

Helms admits Shaw was "CIA contact": Garrison, ibid., p. 251. Marchetti confirms: Groden, *High Treason*, p. 161.

Bethell documents: Flammonde, *The Kennedy Conspiracy*, p. 198; Garrison, *On the Trail of the Assassins*, p. 48.

James Wilcott told the HSCA that Oswald was recruited by the CIA to act as a double agent against the U.S.S.R. Wilcott, a former CIA finance officer, said he handled funding for the Oswald/Soviet mission. Summers in *Conspiracy* (pp. 129–30) notes that Wilcott's story turned out to have some holes, and Wilcott later teamed up with CIA dissident Philip Agee in an anti-CIA campaign. However, Summers notes, "just as most of Agee's allegations are accepted as authentic, there may be some nugget of fact [in Wilcott's story]." Summers also speculates that Wilcott may have been still working for the CIA, in which case his story could be seen as disinformation, perhaps to lead the HSCA down the wrong path.

Helms on Oswald's "dummy file": Groden, *High Treason*, p. 93.

HSCA calls FBI's reaction to Marcello threat "deficient": Summers, *Conspiracy*, p. 259.

Garrison dismisses allegations of mob connections: *On the Trail of the Assassins*, 287–88.

CHAPTER 9

Biographical information on Daniel Sheehan from Rashke, *The Killing of Karen Silkwood;* "The Law and the Prophet," by James Traub, *Mother Jones*, 2–3/88; "Where Have All the Idealists Gone?," by Connie Matthiessen, *Utne Reader* 10–11/86.

Christic lawsuit: *Affidavit of Daniel P. Sheehan.*

Forty thousand dollars per week figure: "The Law and the Prophet."

One million dollar sanction against Christic Institute: "Christic Institute Fights for Its Existence," by Frank Provenzano, Detroit *Metro-Times*, 2/28/89; "Targets of Contra-Conspiracy Suit Awarded $1 million," *San Jose Mercury-News*, 2/4/89.

Reactions of defendants to Christic suit: "The Law and the Prophet."

Chapter 10

Kennedy pullout decision, "determined not to let Vietnam . . .": "How Kennedy Viewed the Vietnam Conflict," *New York Times,* letter to the editor by Roger Hilsman, 1/20/ 92. Hilsman was director of the State Department's Bureau of Intelligence and Research for much of the Kennedy Administration, and was named Assistant Secretary of State for Far Eastern Affairs in the administration's latter months.

Kennedy's troop withdrawal plans are also well documented elsewhere, including: Newman, *JFK and Vietnam:* Scott, *The War Conspiracy;* Prouty, *The Secret Team.*

Johnson's private intelligence: Newman, *JFK and Vietnam,* pp. 225–229. Note that the military distortion of intelligence on Vietnam for Kennedy's consumption, to put the most optimistic possible interpretation on the data even if it involved distorting data, is a major theme throughout Newman's book.

"There seems little doubt . . .": ibid., p. 456; NSAM 273: ibid. p. 446.

Domhoff's comments: "The Cult of Conspiracy," by Tai Moses, *The Sun* (Santa Cruz, CA), 1/26/89.

"It was a different world . . .": my article "Theories on an Assassination," *Worcester Magazine,* 11/23/88.

Secord involvement in Desert One: "The General and the Blonde Ghost," by Ron Rosenbaum, *Vanity Fair,* 1/90. This is an interesting article, interviewing both Secord and the reclusive Ted Shackley, but it perpetuates the odd myth that Vietnam and, in fact, the whole history of CIA and "secret team" malfeasance for the past thirty years are "the tragic legacy of J.F.K.'s Camelot." In light of Prouty's statements above, this curious canard is ironic in the extreme.

Lifton found a plethora of discrepancies, foremost among them that, according to eyewitnesses, the coffin that carried J.F.K.'s body into the Bethesda autopsy room was an ordinary metal shipping casket, not the ornate, expensive ceremonial casket in which his body was loaded onto Air Force One. If Lifton's eyewitnesses are reliable, the body must have been stolen at some point, which leaves wide open the possibility of alterations—a proposition for which Lifton amasses considerable evidence.

Johnson, creating the Warren Commission, also declared that if rumors of a foreign conspiracy were not quelled, the U.S. could be thrown into "a war which could cost 40 million lives." Summers, *Conspiracy*, p. 408.

Nixon in Dallas on day of assassination: Scott, *The Dallas Conspiracy*. Scott cites Earl Mazo and Stephen Hess, *Nixon: A Political Portrait* (New York: Popular Library, 1968), p. 296. Scott notes that Nixon's business likely involved the Pepsi bottling plant planned for Arlington, Texas. If so, says Scott, he would have almost certainly been doing business with Great Southwest Corporation, of which more later in this chapter. The implication that Nixon's presence in Dallas on the two days leading up to the assassination, and, indeed, the very morning of November 22, 1963, is significant may seem farfetched, and it may be. But why, then, did Nixon later deny having been in Dallas on those dates, making him as Groden in *High Treason* quips, the only person of his generation *not* to remember where he was when Kennedy was assassinated?

Nixon death threats: "Guard Not for Nixon," *Dallas Morning News*, 11/22/63.

Trowbridge Ford's comments and background: my interviews with Trowbridge Ford.

"I believe that a full exposure . . .": "From Dallas to Watergate: The Longest Cover-Up," by Peter Dale Scott, *Ramparts*, 11/73.

Nixon, Rebozo, mob links: ibid.

Nixon possible meeting with Murchison: Groden, *High Treason*, p. 243, citing Penn Jones, Jr., *Forgive My Grief* (Rt. 3, Box 356, Waxahachie, TX 75165), vol. 4, p. 114.

H. L. Hunt's death squad: Hougan, *Spooks*, p. 55 (Hougan notes that Hunt denies this allegation, blaming it on a CIA operative out to smear him); Groden in *High Treason* notes that just an hour after the J.F.K. assassination, Hunt was flown from Dallas by the FBI to Mexico, where he stayed for a month. Groden on p. 203 reports Hunt's financing of *Krushchev Killed Kennedy*.

Murchison connections: Groden, *High Treason*, pp. 243, 262–63. Hoover connections: Scott, *The Dallas Conspiracy*, chapter 6.

Marina Oswald and Murchison: Scott, *The Dallas Conspiracy*, chapters 3 and 10. General Walker and German neo-Nazis: ibid., chapters 1 and 4.

Hunt tries to persuade Nixon to pick Ford: Groden, *High Treason*, p. 262; Cabell brothers: ibid., pp. 262–63.

Sturgis plants Cuban conspiracy story: "From Dallas to Watergate."

E. Howard Hunt in Mexico: Summers, *Conspiracy*, pp. 418–19, citing Tad Szulc, *Compulsive Spy* (New York: Viking Press, 1974).

Witness deaths: Penn Jones, Jr., in his book *Forgive My Grief*, cited above, first formulated the "mysterious deaths" theory, calling attention to what appears to be an unusually high rate of untimely demise among witnesses to the assassination and possible participants in a conspiracy. The list of deaths has been oft amended and repeated. I've taken mine from Groden, *High Treason*, chapter 7, simply for the sake of convenience.

Oil companies and Vietnam: Scott, *The Dallas Conspiracy*, chapter 9.

Garrison on Permindex: *On the Trail of the Assassins*, pp. 89–90; *Nomenclature of an Assassination Cabal* was written by William Torbitt, which was a pseudonym for a Houston attorney named David Copeland, now deceased. Re: Permindex, see also Flammonde, *The Kennedy Conspiracy*; "Who Told the Truth about J.F.K.," by Jay Pound, *Critique* #21/22.

Kennedy vow to smash CIA: Groden, *High Treason*, p. 355. Kennedy's true sentiments toward the CIA came to light during the hearings of the House Select Committee on Assassinations. Prouty, in *The Secret Team*, recounts how Kennedy came to the presidency with strong CIA support, even reappointing Allen Dulles as CIA director. But after the Bay of Pigs, he felt he'd been double-crossed. According to Prouty, Kennedy maintained a public show of support for the CIA while in private he plotted against it as he realized that he could not control the intelligence behemoth.

Hoover's friends with underworld ties: Nash, *Citizen Hoover*, pp. 109–13; Messick, *John Edgar Hoover*, pp. 209–11. An example of Hoover's curious links was industrialist Lewis Rosenstiel, who was directly associated in congressional and New York State legislative testimony to the mob's financial overseer Meyer Lansky, and political and gambling boss Frank Costello. Arthur Samish, a liquor industry lobbyist sent to jail for tax evasion, was another mutual friend of Hoover and Lansky.

Interpol, Nazis and Hoover: Foomer, *Interpol*, pp. 49–54. Hoover first joined Interpol in 1938, when the organization was taken over by Nazis. During World War II Interpol was dormant. When it was revived it may or may not have been free of its Nazi links. See Anderson, *Policing the World*, pp. 41–42. Anderson sees "no convincing evidence" that the postwar Interpol was Nazi-influenced, but he does quote from another book, Omar Garrison, *The Secret World of Interpol* (London: Ralston Pilot, 1976). "Several of the committee which reconstituted (Interpol) in 1946 had worked with the Nazis. Four out of seven of Interpol's presidents since the restructuring in 1946 may reasonably be considered carriers of the police state germ."

"Once we decide that anything goes . . .": Moyers, *The Secret Government*, p. 44. Moyers, who could hardly be called a conspiracy theorist (in the same paragraph, he notes, erroneously, that "most of us" dismiss suspicions of conspiracy in J.F.K.'s death—in fact, polls consistently show the majority of Americans *accepting* a J.F.K. assassination conspiracy theory), also marvels at (p. 54) "how easily the Cold War enticed us into surrendering popular control of the government to the national security state."

CHAPTER 11

Robert F. Kennedy conspiracy theories come from a number of sources, notably, Robert Kaiser, *RFK Must Die!* (New York: E. P. Dutton Co., 1970), William Turner and John Christian, *The Assassination of Robert F. Kennedy* (New York: Random House, 1978), and many others. My job, however, was made very easy by a quick look back in the files of my own paper, San Jose *Metro,* for an article, "Unanswered Questions," by Andy Boehm (12/15/88), which is the best summary I've seen of the R.F.K. assassination theories. I also relied on Ted Charach's 1973 documentary film *The Second Gun,* which is in my possession on videotape.

MKULTRA, origins and effects: Marks, *The Search for the "Manchurian Candidate";* Lee and Shlain, *Acid Dreams;* Bowart, *Operation Mind Control.*

Hinckley on Valium: "Hinckley's Psychiatrist Prescribed Disastrous Treatment, Doctor Says," *Miami Herald,* 5/19/82 (with sidebar "Valium Can Cause Rage, Expert Says").

Chapman "could have been programmed": Bressler, *Who Killed John Lennon?,* p. 17. Other details about Chapman, including possible YMCA/CIA connection, from throughout the same book.

Hinckley hoped someone would stop him, felt "relieved": "Hinckley's Psychiatrist Prescribed . . .": op. cit.

Purdy on psychiatric drugs: "A Report to Attorney General John K. Van de Kamp on Patrick Edward Purdy and the Cleveland School Killings," State of California, 10/89.

CIA agent Dwyer at Jonestown: "CIA Agent Witnessed Jonestown Mass Suicide," by Rick Sullivan, San Mateo *Times,* 12/14/79; Dwyer is listed in *Who's Who in the CIA,* p. 152. Dwyer "stripping the dead": Kilduff and Javers, *The Suicide Cult,* p. 176.

Holsinger's story comes from his address to a forum entitled "Psychosocial Implications of the Jonestown Phenomenon," held in San Francisco, 5/23/80.

Statements of Dr. Mootoo, evidence of Jonestown murders: "Coroner Says 700 in Cult Who Died Were Slain," *Miami Herald,* 12/17/78; "Some in Cult Received Cyanide by Injection, Sources Say," *New York Times,* 12/12/78; "Hundreds Were Slain, Survivor Reportedly Says," *Los Angeles Times,* 11/25/78 (from Associated Press).

Death toll jumps: "Question Linger about Guyana," by Sidney Jones, *Oakland Tribune,* 12/9/78.

Layton "a robot": "Cult Reportedly Got Assets from Layton," *Los Angeles Times,* 11/26/78.

Mind control drugs at Jonestown, mentioned in Holsinger's talk, op. cit.; Holsinger quotes, ibid.

"some kind of horrible government experiments . . .": "Cult Defectors Suspect U.S. of a Coverup on Jonestown," by Bella Stumbo, *Los Angeles Times,* 12/18/78.

Jones as Republican: "Jim Jones Was a Republican for 6 Years," *Los Angeles Times,* 12/17/78. In Brazil: "Jones Lived Well, Kept to Himself During Mysterious Brazil Stay," San Jose *Mercury* (date missing from my clipping).

Jones and Lane consider smuggling assassination witness: "Memo Discusses Smuggling Witness into Guyana," *New York Times,* 12/8/78.

Jonestown resettlement: "Resettlement Plan Set Up by Relief Groups," San Francisco *Examiner,* 2/18/80. Hilltown: "Hill Rules Cult with Iron Fist," Cleveland *Plain Dealer,* 12/4/78. Colonia Dignidad: "West German Cultist Concentration Camp in Chile," by Konrad Ege, *Counterspy,* 12/78.

King assassination conspiracy theories: Blumenthal and Yazitian, *Government by Gunplay;* "The Conspiracy to Kill Martin Luther King," by John Sergeant and John Edginton, *Chicago Reader,* 3/2/90.

COINTELPRO against white hate groups: "Vigilante Repression," by Ken Lawrence, *Covert Action Information Bulletin* #31.

Operation Garden Plot and Rex 84: "Blueprint for Tyranny," by Donald Goldberg and Indy Badhwar, *Penthouse,* 8/85; "Variations on a FEMA," by James Ridgeway, *Village Voice,* 11/14/89; "The Take-Charge Gang," by Keenen Peck, *The*

Progressive, 5/85; "Meese-ing with Civil Rights," San Jose *Metro,* 3/28/85.

CIA discusses "how to knock off key guys" with cancer: "CIA's Bizarre Ideas for Assassinations," San Francisco *Chronicle,* 4/2/79.

The Jessica Savitch theory, which usually raises a few eyebrows, is not uncommon among conspiracy researchers. It was relayed to me by John Judge.

The two most comprehensive summaries of the Casolaro case are: "The Last Days of Danny Casolaro," by James Rideway and Doug Vaughn, *Village Voice,* 10/15/91; "The Strange Death of Danny Casolaro," by Ron Rosenbaum, *Vanity Fair,* 12/91. An intial press account was "Writer's Death Called Apparent Suicide But Foul Play Isn't Ruled Out By Examiners," *San Jose Mercury-News* (from *Washington Post*), 9/16/91.

Sarah Jane Moore working for FBI: Blumenthal, *Government by Gunplay.*

Ford assassination allegations: Milan, *The Squad,* pp. 285–90.

The list of "October Surprise" allegedly strange deaths comes from Honneger, *October Surprise,* pp. 283–92.

CHAPTER 12

Black leaders on drug conspiracy: "Talk Grows of Government Being out to Get Blacks," by Jason DeParle, *New York Times,* 10/29/90; "Many Blacks Blame Drug Woes on Conspiracy among Whites," by Howard Kurtz, *San Jose Mercury-News,* 1/1/90 (from *Washington Post*).

John Kerry's opinions on drug conspiracy: my interview with John Kerry.

The best source I have found for a quick summary of the Mafia's early involvement in drugs is in McCoy, *The Politics of Heroin in Southeast Asia,* the definitive work on U.S. government involvement in the drug trade up to 1970. Figures on heroin demand and addict population, pp. 16, 17. Lucky Luciano's heroin entrepreneurship, pp. 18–27.

McCoy's book contains Air America material, but also appeared in a book called *Air America* by Christopher Robbins. However, when a movie of the same title appeared in 1990 (with Mel Gibson), Robbins condemned it in the *New York Times* (8/28/90) as a "half-baked . . . conspiracy theory." As the media-criticism publication *Extra!* noted (11/12/90), "Robbins wasn't always negatively disposed toward the film: he had unsuccessfully petitioned the Writers Guild for a screenwriting credit." As a movie tie-in, a new edition of Robbins's book came out. "Without explanation," *Extra!* observes, "the new version of the book omitted numerous passages about CIA support for dope smugglers that appeared in Robbins's original 1979 text."

Re: *Kiss the Boys Goodbye*, it is worth noting that coauthor William Stevenson is author of *A Man Called Intrepid*, perhaps the most highly respected book on intelligence ever written by an intelligence outsider. William Webster cited the book in the confirmation hearings for his current job, director of the CIA. Stevenson's point of view, while thorough and objective, has always been basically prointelligence, so for him to coauthor a book like *Kiss the Boys Goodbye* is truly astonishing, and has to make one think.

Afghan drug connection: "Afghan Rebels and Drugs," by William Vornberger, *Covert Action Information Bulletin* #28.

"You do not have to be a CIA-hater . . .": Mills, *The Underground Empire*, p. 1142.

John Kerry investigation: my interview with John Kerry; Noriega-contra-CIA links; "Made for Each Other: The Secret History of George Bush and Manuel Noriega," by Murray Waas, *Village Voice*, 2/6/90; "Noriega Has Achieved Least-Favored-Strongman Status," by John M. Goshko, *Washington Post National Weekly Edition*, 3/7/88; see also Cockburn, *Out of Control*; "Is North Network Cocaine Connected?" by Vince Bielski and Dennis Bernstein, *In These Times*, 12/10/86; "Three Committees Track Down Smuggled Drugs, Not Smoking Gun," by Dennis Bernstein and Robert Knight, *In These Times*, 8/5/87.

Drug Tug case: *Napa Sentinel* series ran from 8/4/89 to 10/6/89, with numerous follow-up articles since, including one dated

10/13/89, just a week after the series was supposed to have ended, entitled "It Doesn't End."

History of LSD: Lee and Shlain, *Acid Dreams*; Marks, *The Search for the Manchurian Candidate*. Ronald Stark story appears on pages 279–88 of *Acid Dreams*. Speculation that LSD may have been a CIA tool to destabilize the New Left, ibid., p. 285; Burroughs quote, ibid., p. 282.

CHAPTER 13

Origins of the CIA: Kilpatrick, *The U.S. Intelligence Community*, pp. 45–48; Corson, *The Armies of Ignorance*, pp. 289–91; Prouty, *The Secret Team*, pp. 98–104; Bledowska and Bloch, *KGB/CIA: Intelligence and Counter-Intelligence Operations*, pp. 6–16.

Truman's cloak-and-dagger party: Bledowska and Bloch, *KGB/CIA*, p. 8.

"Other functions" clause: Prouty, op. cit.

CIA charter "must remain secret . . .": Marchetti and Marks, *The CIA and the Cult of Intelligence*, p. 305.

"We are not Boy Scouts . . .": Powers, *The Man Who Kept the Secrets*, p. 159.

Olson incident: Marks, *The Search for the Manchurian Candidate*, chapter 5.

Richard Welch affair and CIA response: Agee and Wolf, *Dirty Work*, pp. 79–105 (this anthology devotes several articles to the Welch assassination, including a full transcript of a "communique" from the "November 17 Revolutionary Organization," which actually "executed" Welch, in which the assassins tell exactly how they planned and carried out the killing —the group issued this communique in response to the vast disinformation campaign surrounding the Welch affair).

Knights of Malta: "Their Will Be Done," by Martin Lee, *Mother Jones*, 7/83.

Licio Gelli and the P2 Lodge: Yallop, *In God's Name*, pp. 129–39. 1987 indictment: Honneger, *October Surprise*, p. 231.

Bologna bombing: ibid., p. 139. Christie, *Stefano Delle Chiaie: Portrait of a Black Terrorist,* pp. 109–12.

Gelli as Knight of Malta: Baigent, Leigh, and Lincoln, *The Messianic Legacy,* p. 360 (authors note that "confirmation is now impossible" of Gelli's Knighthood, but note that his closest associate in P2 is a Knight, so it seems unlikely that the ubiquitous Gelli would neglect to join). Note that Knight of Malta Al Haig, according to the LaRouche intelligence network, played some role in actually founding P2. Gelli, incidentally, was arrested on various charges in Switzerland in 1982. He escaped capture and at last report was said to be living somewhere in South America.

Gelli at Reagan's inauguration: Yallop, *In God's Name,* pp. 359–60. Gelli relayed his offer of help to Reagan through Philip Guarino, a member of the Republican National Committee and of P2. See following note.

Guarino works for Bush: "The Republican Party and Fascists," by Russ Bellant, *Covert Action Information Bulletin* #33; speculation that Bush is a P2 member comes from Honneger, *October Surprise,* p. 240. Honneger says that her mysterious "Informant Y" told her that Bush was inaugurated into the P2 in 1976.

Mino Pecorelli killing: Yallop, *In God's Name,* p. 310.

Gelli and CIA: Yallop, *In God's Name,* pp. 131–32; Brenneke's claim that CIA funded P2 through Amatalia is from *L'Europeo,* 8/25/90. I do not have an original copy of the article, but I do have a handwritten translation that I first heard read by David Emory, 12/17/90.

Gehlen as Knight: "Their Will Be Done." The Knights awarded Gehlen their Grand Cross of Merit, the top honor a Knight can receive.

"He's on our side . . .": Simpson, *Blowback,* p. 53.

"substantial escalation of the Cold War . . .": ibid., p. 54.

Oglesby comments on Gehlen: "The Secret Treaty of Fort Hunt," by Carl Oglesby, *Covert Action Information Bulletin* #35.

CIA's recruitment of SS men: Simpson, *Blowback;* Loftus, *The Belarus Secret;* Infield, *Secrets of the SS,* chapter 15.

"An intelligence service is the ideal vehicle . . .": Wise, *The American Police State*, p. 187.

Skorzeny in Egypt, training terrorists: Infield, *Skorzeny, Hitler's Commando*, pp. 212–17.

Alois Brunner on CIA payroll: Simpson, *Blowback*, chapter 16. Brunner murders 128,500: ibid., p. 249.

Nazi links to Dulles law firm: Lisagor and Lipsius, *A Law Unto Itself*, chapter 8.

Dulles and ITT: Hougan, *Spooks*, p. 425.

CIA in the Golden Triangle: McCoy, *The Politics of Heroin in Southeast Asia*. See notes to previous chapter for numerous citations.

Gelli and P2 linked to KGB: Knight, *The Brotherhood*, chapter 27.

Skull and Bones: "Secret Society," by Steven M. L. Aronson, *Fame*, 8/89. Aronson also reveals that the Skull and Bones headquarters, seen only by initiated Bonesmen, contains "a little Nazi shrine." More on Skull and Bones in the next chapter.

CIA lie-detector exam: McGarvey, *CIA: The Myth and the Madness*, p. 161.

CIA proprietaries: Borsage and Marks, *The CIA File*. Ocean Hunter: Cockburn, *Out of Control*.

"Exxon *is* the CIA": Hougan, *Spooks*, p. 437. A Venezuelan subsidiary of Exxon called Creole was actually founded and operated by the CIA, and eventually consolidated operations with its parent company in Venezuela, thus making the CIA and Exxon indistinguishable in that country.

Speculation that Zapata is CIA linked: "Bush's Boy's Club: Skull and Bones," *Covert Action Information Bulletin* #33. Zapata was an offshore drilling company based in Houston, started by Bush. For more on Zapata, see "The Mexican Connection" by Jonathan Kwitny, *Barron's*, 9/19/88. Kwitny describes Bush's illegal involvement in an oil venture with Jorge Diaz Serrano, one of the most important figures in Mexican politics (he helped write the Mexican constitution), who in 1983 was convicted of defrauding the Mexican government of fifty-eight million dollars while in charge of Mexico's government-owned oil monopoly.

Hughes and CIA: Drosnin, *Citizen Hughes.*

CIA and S&L scandal: *Houston Post* articles by Pete Brewton (note that Brewton's series is ongoing): "S&L Probe Has Possible CIA Links," 2/4/90; "A Bank's Shadowy Demise," with sidebar "Azima No Stranger to Texas Business," 2/8/90; "Lindsay Aided S&L Probe Figure," 2/11/90; "Loan from Texas Thrift Weaves a Tale of Deceit," (note that this article connects the demise of Silverado Savings and Loan, which implicated George Bush's son Neil, to alleged CIA operatives); "Attorney Linked to S&L Crisis Has Ties to CIA, Mafia Figures," 4/4/90; "FBI Points to Insider Fraud as Big Factor in S&L Crisis," 4/12/90.

Other sources on CIA/S&L connection: (note that most other sources rely heavily on Brewton's articles) "Bankrolling Iran-Contra," by John Whalen, San Jose *Metro*, 2/22/90; "Did CIA Raid the S&L's," by Joel Bleifuss, *Los Angeles Reader*, 4/27/90; "Ripoff Savings and Loan of Colorado," with sidebar "Did They Get a Free Toaster, Too?," by Brian Abas, Denver *Westword*, 4/18/90; "S&L Crisis Tied to Mob," by Dave Armstrong, San Pedro *Random Lengths*, 3/15/90; "The Great S&L Robbery," by Dave Armstrong, *Random Lengths*, 4/12/90; "Savings and Loan Sharks," by John Whalen, *Metro*, 5/24/90; "Consensus of Silence?," by Joel Bleifuss, Detroit *Metro Times*, 5/23/90; "Loan Star State," by Joel Bleifuss, *In These Times*, 5/2/90; "Beltway Bandits," by David Corn, *The Nation*, 5/7/90; "The Mob, the CIA and the S&L Scandal," by Steve Weinberg, *Columbia Journalism Review*, 11–12/90; "Cash and Carry: The Banks and the CIA" with sidebar "Who's Spookin' Who? A Cast of Characters," by Paul Muolo and Stephen Pizzo, *Penthouse*, 10/90. See also Pizzo, Muolo, and Fricker, *Inside Job: The Looting of America's Savings and Loans* (book doesn't cover CIA connections, but it's the definitive work on organized crime involvement in the S&L scandal, which appears to be just one step removed from CIA involvement).

Nugan Hand Bank: Kwitny, *The Crimes of Patriots.*

A good history of CIA's foreign intervention is Blum, *CIA: a Forgotten History.*

"Black International," name: Sterling, *The Terror Network,* p. 1. Sterling's book promotes the thesis that the Kremlin is the prime mover behind world terrorism. It became the Bible of the Reagan Administration's terrorism policy. Ironically, on the first page, Sterling acknowledges right-wing terrorism, but dismisses it as a subject she simply chose not to focus on.

Skorzeny, Barbie, Genoud involved in founding right-wing terrorist movement: "Killers on the Right," by Martin Lee and Kevin Coogan, *Mother Jones,* 5/87.

Skorzeny and Palestinian terrorism: Infield, *Skorzeny: Hitler's Commando,* pp. 212–17.

Ali Hassan Salameh: Livingstone and Levy, *Inside the PLO,* pp. 110–12.

Pan Am 103 bombing and CIA connection: much information comes from the Interfor report itself, most of which is in my files, and Johnston, *Lockerbie: The Tragedy of Flight 103,* chapters 4 and 10; characterization of Interfor report as "spitball" is from Emerson and Duffy, *The Fall of Pan Am 103,* a book that, though it contains much useful information, appears to be based almost exclusively on unnamed intelligence and law-enforcement sources and so can't be considered reliable with regard to CIA involvement.

Other sources on Pan Am 103/CIA connection: (most based heavily on Interfor report) "Lawmaker Links Arms Dealer to Bombing of Pan Am Jet," by Frank Greve and Aaron Epstein, *San Jose Mercury-News,* 11/4/89 (first public mention of Interfor report); "Pan Am Blames CIA for Airline Bomb Plot," by John Picton, *Toronto Star,* 11/12/89; "CIA Downs Jet to Protect Drug Pipeline," by Erick Anderson, San Pedro *Random Lengths,* 11/15/89; "Flight 103: The Other Story," by Erick Anderson, *San Francisco Bay Guardian,* 11/6/89; "The Bombing of Pan Am 103," by Jeff Jones, *Covert Action Information Bulletin* #34; "Unwitting Accomplices?," by Maggie Mahar, *Barron's* 12/17/90.

There are interesting parallels between the Pan Am 103 bombing and the crash on December 12, 1985, of an Arrow Air charter jet carrying 248 American servicemen and eight flight crew members (all 256 died), in Gander, Newfoundland. Though a terrorist group claimed immediate credit for bombing the plane, the official cause was listed as "ice on the wings." However, recent revelations suggest that "ice" may have been the Lee Harvey Oswald of this murder. In fact, it appears the plane was bombed. Furthermore, Arrow Air turns out to be a CIA airline (if not owned by the CIA, it was regularly used by them), which shipped arms to the contras as part of the Iran-Contra affair. The cover-up of the bombing, then, would become part of the Iran-Contra cover-up, as would the Pan Am 103 bombing if the Interfor report is credible. See "Crash, Burn, Cover-up," by Joe Conason, *Details*, 12/90; possible bombing was revealed on ABC News *20/20* of 10/13/89.

The allegation that P2 was behind the bombing was read over the air by David Emory, 12/17/90. I don't have a copy of what he was reading.

Bush phones Thatcher: "The Bombing of Pan Am 103"; Bernt Carlsson on board: ibid.

Secord-Shackley-Wilson connections: see Chapter 9.

Gelli and Delle Chiaie: Christie, *Stefano Delle Chiaie: Portrait of a Black Terrorist*, pp. 110–13, 162–63.

Operation Gladio, media coverage and involvement in Moro killing: "Press Clips: Gladio Tiding," by Doug Ireland, *Village Voice*, 11/27/90.

"Black International" summit: Sterling, *The Terror Network*, p. 115.

Links between left and right terrorists, "third position": "Killers on the Right". Jacques Verges background: ibid. Odifried Hepp background, connection to *Achille Lauro* hijackers: ibid.

CHAPTER 14

"I owed Richard Nixon . . .": Bush's autobiography *Looking Forward* quoted in "A Bush Bestiary," by Joe Conason, *San Francisco Bay Guardian*, 12/14/88.

The former CIA operative is Richard Brenneke. A transcript of his testimony is in my files. Brenneke was later tried for perjury for making his accusation against Bush. He was found not guilty.

Bush resigns from the CFR: Silk and Silk, *The American Establishment*, p. 220.

Bush wanted to work for Carter: "A Carter Connection?," by Don Shannon, *Los Angeles Times*, 5/7/88.

Intelligence operatives in Bush campaign: "Agents for Bush," by Bob Callahan, *Covert Action Information Bulletin* #33.

The Neil Bush—Scott Hinckley dinner date was widely reported. It is noted in Honneger, *October Surprise*, p. 244. Honneger notes a series of odd circumstances around the Reagan assassination attempt, including the fact that Hinckley once belonged to an American pro-Khomeni "Islamic Guerilla Army."

Neil Bush's involvement with the Silverado Savings and Loan failure was a major story in 1990. A good summary, including Bush (both Neil and George) and Sun-Flo appears in "S&L Crisis Tied to Mob," cited in Chapter 13 notes; see also, "Neil Bush's Insider Deals," by James Ridgeway, *Village Voice*, 10/2/90.

Casey convinced Reagan to choose Bush: "Agents for Bush," by Bob Callahan, *Covert Action Information Bulletin* #33.

"Casey Investing Again": from a *Newsweek* article of 10/10/83 cited in Johnson, *Shootdown*, p. 115.

Bush/Casey study group: "Agents for Bush."

Skull and Bones: "Secret Society," by Steven Aronson, *Fame*, 8/89; "Skull and Bones," *Covert Action Information Bulletin* #33; Rosenbaum, *Travels With Dr. Death and Other Unusual Investigations*, pp. 375–395.

William Bundy quote: ibid.

"a sinister, unhealthy offshoot . . .": "Secret Society."

Skull and Bones initiations: ibid.; "Yale Society Resists Peeks into Its Crypt," by David W. Dunlap, *New York Times*, 11/4/88.

Bush confesses to Bonesmen: "Bush Opened Up to Secret Yale

Society," by Bob Woodward and Walter Pincus, *Washington Post*, 8/7/88.

"Mr. George Bush of the CIA" memo and subsequent denial: "'63 Bush CIA Link Reported," *New York Times*, 7/11/88, and "Doubts Are Raised in Report on Bush, '63 Memo Seen as Case of Mistaken Identity," *New York Times*, 7/21/88.

"What the fuck do you know . . .": "Company Man," by Scott Armstrong and Jeff Nason, *Mother Jones*, 10/88.

Bush/Colby strategy: ibid.

Crimes allegedly covered up by Bush at CIA: ibid.

Felix Rodriguez and Che Guevara: Rodriguez, *Shadow Warrior*.

Violation of Ford order: "Bush: Covering Up for the CIA," by John Kelly, *San Francisco Bay Guardian*, 12/14/88.

Bush appoints Shackley: "Company Man."

For more on Christic Institute's lawsuit and "The Enterprise," see Chapter Nine.

The best concise summary of the widely reported relationship between Bush and Noriega that I have seen is "Made for Each Other," by Murray Waas, *Village Voice*, 2/6/90. Among other salient details, Waas notes that in 1988, when the Reagan administration was calling for Noriega to resign, Bush told Noriega that he could stay in office until May 1989. Noriega took this as a signal that the U.S. government's call for him to step down was not sincere.

Bush's office in arms-for-drugs operation: "The Dirty Secrets of George Bush," by Howard Kohn and Vicki Monks, *Rolling Stone*, 11/3/88. Rodriguez denial: *Shadow Warrior*.

"Bush by the balls": "The Dirty Secrets of George Bush."

Three million dollars for anti-Noriega operations: "New CIA Plot Reported to Overthrow Noriega," by Robin Wright, *San Francisco Chronicle* (from *Los Angeles Times*), 11/16/89.

"It was an attempt to tick them off . . .": "Flawed Intelligence Let Noriega Escape," by John M. Broder and Robin Wright, *San Jose Mercury-News* (from *Los Angeles Times*), 12/21/89. Almost a year to the day after that *Los Angeles Times* story ran, the *Times* ran another story, "Some Blame Rogue Band of Marines for Picking Fight, Spurring Panama Invasion," by Kenneth Freed, 12/22/90. The story describes "a pattern of aggressive behavior" by a supposedly free-lance group of marines calling themselves "The Hard Chargers," who intentionally provoked Panamanian soldiers. Though the "Hard Chargers" are predictably labeled "rogue," and the entire story was denied by the Pentagon, it could serve to further confirm that the invasion was planned well in advance. Bush simply needed a pretext to put the plan into action.

New Panama government's corruption: "Panama Is Still Besieged by Corruption," by Jack Anderson, *San Francisco Chronicle* (syndicated column), 6/25/90; see also "Press Clips/Jingo Bells," by Doug Ireland, *Village Voice*, 1/2/90. Ireland points out that Panama's American-backed president Guillermo Endara "served for 10 years as a top aide to Arnulfo Arias Madrid, who was three times elected (and three times deposed—by the U.S.) as president of Panama. Arias . . . was identified in 1940 as a 'fascist' by U.S. intelligence reports, which said he had 'reached some understanding with the Rome-Berlin axis.' " Ireland further notes that Endara's former boss, while president, "promulgated racial laws, including one expelling all West Indians. His support came from 'the oligarchies with fascist tendencies' and from the new antiblack class."

"Heritage Council": "The Republican Party and Fascists," by Russ Bellant, *Covert Action Information Bulletin* #33.

Scowcroft and Eagleburger's Kissinger ties: "Nominee Discloses Consulting Income," by Jeff Gerth, *New York Times*, 3/9/89; "Scowcroft Tells of Private Income," *New York Times* (from Associated Press), 3/15/89.

Took orders from Kissinger: "Company Man."

Prescott Bush's business with China: "Firm That Employs Bush's Brother Stands to Benefit from China Deal," by Jim Mann and Douglas Frantz, *Los Angeles Times*, 12/13/89.

Bush sends secret envoy to meet with Iraqi: "U.S. Oil Plot Fueled Saddam," by Helga Graham, London *Observer*, 10/21/90.

Bush orders $1 billion in aid to Iraq: "Bush OK'd aid to Iraq in 1989," by Douglas Frantz and Murray Waas, *San Jose Mercury-News* (from *Los Angeles Times*), 2/23/92.

Peter Dale Scott story: "Project Censored," by Craig Mc-

Laughlin, Syracuse *New Times* (from San Francisco *Bay Guardian*), 7/27/88. The article states that Peter Dale Scott "filed a December 21, 1987 Pacific News Service story that alleged that Vice-President George Bush, a former Texas oilman, actively promoted the Iran-Contra drugs-for-arms deal . . . to stabilize falling oil prices by developing a pricing agreement between the United States and other oil-producing countries, Iran included."

"After much discussion . . .": Salinger and Laurent, *Secret Dossier: The Hidden Agenda Behind the Gulf War*, p. 73; Demarcation of border discussion, ibid., p. 75.

Kuwaiti memo about CIA meeting: ibid., p. 44; Aziz accuses Sabah of being CIA mercenary: ibid. p. 163; War Flag '90: ibid., p. 121.

Bush messages to Jordan, Egypt: ibid., pp. 111–112.

Bribes and threats at United Nations: "Bush's Tool and Victim," by Phyllis Bennis, *Covert Action Information Bulletin #37;* Yemen ambassador bullied: ibid.; Bennis covered the U.N. for WBAI-FM and the Pacifica Radio Network.

Secret American-Saudi military pact: "Eye of the Storm," by Scott Armstrong, *Mother Jones*, 11/91.

Bush pre-war policy toward Iraq: "How America Lost Kuwait," by Murray Waas, San Jose *Metro*, 1/24/91.

Hewlett-Packard sells to Iraq: "The H-P Connection," by Jonathan Vankin, San Jose *Metro*, 1/24/90.

CHAPTER 15

Rockefeller sale to Mitsubishi: "Philanthropy for the 21st Century," *New York Times*, 11/5/89.

Rockefeller's defense of Trilateral Commission: "Foolish Attacks on False Issues," by David Rockefeller, *Wall Street Journal*, 4/30/80.

Kissinger/Bundy feud: Silk and Silk, *The American Establishment*, pp. 218–19.

"If conspiracy means that these men . . .": "Who Rules America," by G. William Domhoff, in Horowitz, ed., *Corporation and the Cold War.*

In the world of David Rockefeller . . .": *Bill Moyers Journal,* Public Broadcasting System, 2/7/80.

"The peace and prosperity of the Trilateral world . . .": "The Grey/Lurid World of the Trilateral Commission," by Richard Brookhiser, *National Review,* 11/13/81.

Carter and Trilateralists: "Jimmy Carter and the Trilateralists: Presidential Roots," by Laurence H. Shoup, in Sklar, ed., *Trilateralism.*

Hamilton Jordan quote: reprinted in *Trilateralism,* p. 89.

Vance and Brzezinski background: "Who's Who on the Trilateral Commission," by Holly Sklar and Ross Everdell, in *Trilateralism.*

Collective management of interdependence: "Trilateralism: Managing Dependence and Democracy," by Holly Sklar, in *Trilateralism.*

Anti-Rockefeller demonstrations: Sklar, *Reagan Trilateralism and the Neoliberals,* p. 11.

History of the Bilderbergers: "Bilderberg and the West," by Peter Thompson, in *Trilateralism.*

Lockheed scandal: Hougan, *Spooks,* chapter 13.

History of the CFR: Schulzinger, *The Wise Men of Foreign Affairs,* pp. 2–3.

CFR membership: "An Elite Group on U.S. Policy is Diversifying," by Richard Bernstein, *New York Times,* 10/30/82.

Casey rejection and subsequent joining of CFR: Woodward, *Veil,* p. 19.

Other CIA directors on CFR: *Trilateralism,* p. 173.

CIA reveals touchy information: Marchetti and Marks, *The CIA and the Cult of Intelligence,* p. 267. Discussing a speech to the CFR in 1968 by CIA Clandestine Services Chief Richard Bissell, Marchetti and Marks note, "When the agency has needed prominent citizens to front for its proprietary companies it has often turned to Council members."

Kissinger on "limited" nuclear war": Kissinger, *Nuclear Weapons and Foreign Policy,* pp. 174–202.

Kissinger sneaking out documents: Hersh, *The Price of Power*, p. 479.

Sklar on Rockefeller family, family's investments: *Trilateralism*, pp. 53–55.

Rockefeller's quotes from his testimony at confirmation hearings.

"If the Illuminati begat . . .": Wilgus, *The Illuminoids*, p. 142.

"Perhaps the most accurate overview . . .": McAlpine, *The Occult Technology of Power*, p. 50.

CHAPTER 16

Urban design of Washington, D.C., based on Masonic principles: Baigent and Leigh, *The Temple and the Lodge*, figure 36 and p. 262.

Russian Skoptski: Daraul, *A History of Secret Societies*, chapter 8.

Templar as bankers: Robinson, *Born in Blood*, pp. 74–77. Robinson says that the term "banking" doesn't quite fit the Templars. He prefers "financial services." But the Templars took money for deposit, loaned money for a fee, issued paper money, and maintained trusts, according to Robinson. While they may not have been "bankers" in the strict, twentieth-century meaning of the word, it seems to me an appropriate description.

Disraeli quote: this is the conspiracy buff's favorite quotation, cited in numerous sources. I culled it from McAlpine, *The Occult Technology of Power*.

History of the Illuminati: Robison, *Proofs of a Conspiracy;* Wilgus, *The Illuminoids;* Wilson, *Cosmic Trigger;* Howard, *The Occult Conspiracy;* Johnson, *Architects of Fear.* The strange bit about Heinz's "57 Varieties" is in Adams, *The Straight Dope*, pp. 196–97. "Fnord" in the *New York Times* is from Robert Shea and Robert Anton Wilson's novel, *The Illuminatus! Trilogy*, intended in jest, of course. Isn't it?

Comte de Mirabeau: Howard, *The Occult Conspiracy*, p. 64.

Hyam Maccoby's views on human sacrifice in the Bible, explication of Cain and Abel story: Tierney, *The Highest Altar*, chapter 21.

Rituals of mystery religion: described throughout Burkert, *Ancient Mystery Cults;* Howard, *The Occult Conspiracy*, chapter 1.

Masonic "third-degree" initiation is described firsthand in Campbell-Everden, *Freemasonry and Its Etiquette*, pp. 222–33; see also Baigent and Leigh, *The Temple and the Lodge*, pp. 124–31.

Abiff as Osiris: *The Occult Conspiracy*, p. 15.

Solomon's temple as tribute to Astarte: *The Temple and the Lodge*, p. 126; Solomon is identified as a "follower" of Astarte at 1 Kings 9:4–5. Note also that Tyre, home of Hiram, was a center of goddess worship. At 1 Kings 3:3, Solomon is said to follow Yahweh, "except that he offered sacrifice and incense on the high places." Howard, in *the Occult Conspiracy* (p. 8), says that the "high places" were traditionally used for sacrifice to the goddess figure. 2 Kings 23 tells how the priest Hilkiah destroyed all the goddess shrines throughout the kingdom, and how King Josiah "desecrated" the high places "which Solomon king of Israel had built for Astarte" and for several other pagan gods.

The Lazarus theory is from Baigent, Leigh, and Lincoln, *Holy Blood, Holy Grail*, pp. 338–44.

Parallels to Jesus: Graham, *Deceptions and Myths of the Bible*, pp. 287–90.

Cult of Attis in Tarsus: Howard, *The Highest Altar*, pp. 441–42.

Jesus as political revolutionary: Schonfield, *The Passover Plot*.

Grail as Shroud of Turin: Currer-Briggs, *The Shroud and the Grail*.

Grail myth as pagan, early "Grail Romances": *Holy Blood, Holy Grail*, pp. 285–303; Matthews and Stewart, *Warriors of Arthur*, pp. 19–21.

Troyes as center of occultism, origin city of Templars: *Holy Blood, Holy Grail*, pp. 87–88.

Destruction of Templars: Robinson, *Born in Blood*, chapter 9; Baigent and Leigh, *The Temple and the Lodge*, chapter 3.

Grail and Celtic head-hunting: Stewart, *Warriors of Arthur*, p. 61.

Jesus substitution on the cross in Gnostic gospels: *The Second Treatise of the Great Seth*, in Robinson, ed., *The Nag Hammadi Library*, p. 365 (this book identifies Simon as the one who actually "bore the cross on his shoulder" and presumably was nailed up in Jesus's place); in Koran: 4:157.

Melding of the Templars into Scottish Freemasons under the protection of Robert Bruce is the theme of both *Born in Blood* and *The Temple and the Lodge*.

Franklin and the "Hell Fire Club": *The Occult Conspiracy*, pp. 78–80.

With regards to the Masonic origins of the U.S., I have always found it ironic that fundamentalist Christians claim that our founding fathers were devout Christians. Christian conspiracy theorists—Joseph Carr, for example (author of *The Lucifer Connection* and *The Twisted Cross*)—see Masonry as an arm of a satanic conspiracy. If Masonry is satanic, then the U.S. is a satanic country.

Masons in the American revolutionary war: *The Temple and the Lodge*, chapter 18.

American Masonry circa 1820s: Formisano, *The Transformation of Political Culture: Massachusetts Parties, 1790's–1840's*, chapter 9.

Reagan Masonic ceremony: *Born in Blood*, p. 325.

Roosevelt in "Ancient Arabic Order": *The Occult Conspiracy*, 92–93.

Ku Klux Klan, Masonic origins: *Born in Blood*, p. 328.

Peasant's revolt backed by "Great Society": ibid., chapters 1–2.

"Secrecy and political power . . .": Bok, *Secrets*, p. 106.

CHAPTER 17

Nazi myths of Aryan origins: Sklar, *Nazis and the Occult*, chapters 2–3.

Order of New Templars and subsequent proto-Nazi occult groups: ibid.; Howard, *The Occult Conspiracy*, chapter 5.

Ostara magazine and psychosexual racism: *Nazis and the Occult,* pp. 17–19.

List adopts founds *Armanen,* adopts swastika: ibid., p. 22.

Thule Society, myths and origins: ibid., chapter 4; *The Occult Conspiracy,* pp. 124–28; Schwarzwaller, *The Unknown Hitler,* pp. 54–55.

Hitler as intelligence agent, possible Thule connection: *The Unknown Hitler,* pp. 52–55.

Dietrich Eckart's character, influence on Hitler: ibid., 56–60. "Follow Hitler! He will dance . . .": ibid., p. 60.

Hitler's crackdown on occultists as cover-up of Hess flight: *The Occult Conspiracy,* p. 137. Hess, Ian Fleming, and Aleister Crowley, their relationship to British intelligence: ibid., pp. 133–37.

"We find it difficult to believe . . .": Pauwels and Bergier, *Morning of the Magicians,* p. 179; "This truth was hidden . . .": ibid., p. 180.

Operation Paperclip is chronicled in Bower, *The Paperclip Conspiracy.*

Wealthy financiers of the Thule Society: Pool and Pool, *Who Financed Hitler,* chapter 1. "It is even partly true . . .": ibid., p. 2. Hitler and Henry Ford: ibid., chapter 3. Rosenberg and Deterding: ibid., p. 319.

"Sullivan and Cromwell thrived . . .": Lisagor and Lipsius, *A Law unto Itself,* p. 125. Dulles using "Heil Hitler" salutation and writing pro-Nazi article for *Atlantic:* ibid., p. 132.

Sosthenes Behn's Nazi links, arranging of Westrick visit: Sampson, *The Sovereign State of ITT,* chapter 2; Hougan, *Spooks,* chapter 12.

Himmler's recruitment of SS members and subsequent purge: Hohne, *The Order of the Death's Head,* pp. 156–62. Wewelsburg Castle: ibid., pp. 172–74.

Multinationals as instruments of foreign policy: Hougan, *Spooks,* p. 427.

"The oligarchs of agricultural kingdoms . . .": Gross, *Friendly Fascism,* p. 54.

For an excellent overview of contemporary American neo-nazism, see "The American Neo-Nazi Movement Today," by Elinor Langer, *The Nation*, 7/16/90. Background on the Identity Church: "The Identity Movement and Its 'Real Jew' Claim," by Michael D'Antonio, *The Alicia Patterson Report*, Spring 1988.

Background on Manson's satanism: Sanders, *The Family*, chapter 3.

Process Church: Terry, *The Ultimate Evil*, chapter 9. Terry's book has the thesis that the Process was the ultimate force behind the Son of Sam murders; see also Lyons, *Satan Wants You*, pp. 88–92.

"Squeaky" Fromme hired to kill Ford: Milan, *The Squad*, pp. 285–90.

Michael Aquino and possible military links to satanic mind control: *Satan Wants You*, chapter 9; Raschke, *Painted Black*, chapter 7.

Bacon quoted in Bok, *Secrets*, p. 172.

Conclusion

"no single, central conspiracy": Gross, *Friendly Fascism*, p. 58.

AIDS as biowarfare conspiracy theories are quite prevalent: see Rappoport, *AIDS Inc.*, chapter 26, for an overview; see also "Is AIDS Non-Infectious? The Possibility and Its CBW Implications," by Nathaniel S. Lehrman, *Covert Action Information Bulletin* #28.

Loftus speculation on Nazi link to Lyme disease: Loftus, *The Belarus Secret*, p. xvii.

For background on eugenics-origins of IQ testing, see Chorover, *From Genesis to Genocide*.

Pellagra cover-up: ibid., p. 47.

Bush envoys sent to China: "Earlier Secret Trip was Made to China," by Owen Ullmann, *San Jose Mercury-News*, 12/19/89.

Sulzberger prints CIA press release: Lee and Solomon, *Unreliable Sources*, p. 116.

CIA blowback in Sterling's book: Woodward, *Veil*, pp. 130–31.

Internal White House "propaganda" memorandum: *Unreliable Sources*, p. 135. The memo is addressed to Pat Buchanan, the syndicated columnist who was then Reagan's Director of Communications, from someone in the State Department's "Office of Public Diplomacy." The OPD was, despite its obfuscating name, a full-blown domestic propaganda operation, which the General Accounting Office concluded in 1987 was engaged in "prohibited, covert propaganda activities." The subject of the memo to Buchanan is " 'White Propaganda' Campaign." "White" propaganda means the undisguised placement of government propaganda in the media. For example, op-ed pieces in the *New York Times* signed by government officials (or, as in the example noted in the memo, contra leaders). "Black" propaganda is the covert placement of propaganda; for example, keeping "legitimate" journalists on a secret CIA payroll would be a "black propaganda" operation.

"large number of Americans . . .": Johnson, *Architects of Fear*, p. 12.

"Sham gives rise . . .": Henry, *On Sham, Vulnerability and Other Forms of Self Destruction*, p. 123.

"I anticipate a geometric increase in madness . . .": *ibid.,* p. 124.

"cannot live in the comfortable, insulated world . . .": Wilson, *The Outsider*, p. 15.

Bibliography

NOTE ON THE BIBLIOGRAPHY

This bibliography contains full citations of books cited in the notes or consulted in preparation of this book. The notes section contains only abbreviated citations. Not listed here are the many articles from newspapers and periodicals from which I drew information. Those are cited in full in the notes. Also not listed are the interviews I conducted. Those from which I took direct quotations are cited in the notes. Others remain as background.

Adams, Cecil. *The Straight Dope.* New York: Ballantine, 1986.

Agee, Philip and Lewis Wolf, eds. *Dirty Work: The CIA in Western Europe.* Secaucus, NJ: Lyle Stuart, 1978.

Allen, Gary. *None Dare Call It Conspiracy.* Rossmoor, CA: Concord Press, 1972.

———. *Say "No" to the New World Order.* Seal Beach, CA: Concord Press, 1987.

Anderson, Jon and Scott Anderson. *Inside the League.* New York: Dodd, Mead and Co., 1986.

Anderson, Malcolm. *Policing the World.* Oxford: Clarendon Press, 1989.

Anti-Defamation League of B'nai B'rith. *Extremism on the Right: A Handbook.* New York: Anti-Defamation League of B'nai B'rith, 1988.

———. *Hate Groups in America.* New York, 1988.

Ashe, Geoffrey. *The Discovery of King Arthur.* New York: Henry Holt and Co., 1985.

Bagdikian, Ben. *The Media Monopoly, Second Edition.* Boston: Beacon Press, 1987.

Baigent, Michael and Richard Leigh. *The Temple and the Lodge.* New York: Arcade, 1989.

Baigent, Michael, Richard Leigh and Henry Lincoln. *Holy Blood, Holy Grail.* New York: Dell, 1983.

————. *The Messianic Legacy.* New York: Dell, 1989.

Bain, Donald. *The Control of Candy Jones.* Chicago: Playboy Press, 1976.

Balsiger, David and Charles Sellier. *The Lincoln Conspiracy.* Los Angeles: Shick Sunn Classic Books, 1977.

Bennett, David. *The Party of Fear.* New York: Vintage Books, 1990.

Bennis, Warren and Ian Mitroff. *The Unreality Industry.* New York: Birch Lane Press, 1989.

Birmingham, Stephen. *America's Secret Aristocracy.* New York: Berkley Books, 1990.

Black, Bob and Adam Parfrey, eds. *Rants and Incendiary Tracts.* New York: Amok Press, 1989.

Bledowska, Celina and Jonathan Bloch. *KGB/CIA: Intelligence and Counter-Intelligence Operations.* New York: Exeter Books, 1987.

Blum, William. *CIA: A Forgotten History.* London and New Jersey: Zed Books, 1986.

Blumenthal, Sid and Harvey Yazitian. *Government by Gunplay.* New York: New American Library, 1976.

Bok, Sissela. *Secrets.* New York: Vintage Books, 1984.

Borosage, Robert and John Marks, eds. *The CIA File.* New York: Grossman Publishers, 1976.

Bowart, Walter. *Operation Mind Control.* New York: Dell, 1978.

Bower, Tom. *The Paperclip Conspiracy.* Boston: Little, Brown and Co., 1987.

Bramley, William. *The Gods of Eden.* San Jose, CA: Dahlin Family Press, 1990.

Bressler, Fenton. *Who Killed John Lennon?* New York: St. Martin's Press, 1989.

Bunzel, John. *Anti-Politics in America.* New York: Vintage Books, 1970.

Burkert, Walter. *Ancient Mystery Cults.* Cambridge, MA: Harvard University Press, 1987.

Calic, Edouard, ed. *Secret Conversations with Hitler.* New York: John Day and Co., 1971.

Campbell-Everden, William. *Freemasonry and Its Etiquette.* New York: Weathervane Books, 1978.

Chorover, Stephan. *From Genesis to Genocide.* Cambridge, MA: MIT Press, 1980.

Christie, Stuart. *Stefano Delle Chiaie: Portrait of a Black Terrorist.* London: Refract Publications, 1984.

Coates, James. *Armed and Dangerous: The Rise of the Survivalist Right.* New York: Noonday Press, 1987.

Cockburn, Leslie. *Out of Control.* New York: Atlantic Monthly Press, 1987.

Collier, Kenneth and James Collier. *Votescam.* Unpublished manuscript.

Commission to Investigate Human Rights Violations. *Railroad!* Washington, DC: Commission to Investigate Human Rights Violations, 1989.

Corson, William. *The Armies of Ignorance: The Rise of the American Intelligence Empire.* New York: Dial Press, 1977.

Curran, Douglas. *In Advance of the Landing: Folk Concepts of Outer Space.* New York: Abbeville Press, 1985.

Currer-Briggs, Noel. *The Shroud and the Grail.* New York: St. Martin's Press, 1987.

Daraul, Arkon. *A History of Secret Societies.* Secaucus, NJ: Citadel Press, 1961.

Drosnin, Michael. *Citizen Hughes.* New York: Bantam Books, 1986.

Dudman, Richard. *Men of the Far Right.* New York: Pyramid Books, 1962.

Dugger, Ronnie. *Reagan: The Man and His Presidency.* New York: McGraw-Hill, 1983.

Ellul, Jacques. *Propaganda: The Formation of Men's Attitudes.* New York: Vintage Books, 1983.

Emerson, Steven and Brian Duffy. *The Fall of Pan Am 103.* New York: Putnam, 1990.

Epstein, Edward Jay. *Counterplot.* New York: Viking, 1969.

Erickson, Paul, ed. *Reagan Speaks.* New York: New York University Press, 1985.

Flammonde, Paris. *The Kennedy Conspiracy.* New York: The Meredith Press, 1969.

Foomer, Michael. *Interpol.* New York: Plenum Press, 1989.

Fort, Charles. *The Book of the Damned.* New York: Ace Books, 1941.

Furneaux, Rupert. *Ancient Mysteries.* New York: Ballantine Books, 1978.

Garrison, Jim. *On the Trail of the Assassins.* New York: Sheridan Square Press, 1988.

Good, Timothy. *Above Top Secret: The Worldwide UFO Cover Up.* New York: Quill, 1988.

Graham, Lloyd. *Deceptions and Myths of the Bible.* New York: Citadel Press, 1975.

Greider, William. *Secrets of the Temple: How the Federal Reserve Runs the Country.* New York: Touchstone, 1987.

Groden, Robert and Harrison Livingstone. *High Treason.* Baltimore: The Conservatory Press, 1989.

Gross, Betram. *Friendly Fascism.* New York: M. Evans and Co., 1980.

Harris, Robert and Jeremy Paxman. *A Higher Form of Killing. The Secret Story of Chemical and Biological Warfare.* New York: Hill and Wang, 1982.

Henry, Jules. *On Sham, Vulnerability and Other Forms of Self-Destruction.* New York: Vintage Books, 1973.

Hersh, Seymour. *The Price of Power.* New York: Summit Books, 1983.

Hoffman, Lance. *Making Every Vote Count.* Washington, DC: George Washington University, 1988.

Hohne, Heinz. *The Order of the Death's Head.* New York: Ballantine Books, 1971.

Honey, Martha and Tony Ayrigan. *La Penca: Report of an Investigation.* Washington, DC: The Christic Institute, 1988.

Honneger, Barbara. *October Surprise.* New York and Los Angeles: Tudor Publishing Co., 1989.

Horowitz, David, ed. *Corporations and the Cold War.* New York: Monthly Review Press, 1969.

Hougan, Jim. *Spooks.* New York: Bantam Books, 1978.

Howard, Michael. *The Occult Conspiracy.* Rochester, VT: Destiny Books, 1989.

Infield, Glenn. *Secrets of the SS.* New York: Jove Books, 1990.

———. *Skorzeny: Hitler's Commando.* New York: Military Heritage Press, 1981.

James, Rosemary and Jack Wardlaw. *Plot or Politics?* New Orleans: Pelican Publishing House, 1967.

Jensen-Stevenson, Monica and William Stevenson. *Kiss the Boys Goodbye.* New York: Dutton Books, 1990.

Johnson, George. *Architects of Fear: Conspiracy Theories and Political Paranoia.* Los Angeles: Jeremy P. Tarcher, Inc., 1983.

Johnson, R. W. *Shootdown: Flight 007 and the American Connection.* New York: Penguin Books, 1987.

Johnston, David. *Lockerbie: The Tragedy of Flight 103.* New York: St. Martin's Press, 1989.

Jones, Alexander, ed. *The Jerusalem Bible: Reader's Edition.* Garden City, NY: Doubleday and Co., 1968.

Keel, John. *Disneyland of the Gods.* New York: Amok Press, 1988.

———. *UFOs: Operation Trojan Horse.* New York: G.P. Putnam's and Son's, 1970.

Kilduff, Marshall and Ron Javers. *The Suicide Cult.* New York: Bantam Books, 1978.

King, Dennis. *Lyndon LaRouche and the New American Fascism.* New York: Doubleday, 1989.

Kirkpatrick, Lyman. *The U.S. Intelligence Community: Foreign Policy and Domestic Activities.* New York: Hill and Wang, 1973.

Kissinger, Henry. *Nuclear Weapons and Foreign Policy.* New York: Council on Foreign Relations, 1957.

Knight, Stephen. *The Brotherhood: The Secret World of the Freemasons.* New York: Dorset Press, 1986.

———. *Jack the Ripper: The Final Solution.* Chicago: Academy Chicago Publishers, 1986.

Krause, Charles. *Guyana Massacre: The Eyewitness Account* New York: Berkley Books, 1978.

Kwitny, Jonathan. *The Crimes of Patriots.* New York: Touchstone Books, 1988.

LaRouche, Lyndon. *The Power of Reason: A Kind of Autobiography.* New York: New Benjamin Franklin House, 1979.

———. *There Are No Limits to Growth.* New York: New Benjamin Franklin House, 1983.

Lee, Martin and Bruce Shlain. *Acid Dreams.* New York: Grove Press, 1985.

Lee, Martin and Norman Solomon. *Unreliable Sources: A Guide to Detecting Bias in News Media.* New York: Lyle Stuart, 1990.

Lifton, David. *Best Evidence: Disguise and Deception in the Assassination of John F. Kennedy.* New York: Carroll and Graf, 1988.

Lisagor, Nancy and Frank Lipsius. *A Law unto Itself: The Untold Story of the Law Firm Sullivan and Cromwell.* New York: Paragon House, 1989.

Livingstone, Neil and David Levy. *Inside the PLO.* New York: William Morrow and Co., 1990.

Loftus, John. *The Belarus Secret.* New York: Paragon House, 1989.

Lyons, Arthur. *Satan Wants You.* New York: Mysterious Press, 1989.

Mader, Julius. *Who's Who in the CIA.* Berlin: Julius Mader, 1968.

Malaclypse the Younger. *Principia Discordia.* Port Townsend, WA: Loompanics Unlimited.

Marchetti, Victor and John Marks. *The CIA and the Cult of Intelligence.* New York: Dell, 1975.

Marks, John. *The Search for the "Manchurian Candidate."* New York: Dell, 1979.

Matthews, John and Bob Stewart. *Warriors of Arthur.* London: Blandford Press, 1987.

McAlpine, Peter. *The Occult Technology of Power.* Port Townsend, WA: Loompanics Unlimited (reprinted from Alpine Enterprises, 1974).

McCoy, Alfred W. *The Politics of Heroin in Southeast Asia.* New York: Harper and Row, 1972.

McGarvey, Patrick. *CIA: The Myth and the Madness.* Baltimore: Penguin Books, 1972.

McManus, John. *The Insiders.* Belmont, MA: John Birch Society, 1983.

Messick, Hank. *John Edgar Hoover.* New York: David McKay Company, 1972.

Milan, Michael. *The Squad: The U.S. Government's Secret Alliance with Organized Crime.* New York: Shapolsky Publishers, 1990.

Miller, Nathan. *Spying for America.* New York: Paragon House, 1989.

Mills, James. *The Underground Empire.* New York: Dell, 1987.

Moldea, Dan. *Dark Victory: Ronald Reagan, MCA and the Mob.* New York: Penguin Books, 1987.

Moore, Alan and Bill Sienkiewicz. *Brought to Light.* Forestville, CA: Eclipse Books, 1989.

Moyers, Bill. *The Secret Government.* Washington, DC: Seven Locks Press, 1988.

Nash, Jay Robert. *Citizen Hoover.* Chicago: Nelson Hall, 1972.

Newman, John M. *JFK and Vietnam.* New York: Warner Books, 1992.

Oglesby, Carl. *The Yankee and Cowboy War: Conspiracies From Dallas to Watergate.* Kansas City: Sheed Andrews and McMeel, 1976.

Ouides, Bruce, ed. *From: The President: Richard Nixon's Secret Files.* New York: Perennial Library, 1990.

Pagels, Elaine. *The Gnostic Gospels.* New York: Vintage Books, 1979.

Parfrey, Adam, ed. *Apocalypse Culture.* New York: Amok Press, 1987.

Pauwels, Louis and Jacques Bergier. *The Morning of the Magicians.* New York: Dorset Press, 1988.

Pizzo, Stephen, Paul Muolo and Mary Fricker. *Inside Job: The*

Looting of America's Savings and Loans. New York: McGraw Hill, 1989.

Pool, James and Suzanne Pool. *Who Financed Hitler?* New York: The Dial Press, 1978.

Powers, Thomas. *The Man Who Kept the Secrets: Richard Helms and the CIA.* New York: Alfred A. Knopf, 1979.

Prouty, L. Fletcher. *The Secret Team.* Englewood Cliffs, NJ: Prentice-Hall, 1973.

Rand, Ayn. *Atlas Shrugged.* New York: New American Library, 1959.

Randle, Kevin D. *The UFO Casebook.* New York: Warner Books, 1989.

Rappoport, Jon. *AIDS, Inc. Scandal of the Century.* San Bruno, CA: Human Energy Press, 1988.

Raschke, Carl A. *Painted Black.* San Francisco: Harper and Row, 1990.

Rashke, Richard. *The Killing of Karen Silkwood.* Boston: Houghton Mifflin Co., 1983.

Ravenscroft, Trevor. *The Spear of Destiny.* York Beach, ME: Samuel Weiser, Inc., 1973.

Reed, Sally D. *NEA: Propaganda Front for the Radical Left.* 1984.

Robbins, Christopher. *Air America: The Story of the CIA's Secret Airlines.* New York: Putnam's, 1979.

Robinson, James M., ed. *The Nag Hammadi Library.* San Francisco: Harper and Row, 1988.

Robinson, John. *Born In Blood: The Lost Secrets of Freemasonry.* New York: M. Evans and Co., 1989.

Robison, John. *Proofs of a Conspiracy.* Boston: Western Islands Press, 1967.

Rodriguez, Felix and John Weisman. *Shadow Warrior.* New York: Pocket Books, 1989.

Rosenbaum, Ron. *Travels With Dr. Death and Other Unusual Investigations.* New York: Penguin, 1991.

Salinger, Pierre and Eric Laurent. *Secret Dossier: The Hidden Agenda Behind the Gulf War.* New York: Penguin Books, 1992.

Sampson, Anthony. *The Sovereign State of ITT.* Greenwich, CT: Fawcett Crest, 1974.

Sanders, Ed. *The Family: Revised and Updated Edition.* New York: Signet, 1989.

Scheflin, Alan and Edward Opton, Jr. *The Mind Manipulators.* London: Paddington Press, 1978.

Schomp, Gerald. *Birchism Was My Business.* New York: MacMillan, 1970.

Schonfield, Hugh. *The Passover Plot.* New York: Bantam Books, 1967.

Schulzinger, Robert A. *The Wise Men of Foreign Affairs: The History of the Council on Foreign Relations.* New York: Columbia University Press, 1984.

Scott, Peter Dale. *The Dallas Conspiracy.* Unpublished manuscript, 1971.

——. *The War Conspiracy: The Secret Road to the Second Indochina War.* New York: Bobbs-Merrill, 1972.

Scwarzwaller, Wulf. *The Unknown Hitler.* New York: Berkley Books, 1990.

Shackley, Theodore. *The Third Option.* New York: Dell, 1988.

Shea, Robert and Robert Anton Wilson. *The Illuminatus Trilogy.* New York: Dell, 1988.

Shoup, Laurence and William Mintier. *Imperial Braintrust: The CFR and U.S. Foreign Policy.* New York: Monthly Review Press, 1977.

Silk, Leonard and Mark Silk. *The American Establishment.* New York: Avon/Discus Books, 1981.

Simpson, Christopher. *Blowback.* New York: Weidenfeld and Nicholson, 1988.

Sklar, Dusty. *Nazis and the Occult.* New York: Dorset Press, 1989.

Sklar, Holly. *Reagan Trilateralism and the Neoliberals.* Boston: South End Press, 1986.

Sklar, Holly, ed. *Trilateralism: The Trilateral Commission and Elite Planning for World Management.* Boston: South End Press, 1980.

Smoot, Dan. *The Invisible Government.* Boston: Western Islands Press, 1965.

Sorman, Guy. *The Conservative Revolution in America.* Chicago: Regenery, 1985.

Sterling, Claire. *The Terror Network.* New York: Holt, Rinehart and Winston, 1981.

Stormer, John. *None Dare Call It Treason.* Florissant, MO: Liberty Bell Press, 1964.

Summers, Anthony. *Conspiracy.* New York: Paragon House, 1989.

Sutton, Anthony. *Wall Street and the Rise of Hitler.* Seal Beach, CA: '76 Press, 1976.

Terry, Maury. *The Ultimate Evil.* Garden City, NY: Dolphin Books, 1987.

Thornley, Kerry. *The Dreadlock Recollections.* Unpublished manuscript, 1984.

———. *The Idle Warriors.* Avondale Estates, GA: IllumiNet Press, 1991.

———. *Oswald.* Chicago: New Classics House, 1965.

Tierney, Patrick. *The Highest Altar: The Story of Human Sacrifice.* New York: Viking, 1989.

Tudhope, George. *Bacon-Masonry.* Mokelumne Hill, CA: Health Research, 1989.

United States Senate. *Hearings Before the Subcommittee on Terrorism, Narcotics and International Communications,* 1988.

U.S. Labor Party Investigating Team. *Dope Inc.: Britain's Opium War against the United States.* New York: New Benjamin Franklin House, 1978.

Vahan, Richard. *The Truth about the John Birch Society.* New York: MacFadden Books, 1962.

Vallee, Jacques. *Messengers of Deception.* Berkeley, CA: And/Or Press, 1979.

Welch, Robert. *The Blue Book of the John Birch Society.* Belmont, MA: Western Islands Press, 1959.

———. *And Some Ober Dicta.* Belmont, MA: American Opinion, 1976.

Whyte, William. *The Organization Man.* Garden City, NY: · Doubleday/Anchor, 1957.

Wilgus, Neil. *The Illuminoids: Secret Societies and Political Paranoia.* Santa Fe, NM: Sun Books, 1978.

Wills, Garry. *Reagan's America.* New York: Penguin Books, 1988.

Wilson, Colin. *The Encyclopedia of Unsolved Mysteries.* Chicago: Contemporary Books, 1988.

——. *The Outsider.* Los Angeles: Jeremy P. Tarcher, Inc., 1982.

Wilson, Robert Anton. *Cosmic Trigger: Final Secret of the Illuminati.* Phoenix, AZ: Falcon Press, 1986.

Winrod, Gerald. *Adam Weishaupt: A Human Devil.*

Wise, David. *The American Police State.* New York: Random House, 1976.

Woodward, Bob. *Veil: The Secret Wars of the CIA, 1981–1987.* New York: Pocket Books, 1987.

Yallop, David. *In God's Name.* New York: Bantam Books, 1985.

INDEX